Robert the Burgundian
and the Counts of Anjou,
ca. 1025–1098

Robert the Burgundian
and the Counts of Anjou,

ca. 1025–1098

W. Scott Jessee

The Catholic University of America Press

Washington, D.C.

Copyright © 2000

The Catholic University of America Press

All rights reserved

Printed in the United States of America

The paper used in this publication meets the minimum requirements of American National
Standards for Information Science—Permanence of Paper for Printed Library materials,

ANSI Z39.48—1984.

∞

Library of Congress Cataloging-in-Publication Data

Jessee, W. Scott, 1949—

    Robert the Burgundian and the Counts of Anjou, ca. 1025–1098 /
W. Scott Jessee.

        p.   cm.

    Includes bibliographical references and index.

    1. Robert, the Burgundian, d. 1098. 2. Anjou (France)—History
—Sources. 3. France—History—Medieval period, 987–1515—Sources.
4. Nobility—France—Anjou—Biography. I. Title.

DC611.A607 J47 2000

944'.1802'092—dc21

[B]

99-048573

ISBN 0-8132-0973-0

To Laura
"Unico mihi amore dilectissima uxor"

Contents

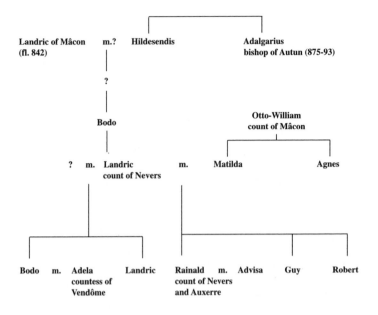

Figure 1. Genealogy of the Counts of Nevers

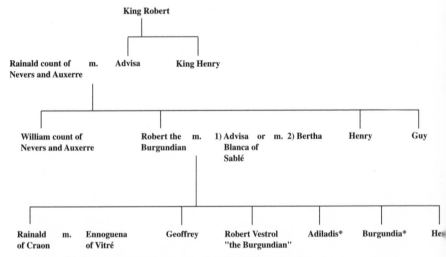

*(possibly the same) one of whom marries Rainald of Château-Gontier

Figure 2. Robert the Burgundian and His Family

Acknowledgments

It is only now that the work is done that I fully understand how much I owe to so many. First and foremost to Bernard S. Bachrach for first introducing me to Robert the Burgundian and firmly (and patiently) teaching me the skills I needed to make sense of the evidence of the man's life. He has also read through one or another version of the manuscript and offered much good advice. Others from the University of Minnesota to whom I owe much include Fredrick Suppe, for good advice and conversation about things medieval and otherwise, Steven Fanning for advice and help with some key documents, and Peter Burkholder for useful discussions of his work on Durtal. From an earlier time at Florida State I am indebted to Ralph Turner for introducing me to both the medieval world and the world of the scholar.

I was twice able to visit archives in France for vital research among unpublished documents with grants from the University of Minnesota and Appalachian State University. While in France I was unfailingly assisted by Madam Poirier-Countansais and her staff at the Archives de Maine-et-Loire as well as the staffs of the Archives de Sarthe, the Archives de Indre-et-Loire and the Bibliothèque nationale. I owe special thanks to Noël-Yves Tonnerre of the Université d'Angers for his warm welcome and assistance in obtaining the published version of the cartulary of Saint-Serge. Christopher Lewis of the University of Leeds was kind enough to check one particularly troubling but very meaningful letter of one word of one manuscript in the British Museum. Kathleen Thompson and Hendrick Teunis have also provided generous advice on questions I had.

Here at Appalachian State University I would like to thank my colleagues in the History Department for providing me with, need it be said, employment at my craft, and a place where I could continue to learn it. All have contributed, but I owe much in particular to Jeff Bortz, Mike Wade, Tim Silver and John Jackson. It is unusual at a university the size of mine to have colleagues who are fellow medievalists, and I have had two of the best: H. Lawrence Bond and Thomas K. Keefe. I am delighted to publically acknowledge their shared advice, thoughts and friendship and saddened that Tom is not here to see this work on a period and place he loved finally make its appearance.

As a former confirmed bachelor, I have always wondered about the fulsome praise and gratitude heaped on authors' spouses at this point in the acknowledgments. Now I know. They have not done them justice. The dedication of this book to my wife, Laura del Carmen Yanes, does not begin to cover my debt to her.

Robert the Burgundian
and the Counts of Anjou,
ca. 1025–1098

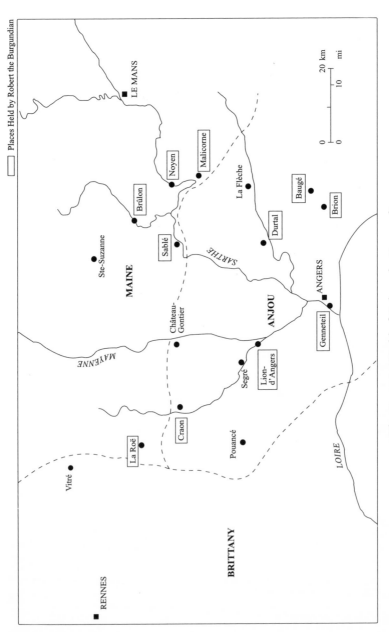

The Angevin World of Robert the Burgundian

Introduction

In the course of the tenth century the western realm of the Franks split into several territorial principalities, each with its ruler, the duke or count, who operated virtually independently of whichever Carolingian or Robertian claimed the kingship. The election of Hugh Capet on 1 June 987 ratified this situation. Although we should not underestimate the genuine power of the first Capetians, the family came to the throne only with the support of key territorial princes, the count of Anjou chief among them. While willing to concede their obedience to the Capetian king in theory, the princes comported themselves as the real rulers of their principalities and took every opportunity to expand their territory at the expense of their neighbors.[1] During the first half of the eleventh century Anjou, under the leadership of Count Fulk Nerra (987–1040) and his son Count Geoffrey Martel (1040–1060), developed into one of the most powerful and cohesive of the principalities. From relatively modest beginnings the Angevin territory had expanded into a prosperous and well-ordered state able to contend with the duchy of Normandy for domination of western *Francia*. In doing this the two Angevin counts had displayed considerable skill. Nowhere was this skill more evident than in their construction of an interlocking network of castles carefully designed for defensive and offensive action. The castles, called *castella* or *castra* in Latin, were put under the command of castellans appointed by the count. The most powerful of these castel-

---

1. For the creation of the territorial principalities see Jan Dhondt, *Étude sur la naissance des principautés territoriales en France: IXe–Xe siècle* (Bruges: De Tempel, 1948).

lans held their castles and the surrounding territory by hereditary right. To distinguish them from commanders serving at the count's discretion they were called *domini,* or "lords."[2] Angevin power remained intact as long as the castle *domini* and castellans remained loyal to the house of Anjou.

The *domini* formed a rank of nobility second only to the count and were the bedrock of Angevin military and political organization. Yet despite their importance little is known about them. Few contemporary Angevin histories have survived. Nineteenth century historians of the Angevin nobility produced little more than genealogical studies. Twentieth century works give only a bit more information. Two of the best, Louis Halphen's *Le comté d'Anjou* and Olivier Guillot's *Le comte d'Anjou et son entourage,* do provide a solid historical framework for examining the nobility.[3] By their nature, however, these works focus on the juridical and political power of the counts. They offer only general descriptions of the role of the *domini* in relation to the counts of Anjou. No clear picture of the *domini* emerges.

More recently Bernard Bachrach has published a study of Count Fulk Nerra that used the technique of biography to reveal the development of the Angevin state under its chief architect.[4] In an earlier article, "The Angevin Strategy of Castle Building in the Reign of Fulk Nerra, 987–1040," Bachrach examined the strategic and tactical characteristics of the Angevin castles as part of this process.[5] While he focused briefly on numerous individual *domini* and castellans, his purpose was not to elucidate their role so much as Fulk Nerra's consummate skill in utilizing each castle in a complex system of defense in depth. He concluded

2. In eleventh-century documents from the Angevin region the word *senior,* modern French *seigneur,* is almost never used to designate a man's lordship over a castle. An individual might have a *senior,* but a *castrum* or *castellum* was possessed by a *dominus.*

3. Louis Halphen, *Le comté d'Anjou au XIe siècle* (Paris: A. Picard et Fils, 1906; reprint, Geneva: Slatkine-Megariots Reprints, 1974); Olivier Guillot, *Le comte d'Anjou et son entourage au XIe siècle,* 2 vols. (Paris: A. and J. Picard, 1972). Brief but useful accounts in English of the development of the Angevin state are found in Jean Dunbabin, *France in the Making, 843–1180* (Oxford: Oxford University Press, 1985), 184–90, and R. W. Southern, *The Making of the Middle Ages* (New Haven: Yale University Press, 1968), 81–90, although now dated.

4. Bernard S. Bachrach, *Fulk Nerra the Neo-Roman Consul, 987–1040: A Political Biography of the Angevin Count* (Berkeley: University of California Press, 1993).

5. Bernard S. Bachrach, "The Angevin Strategy of Castle Building in the Reign of Fulk Nerra, 987–1040," *American Historical Review* 88 (1983): 533–60.

that "Fulk Nerra's strategy of castle building provided the foundation upon which his descendants built nothing less than the Angevin empire."[6]

Under the weak and unpopular leadership of Count Geoffrey the Bearded (1060–1068), however, the system broke down. The castle commanders were no longer able to depend on the count for leadership and protection. Aided by the civil war that broke out between Geoffrey and his younger brother, Fulk Rechin, they began to augment their own power to the detriment of the count. By the time Fulk finally seized the countship (abortively in 1067, definitively in 1068), the Angevin state had been seriously weakened. Until his death in 1109, Fulk spent most of his reign desperately reasserting authority over his *domini* while fighting off Norman advances into Maine.[7] It would only be the heroic efforts of Fulk's grandson, Count Geoffrey Plantagenet (1131–1151), that would restore comital power to the point where Geoffrey's son, Henry II Plantagenet, could become the first Angevin king of England (1154–1189) and create the vast Angevin empire.

Such is the traditional view of the situation as developed by Halphen in the nineteenth century and generally followed by recent historians. Yet the scenario does not ring true. In light of Bachrach's insistence on the ultimate strength of the eleventh century defensive structure, understanding the motives and interests of the *domini* becomes pertinent

6. Bachrach, "Angevin Strategy," 560.

7. This view of the breakdown of Angevin comital authority fits into the general notion that around AD 1000 western Europe fell into a period of feudal anarchy in which first the major castle-holders and then lesser figures seized control of public power and used it to virtually enslave the rural population under a seigneurial regime. The clearest synthesis of this view is Jean-Pierre Poly and Eric Bournazel, *La mutation féodale, Xe–XIIe siècles* (Paris: PUF, 1980), trans. Caroline Higgit as *The Feudal Transformation, 900–1200* (New York: Holmes and Meier, 1991). Dominique Barthélemy has criticized this view in "La mutation féodale a-t-elle eu lieu? (Note critique)," *Annales: économies, sociétés, civilisations* 3 (1992): 767–77. His theme was developed in more detail in *La société dans le comté de Vendôme de l'an Mil au XIVe siècles* (Paris: Fayard, 1993), in which he argued for essential continuity from the ninth to the early twelfth centuries, with only a gradual change in a region that was an integral part of the Angevin state. The "Mutationists," as Barthélemy calls them, were quick to respond. For a good overview of this dispute with appropriate selections from the literature see Lester K. Little and Barbara H. Rosenwein, "Feudalism and its Alternatives," in their *Debating the Middle Ages: Issues and Readings* (Oxford: Blackwell, 1998). It is worth noting that even the most exteme "mutationist" does not see such a feudal transformation in Anjou until after 1060, precisely the focus of the present study.

to understanding the phenomenal success of the Angevin dynasty in the following century.[8] The question is this: did the *domini* very nearly wreck the Angevin state, only to be brought to heel by a resurgent comital policy of the Plantagenets, or was it the *domini* themselves who remained loyal to the house of Anjou and maintained the integrity of the state during a period of comital weakness. One must always keep in mind that in their struggle for Maine the Angevin *domini* faced the greatest captain of the age, William the Conqueror, who after 1066 had at his command the considerable resources of both England and Normandy. Despite this it was Angevins who ultimately controlled Maine.

Biographical studies similar to Bachrach's work on Fulk Nerra but focusing on individual *domini* would do much to illuminate this crucial period in Angevin history. The value of such studies of powerful nobles, second only among laymen to dukes and counts, has been demonstrated for a later period in English history. John Horace Round first brought to light many aspects of the so called "Anarchy" period in England (1036–1054) by examining the charters of one such lord, Geoffrey de Mandeville.[9] Sidney Painter did much the same thing with his study of William Marshal, although here he had the unique source of a rhymed chronicle of William's life.[10] The source is so rich, indeed, that two further studies of William have since been written by Georges Duby and David Crouch, demonstrating the continuing value and fascination of a biographical study when the sources permit.[11] More recently a pair of complimentary works have appeared, David Crouch's *The Beaumont Twins* and Sally Vaughn's study of both the father of the twins, Robert of Meulan, and Anselm of Bec.[12] Between them the two

---

8. Jim Bradbury, "Fulk le Réchin and the Origins of the Plantagenets," *Studies in Medieval History Presented to R. Allen Brown*, eds. Christopher Harper-Bill and others (Woodbridge, Suffolk: Boydell Press, 1989), 27–41, calls for a serious reassessment of Fulk's rule for these and other reasons.

9. John Horace Round, *Geoffrey De Mandeville: A Study of the Anarchy* (New York: Burt Franklin, 1892).

10. Sidney Painter, *William Marshal, Knight-errant, Baron, and Regent of England* (Baltimore: John Hopkins Press, 1933).

11. Georges Duby, *William Marshall: the Flower of Chivalry*, trans. Richard Howard (New York: Pantheon Books, 1985); David Crouch, *William Marshall: Court, Career, and Chivalry in the Angevin Empire, 1147–1219* (London: Longman, 1990).

12. David Crouch, *The Beaumont Twins: The Roots and Branches of Power in the Twelfth Century* (Cambridge: Cambridge University Press, 1986); Sally N. Vaughn, *Anselm of Bec and*

authors cover the period of roughly 1088–1168. All of these works suggest the possibilities awaiting a thorough study of important individuals in eleventh century Anjou.

Following this lead then, the beam of the present inquiry is narrow, but intense, illuminating the life of one unusually well-documented individual, Robert the Burgundian. Robert is the focus for several reasons. As a younger son of the count of Nevers and grandson of the king of France, he was of high birth. He entered the service of Count Geoffrey Martel around 1040 and was rewarded with the command of two strategically important strongholds on the Maine frontier. Thus he was one of the all important *domini*. By the early 1050s Robert was clearly preeminent among Angevin nobles. He maintained this position until his departure on the First Crusade in 1098. Because of his importance and longevity Robert left behind an unusually large number of documents relating to his activities.

Remarkably, a major portion of this evidence comes down to us in Robert's own words. In 1076 he became involved in a bitter and protracted dispute with the bishop of Le Mans over the disposition of his churches at Sablé. As explained in Chapter 5, it was an important case both to Robert and the Church. In the ensuing process Robert narrated his version of the history of Sablé and its churches in two lengthy documents preserved by the monks of Marmoutier.[13] In the presence of the judges of the case, all of Robert's followers dutifully certified that his testimony was accurate. At the end of his life, in 1098, Robert stopped at the monastery of Marmoutier in Tours on his journey to the Holy Land. There he had the monks write several charters purporting to be in his own words, describing his motives and preparations for his final adventure.[14]

While Robert's name is not well known to many modern students of the age, his life has been the object of an impressive number of

---

Robert of Meulen: The Innocence of the Dove and the Wisdom of the Serpent (Berkeley: University of California Press, 1987).

13. Two versions of Robert's account have survived, *Cartulaire manceau de Marmoutier*, ed. E. T. Laurain, 2 vols. (Laval: Librairie Goupil, 1945), 2: 67–76, nos. 4 and 5 from Sablé. No. 4 is hereafter referred to as "Testimony" and no. 5 as "Judgement" for reasons explained in Chapter 5.

14. *Carulaire manceau*, 2: 86–91, nos. 13 and 14.

works. Barely two decades after Robert's death, Orderic Vitalis wrote of Robert's participation at the siege of Sainte-Suzanne in some detail.[15] Nearly 150 years later Robert's life had become the subject of legends recounted in the modest chronicle of an obscure priest of Parcé, an area once subject to Robert's domination.[16] At the end of the fifteenth and the beginning of the sixteenth centuries Robert appeared under the name of "Hugh" the Burgundian in several works of local history, two by the Breton chronicler Pierre Le Baud and another by Jehan de Bordigné, an Angevin.[17] Unfortunately these early works are very brief, like Orderic's, or almost entirely legendary with major and obvious errors of chronology and fact.

The most serious historical work on Robert the Burgundian was by the prolific writer from Sablé, Giles Ménage. In 1683 he published the first part of his *Histoire de Sablé,* a massive work that is at once erudite, charming, and scatterbrained.[18] It gives the impression of an extended letter written to a friend regarding the history of his hometown, with the author occasionally correcting himself as he discovers new material and remembers that he had forgotten to make a point earlier. Ménage did an admirable job of searching the sources that were available to him including chronicles and charters that have since disappeared. Yet he was writing at a time when many basic facts of French history were still obscure or confused and this led him into many errors.

15. Orderic Vitalis, *The Ecclesiastical History,* ed. and trans. by Marjorie Chibnall, 6 vols. (Oxford: Clarendon Press, 1969–1973) 4: 48–49. Hereafter cited as Orderic. All translations are Chibnall's unless otherwise noted.

16. *Chronique de Parcé,* ed. by H. de Berranger, Archives Départmentales de la Sarthe: Inventaires et Documents (Le Mans: Imprimerie Monnoyer, 1953).

17. Pierre Le Baud, *Chronique de Vitré* and *Histoire de Bretagne,* both published in *Histoire de Bretagne avec les Chroniques des maison de Vitré et de Laval* (Paris: Gervais Alliot, 1638), 10–13 and 157; Jehan de Bordigné, *Hystoire agregative des annales et croniques daniou* (Paris: C. de Boingne et C. Alexandre, 1529), chapter 37, fueillets 77–78. Republished with modernized spellings and commentary, *Chroniques d'Anjou et du Maine par Jehan de Bourdigné* (Angers: Cosnier et Lachèse, 1842).

18. Giles Ménage, *Histoire de Sablé: premiere partie* (Paris: Pierre le Petit, 1683). Although called "the first part," Ménage had planned six parts to his history. Only the first part was published in 1683. Something called the *Second partie de l'histoire de Sablé* was published in Le Mans in 1844. Later the "Description de la ville de Sablé par Giles Ménage" was published in *Revue de l'Anjou* 2 (1868): 93–103. These two nineteenth-century publications seem to represent Ménage's projected part six and contain no material relevant to the eleventh century.

In the nineteenth century one amateur and two scholars wrote works that included short studies on Robert the Burgundian. The amateur, Bodard de la Jacopière, produced a history of Craon, the site of one of Robert's major castles, entitled *Chroniques craonaises*.[19] A marvelous book in appearance, with plates, maps, and a seemingly sound critical apparatus, the work was riddled with faulty readings of documents, an overactive imagination, and an inability to discern fact from fiction. Bertrand de Broussillon took note of these shortcomings when he published the more scholarly *La maison de Craon* in 1893, in which he included a short history of Robert the Burgundian.[20] The Abbé Angot wrote a lengthy chapter on the lords of Sablé in his monumental *Généalogies féodales mayennaises* that focused almost exclusively on Robert.[21] Both authors labored to correct many earlier errors and misconceptions, but neither was able to place Robert within the context of either the Angevin or Norman states. Robert appeared almost as an actor without stage or supporting cast.

Recently the French writer Jacques Lalubie has published a study of Sablé entitled *Une baronnie médiévale*.[22] Based on original documents, this is the most detailed reconstruction of Robert's life produced since Angot. While it falls short as a rigorous historical study, and I certainly disagree with many of the author's interpretations, it remains an interesting attempt at reconstructing Robert the Burgundian's career with verve and imagination.

Building on this historiographical base, the aim of the present work is to focus closely on Robert the Burgundian by using charters and chronicles of Robert's time, to make use of later historical works, and to put the results within the scope of our greatly expanded apprecia-

19. Didacus Antoine de Charpentier de Bodard de la Jacopiére, *Chronique craonaises,* 2d ed. (Le Mans: Monnoyer, 1871).

20. Arthur Bertrand de Broussillon, *La Maison de Craon, 1050–1480: Étude historique accompagné du cartulaire de Craon,* 2 vols. (Paris: Picard et Fils, 1893).

21. Alphonse Angot, *Généalogies féodales mayennaises de XIe au XIIIe siècle* (Laval: Librairie Goupil, 1942). The section on Robert and Sablé was published earlier as "Sablé," *Bulletin de la commission historique et archéologique de la Mayenne,* 2d series 35 (1919): 166–89. Although not often cited and prone to error, Angot's work is a treasure house of prosopographical information on the nobility of Maine.

22. Jacques Lalubie, *Une baronnie médiévale: Sablé-sur-Sarthe de l'an 1000 à l'an 1500* (Sablé-sur-Sarthe: J. Lalubie, 1994).

tion of the early development of Anjou, Maine, and Normandy.[23] This task is bolstered by studies of the surrounding territories dominated by the Angevins.[24] However, as Round said regarding his study of Geoffrey de Mandeville, "the charters granted to Geoffrey are the very backbone of my work. By those charters it must stand or fall: for on their relation and their evidence the whole narrative is built."[25]

The charters used in the present work are documents recording one or more juridical acts performed by someone in authority such as a count or a *dominus* like Robert. The texts of thousands of these charters have survived from the eleventh century. Over a hundred relate to acts involving Robert. Some of these have been edited and published, yet many exist only in manuscript form at the Bibliothèque nationale and in various departmental archives in France. The examination of these documents using the rigorous techniques developed by French medievalists for the study of charters is the cornerstone for this study.

This process produced the raw material for a study that will, it is hoped, answer a number of questions. Where did this *dominus* come from and how was he recruited? How did Robert obtain his rank? Having gained an *honor*, that is, at least one castle with the associated office, power, and wealth that went with it, how did he hold on to it? And finally, how did a *dominus* like Robert interact with the count of Anjou,

---

23. For Anjou see the works by Halphen, Guillot, and Bachrach cited above. For Normandy, studies in English include David C. Douglas, *William the Conqueror: The Norman Impact Upon England* (Berkeley: University of California Press, 1967); David Bates, *Normandy Before 1066* (New York: Longman, 1982); Eleanor Searle, *Predatory Kinship and the Creation of Norman Power, 840–1066* (Berkeley: University of California Press, 1988); John Le Patourel, *The Norman Empire* (Oxford: Clarendon Press, 1976). For a comparison of the two, see Le Patourel, *Feudal Empires: Norman and Plantagenet* (London: Hambledon Press, 1984). Little has been done with Maine since Robert Latouche, *Histoire du comté du Maine: pendant le Xe et le XIe siècle* (Paris: H. Champion, 1910; reprint, Geneva: Slatkine Reprints, 1977), but see André Bouton, *Le Maine: Histoire Économique et sociale des origines au XIVe siècle*, 2d ed., vol. 1 (Le Mans: A. Bouton, 1975), and Richard E. Barton, "Lordship in Maine: Transformation, Service and Anger," *Anglo-Norman Studies XVII: Proceedings of the Battle Conference 1994*, ed. Christopher Harper-Bill, 17: 41–63 (Woodbridge: Boydell Press, 1995).

24. For example, Barthélemy, *Société dans le comté de Vendôme*; George Beech, *A Rural Society in Medieval France: The Gâtine of Poitou in the Eleventh and Twelfth Centuries* (Baltimore: John Hopkins Press, 1964); and Noël-Yves Tonnerre, *Naissance de la Bretagne: Géographie historique et structures sociales de la Bretagne méridionale* (Angers: Presses de l'Univerité d'Angers, 1994).

25. Round, *Geoffrey de Mandeville*, v–vi.

and what effect, if any, did this have on the development of the Angevin state?

The intense scrutiny of contemporary Angevin documents produces two interesting, and I believe salutary, tendencies. One is an escape from the existing historiography centered on Normandy and William the Conqueror. Whatever the undoubted qualities of the Normans and their most renowned warlord, they were not as exceptional as past writers would have us believe.[26] Their inability to make any headway against the Angevins at a time when the Angevin state was supposedly disintegrating thus becomes a central issue. Secondly, the reader will find little discussion of "feudalism" or the "seigneurial order." These terms, however useful, are modern constructs adopted from nineteenth century scholars using sixteenth century legal conceptions of twelfth century realities.[27] By a strict reading of the evidence from Robert's own time I hope to reach a little closer to the realities of his world in the eleventh century frontier between Angevin and Norman power.

One final word about the materials used here. The language of the documents is, of course, medieval Latin. The crisp Latin of the original documents introduces us to a world that is harsher and more down to earth than the romantic imaginings of a chivalric society, but also curiously legalistic and earnestly religious. To use standard translations of key terms is to mislead; to not translate such terms leads to confusion. I have found no easy way around this problem. Most Latin terms are translated: for *miles* I have used "knight," although the reader should keep in mind that during Robert's lifetime *miles* meant nothing grander than "professional cavalry soldier."[28] *Castrum* and *castellum* I have translated as "castle," though few were of stone, and none would match the image implied by the English word. On the other hand, I have kept the Latin word *dominus* (*domini* in the plural), since Robert and the other

---

26. David Bates, *William the Conqueror* (London: G. Philip, 1989), 8–9, for example, makes the point that William can best be appreciated as one of several successful leaders in France.

27. Susan Reynolds, "The historiography of Feudalism," in her *Fiefs and Vassals: The Medieval Evidence Reinterpreted* (Oxford: Oxford University Press, 1994), 3–14.

28. P. Van Luyn, for example, in "Les *milites* dans la France du XIe siècle," *Moyen Age* 77 (1977): 8, refuses to translate *miles* and chides both Duby and Lemarignier for translating the word as *chevalier.*

Angevin holders of this rank are a central focus of this study. To translate it by the English "lord" or even French "seigneur" would make no more sense than translating "samurai" in a study of Japanese military history. I have also not translated *casamentum,* the totality of territory a *dominus* held, nor *feodum* (sometimes *fevum*) although both terms are usually translated as "fief." For somewhat the same reasons I have not modernized most of the personal names—Geoffrey for Gosfredus being one major exception.

CHAPTER ONE

Family Origins

Countess Agnes of Anjou, in a formal ceremony sometime between 1 July 1046 and 15 August 1052, bought a mill from Salomon son of Otred with the assent of the sons of Lancelin of Beaugency, Salomon's lord. It was apparently an elaborate ceremony since Agnes then gave the mill to the monastery of the Trinity of Vendôme, which had been personally founded by her and her husband, Geoffrey Martel count of Anjou. As the monk scribe labored to draw up the charter commemorating this important donation to the monastery, he came to the list of witnesses, those whose presence and memory could be relied upon to enhance the validity of the act. As he drew near the end of his list he saw a young man standing among the glittering entourage surrounding the countess and her husband. Adding him to the list of sixteen men he thought worth recording, the scribe carefully identified him for posterity as "Robert the nephew of the countess."[1] This young man would come to be known as Robert the Burgundian, *dominus* of the fortresses of Craon and Sablé, a man occupying the highest rank within the entourage of the counts of Anjou for nearly half a century.

Yet the scribe's description of him simply as "nephew of the countess" underlines a fundamental truth about the society of eleventh century France. If the people of that time were asked to identify themselves, they would likely first reply that they were Christians, and there-

1. "Rotbertus nepos comitissa," *Cartulaire de l'abbaye cardinale de la Trinité de Vendôme,* ed. Charles Métais, vol. 1 (Vendôme: Clovis Ripé, 1893), 155–56, no. 85; Guillot, *Comte d'Anjou* 2: 103–4, C 139. The word *nepos* has a broader meaning than English "nephew." Robert was Agnes's grandnephew.

after that they were members of a specific family. Their concept of "the family" might require some elucidation and might even shift as occasion demanded, but only after they had disposed of their blood connections would they start talking in the terms of ethnicity, regional origin, or political allegiance that people of our own time find so important.[2] To a large extent family in medieval society defined who a person was and the scope of the opportunities open to the individual. Family and birth mattered, and they mattered very much to Robert the Burgundian, no matter how crucial other ties and obligations might be.[3] Robert, in fact, was worth noting in the act because he was related to the countess. Descent and kinship would shape Robert, and he spent his entire career insuring that his own offspring were placed in positions of power and influence. To do this required something more than mere birthright—Robert would have to perform.

In fact it was Robert's deeds against the Normans that drew him to the attention of the Anglo-Norman historian Orderic Vitalis, who noted that Viscount Hubert of Le Mans had married Ermengard, daughter of Count William I of Nevers and niece of Robert the Burgundian.[4] Robert, whose adult life was spent in Anjou, was therefore the brother of the count of Nevers and thus a member of an illustrious family.[5] It was also an unusual family, continually casting up striking individuals who left a distinct trail in the historical record. Not the least unusual aspect was that many of these individuals were women. Indeed, one of the most striking figures of the twelfth century Angevin dynasty, Eleanor of Aquitaine, was descended from one of them.[6] Robert's political

2. In this period "kinship was a fluid concept that could be construed and employed in many different ways." Stephen D. White, *Custom, Kinship, and Gifts to Saints: The "Laudatio Parentum" in Western France, 1050–1150* (Chapel Hill: University of North Carolina Press, 1988), 16.

3. W. Scott Jessee, "The Family of Robert the Burgundian and the Creation of the Angevin March of Sablé and Craon," *Medieval Prosopography* 16 (1995): 31–67. Some of the material presented in this chapter appeared in this article.

4. Orderic, 48–49.

5. There are several studies of this family: Ferdinand Lot, "La chanson de Landri," *Romania* 32 (1903): 1–17; René de Lespinasse, *Le Nivernais et les comtes de Nevers*, vol. 1 (Paris: H. Champion, 1909); Léon Mirot, "Les origines des premiers comtes héréditaires de Nevers," *Annales de Bourgogne* 17 (1945): 7–15; Constance Brittain Bouchard, *Sword, Miter, and Cloister: Nobility and the Church in Burgundy, 980–1198* (Ithaca: Cornell University Press, 1986), 340–46.

6. D. D. R. Owen, *Eleanor of Aquitaine: Queen and Legend* (Oxford: Blackwell, 1993).

and social life would be shaped by this family and its densely woven connections with the nobility of western *Francia*.

In the twelfth century it became something of a fad to produce elaborate genealogies purporting to show the origins of important families.[7] Around 1160 Hugh of Poitiers, a monk of Vézelay, wrote such an account of the family of the counts of Nevers, the *Origo et historia brevis Nivernensium comitum*.[8] Despite its deficiencies as an historical document, it is the most complete account surviving of the family and is examined in more detail in the Appendix.

Hugh traced the origins of this family back to a member of Charles the Bald's court, Bishop Hildegarius of Autun, whose patronage allowed his nephew Landric to win the lordship of a castle in the Nivernais. This nephew's son Bodo extended the family territory and married an Angevin woman. Their son Landric then so impressed the count of Burgundy that he was made count of Nevers. How much truth is in this account has been debated, but the figure of Hildegarius seems to the be the real chancellor of Charles the Bald, Adalgarius, who was bishop of Autun by 23 February 877.[9] When compared with the surviving documentation one can postulate that the origins of the counts of Nevers go back to a supporter of Charles the Bald named Landric who held considerable land in the Mâconnais in the mid ninth century and was probably related to the bishop of Autun. There is indeed a Landric active in the Mâconnais during the ninth century, although there is no proof that he was an ancestor of the count of Nevers.[10]

The family begins to emerge more clearly in the next generation. A Bodo appears as a witness along with a Landric (eight names later) in

---

Robert's great-aunt Agnes was Eleanor's great-great-grandmother. Robert's niece, Hewise, countess of Évreux, impressed Orderic Vitalis as an extraordinary personality. See Orderic, 4: 212–13.

7. For the comital house of Anjou, see Bernard S. Bachrach, "Some Observations on the Origins of the Angevin Dynasty," *Medieval Prosopography* 10 (1989): 1–23.

8. Ferdinand Lot published a complete edition of Hugh's work in "Chanson de Landri," 1–17. The latest and best edition is in R. B. C. Huygens, *Monumenta Vizeliacensia: Textes relatifs à l'histoire de Vézelay* (Turnhout: Brepols, 1976), 235–39, hereafter cited as "Origo."

9. *Recueil des actes de Charles II, le Chauve, roi de France,* ed. Arthur Giry, Maurice Prou, and Georges Tessier, 3 vols. (Paris, 1943–55), 2: no. 382, August 867–75, and no. 420, 23 February 877.

10. The document and its implications to the family of the counts of Nevers are discussed in the Appendix.

an act of donation by Bishop Herveus to the church of Autun of land in the Nivernais on 23 April 920.[11] Several elements of Hugh's genealogy appear: a Bodo and a Landric witness an act of a bishop of Autun regarding property near Nevers. The same names reappear in an act of November 950 in which Bodo donates to the monastery of Cluny some properties in the Mâconnais he had received from his kinsman Rainald. Landric is a witness.[12] In both documents we are probably dealing with Robert the Burgundian's ancestors. Certainly all three names, Bodo, Landric, and Rainald, appear in his family. The Bodo of 920 and 950 would represent the Bodo in Hugh's account whose mother was an Angevin while Landric could be either his brother or his father.[13]

The next member of the family to appear is Robert the Burgundian's grandfather, the remarkable Landric, first hereditary count of Nevers. There is no doubt that this Landric is an historical character, nor that his father's name was Bodo, just as the *Origo et historia* claimed.[14] Landric, *gloriosus miles,* appears at Otto-William's side attesting the bishop of Nevers's donation of April 986 to the church of Saint-Cyr of Nevers.[15] Otto-William was count of Mâcon, and the charter evidence suggests a Mâconnais origin for the Landrican family.

At the time, Burgundy was almost a kingdom in its own right ruled by Duke Henry, brother of Hugh Capet. Landric appears to have risen to power as a member of the entourage of Otto-William, the duke's stepson. Otto-William was the son of Adalbert king of Lombardy and his wife Gerbergis. When Adalbert was deposed from the throne, Gerbergis fled with her son to Burgundy where she married Duke Henry.

---

11. *Cartulaire de l'Église d'Autun,* ed. Anatole de Charmasse, vol. 1 (Paris: Auguste Durand, 1875), no. 43, "Datum IX kalendas Maii, indictione VIII, anno XXIV Karoli regis."

12. *Recueil des chartes de l'abbaye de Cluny,* eds. Auguste Bernard and Alexandre Bruel, 6 vols. (Paris: Imprimerie nationale, 1876–1903) 1: no. 783, "S. Bodoni . . . S. Gisoni, S. Attoni, S. Landrici."

13. Bouchard, *Sword,* 341 n. 180.

14. He is called Landric son of Bodo by Adalbero of Laon, "Rythmus satiricus," in Claude Hohl, "Landri de Nevers dans l'histoire et dans le *Girart de Roussillon,*" published in *Chanson de geste et le mythe Carolingian: Mélanges René Louis,* vol. 2 (Saint-Père-sous-Vézelay: Musée archéologique regional, 1982), 791–806.

15. *Cartulaire de Saint-Cyr de Nevers,* ed. René de Lespinasse (Paris: Champion, 1916), no. 23; Christian Pfister, *Étude sur le règne de Robert le Pieux (996–1031)* (Paris: F. Viewig, 1885), 254; Ferdinand Lot, *Les derniers Carolingiens: Lothaire, Louis V, Charles de Lorraine, 954–991* (Paris: E. Bouillon; reprint, Geneva: Slatkine Reprints, 1975), 175 n. 5.

Having no children of his own, Henry made young Otto-William his heir to the duchy of Burgundy.[16]

When the count of Mâcon died around 980, Otto William took over the county by marrying the young widow, Ermentrude.[17] A number of scholars have believed that Duke Henry gave Otto-William the county of Nevers because the latter attested the donation of April 986 at Nevers in which Landric first appears.[18] It is more likely, however, that Otto-William attested to it merely as Duke Henry's adopted son, since the duke heads the witness list immediately after the bishop. There is no evidence that Otto-William held any title other than count of Mâcon at this time.[19] Landric's inclusion among the witnesses may simply indicate his high standing in either the duke's or the count's entourage, or it may suggest that already he had some interest in Nevers, perhaps as castellan. He definitely was not yet count of Nevers, although by 12 August 990 he is given that title by the author of the annals of Nevers.[20]

As a further mark of Otto-William's regard, Landric married the count's daughter Matilda, apparently at the same time he received the countship.[21] It would seem then that Landric owed his advance to Otto-William, who played the role ascribed to the "count of Burgundy" by Hugh of Poitiers. Landric and Matilda had three sons, Rainald his heir, Guy, and Robert.[22] Apparently he had already fathered two sons, Bodo

16. Constance Brittain Bouchard, "Laymen and Church Reform around the Year 1000: The Case of Otto-William, Count of Burgundy," *Journal of Medieval History* 5 (1979): 2. For Gerbergis's family see Bouchard, "The Origins of the French Nobility: A Reassessment," *American Historical Review* 86 (1981): 516–17.

17. René Poupardin, *Le royaume de Bourgogne (885–1038), Étude sur les origines du royaume d'Arles* (Paris: H. Champion, 1907), 414–19. For Ermentrude see Bouchard, "Origins of French Nobility," 518.

18. *Cartul. de Saint-Cyr*, no. 23; Pfister, *Règne de Robert le Pieux*, 254; Lot, *Derniers Carolingians*, 175, n. 5.

19. Poupardin, *Royaume de Bourgogne*, 233.

20. "Annales Nivernensis," in *Monumenta Germania Historica, Scriptores*, 30 vols. (Hanover, 1824–1924), 13: 89, under year 991, which Lot, "Chanson de Landri," 3, n. 2, corrects to 990 in agreement with the "Annales Vezeliacensis," published in Huygens, *Monumenta Vizeliacensia*, 218.

21. Raoul Glaber, *Rodulfi Glabri Historiarum libri quinque* 3.ii.6, in *Rodulfus Glaber Opera*, ed. John France (Oxford: Oxford University Press, 1989), 105, hereafter cited as "Raoul Glaber."

22. Rainald and Guy appear in *Chartes de Cluny* 4: 13–14, no. 2811. For Robert, see Bouchard, *Sword*, 341–43.

and Landric, but nothing is known of their mother. They first appear ten years later, too soon to be sons of Matilda, and had no claim to the countship of Nevers.[23]

Landric was now a very powerful and influential man. The *Rythmus satiricus* of Bishop Adalbero of Laon in 996, for example, refers to Landric as *architriclinus* and *dapifer,* titles indicating that Landric played an important role in Hugh Capet's court, if not actually as the count of the palace than certainly as seneschal.[24] In 993 there was a plot against the Capetian monarchy by Count Odo I of Blois and Bishop Adalbero of Laon to hand over the throne to King Otto III of Germany. Odo's reward would be the title of "Duke of the Franks," while Adalbero would receive the archbishopric of Reims. The plot was discovered. When Adalbero was accused before King Hugh and his son Robert, one of his supporters offered to defend the bishop's honor by combat. Count Landric intervened, coolly advising the bishop's man to wait until he had heard the truth from Adalbero's own lips before risking his life. When Adalbero refused the combat it was taken as an admission of guilt and he was arrested.[25]

According to Adalbero's obscure poem, Landric was involved in two scandals at the royal court. One occurred when Count Odo of Blois died on 12 March 995 and Robert the Pious decided to marry his widow Bertha, even though she was his cousin. The poem implies that Landric played a role in introducing Bertha to Robert's bed in the face of the disapproval of the church and King Hugh. In return Landric expected to receive the town of Provins as promised him by the new royal mistress. Once Bertha slept with the king, though, her promise slept also. Landric was furious.[26] Adalbero, who throughout the poem maliciously

23. *The Cartulary of Flavigny, 717–1113,* ed. Constance Brittain Bouchard (Cambridge: Medieval Academy of America, 1995), 86–88, no. 29; *Cartul. de St-Cyr,* 88–89, no. 47.

24. Ferdinand Lot, *Études sur le règne de Hughes Capet et la fin du XIe siècle* (Paris: E. Bouillon, 1903; reprint, Geneva: Slatkine Reprints, 1975), 421–22 n. 6.

25. Richer, *Histoire de France,* ed. and trans. R. Latouche, 2 vols. (Paris, 1937), I.IV, c. 95–98. Although the bishop's refusal could have several interpretations, it was taken by contemporaries to be an admission of guilt; see *Hugues Capet,* 170–72.

26. *Rythmus satiricus,* str. 24, ed. G. A. Hückel, "Les Poèmes de Adalbéron," in *Mélanges d'histoire du Moyen Age,* ed. R. Luchaire, vol. 13 (Paris, 1901). The interpretation is Lot's, *Hugues Capet,* 108–10 and n. 4 for str. 22–26.

refers to Landric as Achitophel, Absalom's unfortunate counselor, obviously took great delight in Landric's frustrated anger.[27]

The second affair involved Landric's Burgundian father-in-law, Otto-William. Duke Henry's first wife, Gerbergis, the mother of Otto-William, no longer appears after April 986. By 11 May 993 Henry had married Gersende, daughter of William-Sancho, duke of Gascony.[28] According to the *Rythmus satiricus,* Landric somehow induced the duchess to return to her homeland, either by her own will or because Duke Henry repudiated her.[29] It is almost certain that Otto-William was behind Landric's meddling in the duke's marriage. As Henry's adopted heir he would naturally fear and resent Henry's second marriage with its possibility of producing a direct heir. Landric's motivation is easy to understand since he seems to have owed his advancement to Otto-William and would always remain one of his staunchest supporters.[30]

Landric's loyalty to his benefactor soon involved the family in a major crisis. When Duke Henry died on 15 October 1002, Otto-William claimed the duchy of Burgundy as the duke's adopted son and heir. King Robert would not accept this and invaded Burgundy with a large army of Normans. In the ensuing war Landric distinguished himself as Otto-William's chief supporter. He quickly seized the fortress of Auxerre from Bishop Hugh, a staunch royalist. When King Robert invaded Burgundy in the spring of 1003, Landric was able to resist all attempts to retake Auxerre and the royalist forces were forced to retreat.[31]

Nevertheless, Otto-William felt constrained to come to some sort of agreement with the king.[32] Apparently on his own, Landric continued to resist until the king laid siege to Auxerre a second time and took it in

---

27. Achitophel advised Absalom to revolt against his father, King David. When his advice was ignored he hanged himself in frustration. See 2 Samuel 16–17.

28. She is mentioned in a charter dated "anno dominicae incarnationis DCCCCXCIII, regnantibus Hugone et Rotberto," published by Chifflet, *Lettre touchant Beatrix, comtesse de Chalon,* 198, no. 170. A knight named Bodo also attests the act and is probably Landric's son. Cf. Lot, *Hugues Capet,* 417–18, n. 6.

29. Lot, *Hugues Capet,* 416.

30. Maurice Chaume, *Les origines du duché de Bourgogne,* 2 vols. (Dijon: Imprimerie Jobard, 1925), 1: 458–59; Lot, *Hugues Capet,* 419; Poupardin, *Royaume de Bourgogne,* 223.

31. Chaume, *Origine du duché de Bourgogne,* 1: 476; Raoul Glaber, *Historia,* 78–81, 2.viii.15.

32. Raoul Glaber, 80–81, 2.viii.15.

November 1005.[33] Robert, however, felt it was still necessary to reconcile himself to such an obdurate foe and promised Landric his daughter
Advisa as a wife for Landric's eldest son Rainald.[34] This couple would be
the parents of Robert the Burgundian.

It is unlikely that the final arrangements for the wedding took place
until after January 1016, when the king felt secure enough in the duchy
to visit Dijon.[35] Since in 1016 Advisa could only have been twelve or thirteen years old, at the oldest, it may be assumed that the marriage was
not actually consummated until several years later, probably 1020–
1023.[36] The birth of her first child, William, would probably be around
1020 at the earliest. Robert, the second son, was born then a few years
after 1021 at the absolute earliest and probably several years later.[37]
Robert was followed by two more brothers, Henry and Guy. This
scheme of births obviously does not allow for daughters, miscarriages,
or deaths in infancy, about which nothing is known. Ties to his family
evidently remained strong throughout Robert's life. He would work
closely with Guy and remembered him and Henry in his pious donations. Evidence of attachment to William is difficult to document, but
it is telling that the marriages of William's children served to benefit
Robert's political and diplomatic plans.

Of Robert's relations with his parents we know nothing. He certainly would have been raised with stories of his grandfather, the glorious
knight who first won a countship, then battled a king to a standstill and
inspired hatred in the heart of a bishop.[38] Nearly two centuries after

33. Chaume, *Origines du duché de Bourgogne*, 1: 478, citing *Chronicon breve Autissiodorense*,
"Anno MV, Robertus rex civitatem Autissiodorum obsedit in vigilia sancti Martini, IV idus no-
vembris."

34. See W. Scott Jessee, "A Missing Capetian Princess: Advisa Daughter of King Robert II
of France," *Medieval Prosopography* 11 (1990): 1–16, for the identity of the bride.

35. Jessee, "Missing Capetian Princess," 13 n. 44.

36. By September 1001 Bertha was no longer married to the king; by 25 August 1003 Constance was Robert's new bride. See Pfister, *Robert le Pieux*, 64. Guillot, in *Comte d'Anjou* 1: 26,
however, sees the end of 1003 as merely the *earliest* date the marriage could have taken place.
It probably occurred in 1004. For the likely date of Rainald's wedding, see Yves Sassier,
Recherches sur le pouvoir comtal en Auxerrois du Xe au début du XIIe siècle, vol. 5 of *Cahiers
d'Archéologie et d'histoire* (Auxerre: Société des Fouilles Archéologiques et des Monuments
Historique de l'Yonne, 1980), 40.

37. Jessee, "Origins," 47.

38. In his *Rythmus satiricus* Bishop Adalbero called Landric the new Eglon, king of Moab,

Landric's death his reputation had entered the realm of popular legend and *chansons de geste*.[39] The personalities of his parents are unrecoverable, except that Raoul Glaber refers to Rainald as "bold" *(audax)*, a man who feared that his own "boldness" *(audatia)* would hasten his death after being wounded in combat.[40] One other hint concerns Robert's maternal great aunt Agnes. Years later when she was countess of Poitou a charter remarks that she laid seige to a castle and took it, "as was her custom." She was clearly a forceful, competent personality. In such a family Robert would certainly have been raised in a tradition of military accomplishment combined successfully with great daring and audacity. More than lands and titles, this would be his heritage.

There can be no doubt, at any rate, that he was raised to be what the people of the time called simply a *miles*, a "soldier." It meant the type of armed horseman usually translated as "knight." In his adult life charters often referred to Robert as one of the Angevin count's *fideles*, his "faithful"; *meus fidelis* Geoffrey Martel calls him.[41] There is no adequate English translation for this term—it does not mean "vassal," for example. One of his chief duties as a *fidelis* is clear from the documents. He is called a *miles, de meis militibus*, "one of my soldiers."[42] It is likely that Robert was regarded as a "knight" as soon as he was of age, that is, his fifteenth year. We underestimate the level of military and political skill eleventh century men (and a few women) of the arms-bearing class had at their command. The training they received from an early age was rigorous and broad, involving whatever techniques of command deemed necessary. This training, like medieval warfare in general, has been seriously misunderstood by scholars.[43] Robert would have learned to ride well, to handle the equipment of a mounted warrior (hauberk,

---

who ruled the Israelites until assassinated. See Judges 3: 12–23 to fully appreciate Adalbero's hatred.

39. Lot, "Chanson de Landri," 13.

40. Raoul Glaber, 212–13, 4.ix.26.

41. *Cartul. Trinité de Vendôme*, I: 175–77, no. 96.

42. Paul Marchegay, *Bibliothèque de l'École de Chartes* 36: 396–97. See also Livre noir de Saint-Florent, Bib. nat. n.a. lat. 1930, fol. 137v.

43. For a well documented refutation of the opinion that medieval warfare was little more than a brawl see John Gillingham, *Richard Coeur de Lion: Kingship, Chivalry and War in the Twelfth Century* (London: Hambledon Press, 1994), 211–41. Gillingham is speaking of the twelfth century but his comments apply to the eleventh as well.

helmet, shield, lance, and sword) and the basic techniques of command, tactics, and strategy, at least as they were perceived in the second quarter of the eleventh century. Robert, the son of a count and grandson of a king was no mere knight. When he is called a *miles* the title should be construed as a function he fulfilled when needed, not as a rank.

This training aside, all that is known about Robert's early years within the comital family of Nevers is his reconstructed birth order and his name, both of which may have stories to tell. The eldest son was named William, after Otto-William his great grandfather, called simply William by contemporaries. At first glance this is odd. Why not name him after the traditional Landrican names of Landric and Rainald or the traditional names of the royal family of his mother? The name may have served two purposes, the first to indicate that in their hearts the Landricans still adhered to the party of their benefactor, Otto-William. More certainly it was to indicate that William was the intended heir to at least the county of Nevers, since it had probably been a part of Matilda's dowry.[44]

Robert, the second son, was named after his maternal grandfather, King Robert II. This name might well indicate that Robert was expected to inherit from the maternal inheritance, which in this case would be the county of Auxerre.[45] Such an arrangement would be in keeping with the common, although by no means universal, practice of the eleventh century whereby the chief honor with the patrimonial lands went undivided to the eldest son, leaving the maternal or collateral lands to at least one of the younger sons.[46] Robert grew up knowing

44. Ernest Petit, *Histoire des ducs de Bourgogne de la race capétienne*, vol. 1 (Paris: E. Thorin, 1885), 71; Poupardin, *Royaume de Bourgogne*, 224–25; Pfister, *Robert le Pieux*, 254.

45. Although Landric had taken Auxerre by force, the royal recognition of his son Rainald as count of Auxerre has been assumed to be included in Advisa's dowry as part of the peace settlement. The "Annales Vizeliacenses," in Huygens, *Monumenta Vizeliacensia*, 218, is explicit on this point, "Robertus rex Altisiodorum obsedit et dedit cum sorore Rainaldo filio comitis Nivernensis Landrici." Petit, in *Hist. des ducs de Bourg.* 1:90–91, believed that Auxerre was actually divided, with Landric's family retaining only the northern part with the town of Auxerre. This would include the title of "count of Auxerre." Sassier, however, in *Pouvoir comtal*, 31–41, argues that Rainald only received the countship of Auxerre in 1032.

46. Andrew W. Lewis, *Royal Succession in Capetian France: Studies on Familial Order and the State* (Cambridge: Harvard University Press, 1981), 30. Lewis observed, however, that cadets could also be married to heiresses, put into church office, or even disinherited.

that he was only one step away from inheriting the patrimonial inheritance of Nevers. Possibly he even expected to receive the countship of Auxerre for himself.

If Robert truly expected the Auxerrois or some other holding in his father's honor, such hopes were frustrated when Count Rainald was killed by a "knight of low birth" while battling against Duke Robert of Burgundy over control of Auxerre on 24 May 1040.[47] Rainald's sudden death left his eldest son, William, as count of Nevers. In this instance the succession followed strict primogeniture for there is no evidence of Robert, Henry, or Guy holding any property anywhere in Burgundy. This is odder than might first appear. It is true that their grandfather Landric had left all that he had gained at Nevers to Rainald, his eldest son by Advisa, but he was careful to see that Bodo, a son by another woman, was married to the heiress of Vendôme. At about the same time Landric's patron, Otto-William, divided his inheritance, giving the county of Mâcon to his eldest son and Burgundy to his second son.[48]

It is clear that both Robert and his brother William were comfortable with this habit of making provision for younger sons, since both of them did this for their own children. Robert much later was to divide his honor, consisting of two separate inheritances, between his two eldest sons, Rainald and Robert. William went even further and associated his eldest son Rainald with the comital title of Nevers, made his second son William the count of Tonnere, and made his youngest son Robert both bishop and count of Auxerre.[49]

The Landrican family then, for the generations of Robert and his grandfather, followed the general rule of succession as described in Andrew Lewis's study of Capetian inheritance patterns. The father provided for cadets in order to keep them loyal to the eldest, who was the principle heir. "It was necessary to endow [the younger sons] as befitted their birth and to satisfy their ambitions, yet not to dismember the duchy or strip the heir to the honor."[50]

47. Raoul Glaber, 212–13, 4.ix.26; "Annales Vizeliacenses," 220–21; "Origo," 238.
48. Lewis, *Royal Succession*, 31. For a slightly different interpretation of Otto-William's inheritance see Petit, *Hist. des ducs de Bourg.*, 1: 110–11.
49. Bouchard, *Sword*, 346, and Lespinasse, *Nivernais*, 258–59.
50. Lewis, *Royal Succession*, 41.

Landric, Robert the Burgundian, and William I were all extraordinarily long-lived and had time to associate their own adult sons with them in their titles, as Rainald had time to do with William.[51] Rainald was killed, however, before definite arrangements could be made for his second son, Robert. William emerged as the sole heir to his father's lands and titles. Either Robert was not yet old enough to assume the comital title to Auxerre (if such were the plan), or the family judged it unwise to split the two titles in a time of crisis. More likely William was simply too inexperienced and his hold on Nevers too weak to prosecute the war and he was forced temporarily to leave the Auxerrois in the hands of Duke Robert as the price of peace in 1041.[52] Whatever actually happened, William became count while Robert and his younger brothers Henry and Guy were left with nothing in the Nivernais. The cadets of the Landrican family were to have no future in the land of their father and had to seek their careers elsewhere.

Robert, or his adult guardians, saw to it that his future home would be in Anjou. This move to western *Francia* had a solid foundation in his family's connections with the Angevin region that perhaps stretched back to the time of Robert's grandfather. According to the *Origo et historia,* the original ninth-century Landric had married an Angevin.[53] The same source claims that the count of Anjou, who in this case must be either Geoffrey Greymantle or Fulk Nerra, was present when Otto-William made Landric count of Nevers.[54] True or not, this represents a family tradition of Angevin ties with the house of Nevers stretching back to its founding by Landric. There is no doubt that Count Landric, Robert's grandfather, had close ties with Fulk Nerra. A brief overview centered on Robert's grandmother, Matilda, reveals just how intertwined the family relations were. Matilda had a stepson who married Fulk Nerra's daughter, a sister who married Fulk's son, two grandsons who served Fulk's son and grandsons, and a half-sister whose son married another of Fulk's daughters and consequently was the grandmoth-

51. Lespinasse, *Nivernais,* 224.
52. Petit, *Hist. des ducs de Bourg.,* 1: 143, 160; Sassier, *Pouvoir comtal,* 46.
53. "Origo," 237, although Lot, "Chanson," 9, doubts the validity of this story.
54. "Origo," 238.

er of two of Fulk's grandsons, each of whom would be count of Anjou.[55]

To start with the first of these, Landric's son Bodo married Fulk's daughter Adele around 1005. This marked an alliance between Landric and Fulk to meet the Blésois-Capetian threat on Fulk's eastern border. Seen through Angevin eyes, Landric's exploits in the Burgundian war of 1003–1005 were the efforts of a brave ally relieving pressure on the Angevins.[56] Since Adele's mother was Elizabeth, daughter of Count Burchard the Venerable of Vendôme, Bodo's wife was the heiress of the county of Vendôme. When Burchard's son and heir, Bishop Rainald of Paris, died sometime between 1016 and 1020, Adele became the sole heir to the county. Instead of Bodo receiving any rights to Vendôme, however, Adele transferred the whole honor of Vendôme to her father, Fulk, during the minority of Bodo's eldest son, Burchard II the Bald.[57]

In 1031, supposedly at the will of the "boy" Burchard, his mother, Adele, and King Henry I of France, the honor of Vendôme was given to Fulk Nerra's son, Geoffrey Martel. Burchard and his mother henceforth held the county from Geoffrey.[58] Shortly thereafter first Burchard and then his father Bodo died, leaving the second son, Fulk l'Oison, to hold Vendôme from Geoffrey Martel.[59] Fulk l'Oison would eventually become count of Vendôme.

55. The half-sister Beatrix was the daughter of Matilda's mother's first marriage to Alberic count of Mâcon. Beatrix married Geoffrey of Château-Landon and had a son named Geoffrey. This Geoffrey married Ermengard, Fulk Nerra's daughter, who in turn bore Geoffrey the Bearded and Fulk Rechin. Robert the Burgundian and the two counts therefore shared the same great-grandmother. Bouchard, "Origin of French Nobility," 511. The other relations are explained below.

56. See Bachrach, *Fulk Nerra*, 73–74, for the Angevin view of this alliance.

57. Guillot, *Comte d'Anjou* 1:27 and Halphen, 63, both basing their reconstruction of events on charters nos. 1 and 6 of the *Cart. Trinité de Vendôme*. Bodo was never styled count. Angevin lack of regard for Bodo's position may have been because Bodo's mother was Landric's first wife or mistress and lacked the status of Matilda's sons born after Bodo's marriage to Adele. The transference of Vendôme to Adele's father could only have been done with the full support of King Robert. See Bachrach, *Fulk Nerra*, 159, for the bargaining that secured this support.

58. *Cartul. Trinité de Vendôme* 1: 14–18, no. 6. Guillot, *Comte d'Anjou*, 1: 44, explains that Henry thought it better to give Vendôme to the house of Anjou than to have it held by the house of Blois, whom he perceived as the more immediate threat. At this time Blois also had claims on Vendôme.

59. *Cartul. Trinité de Vendôme* 1: 14–18, no. 6. Guillot, *Comte d'Anjou*, 1: 48–49; Penelope Johnson, *Prayers, Patronage, and Power: The Abbey of la Trinité, Vendôme, 1032–1187* (New York: New York University Press, 1981), 3–5 and genealogy on 191.

It is important to keep in mind that King Henry was Robert the Burgundian's uncle, and that Robert, Burchard the Bald, and Fulk l'Oison were first cousins. Control of Vendôme was an essential part of Fulk Nerra and his son's strategy, so that their relationship with this branch of the Landrican clan was of paramount importance. Robert's brother Guy was later to exploit this connection brilliantly by serving as count of Vendôme during the minority of Burchard III, son of Fulk l'Oison.[60]

This important connection to the house of Anjou was greatly strengthened by the marriage of Agnes, daughter of Otto-William and thus Robert's great-aunt, to Geoffrey Martel. Agnes's first husband, William the Great duke of Aquitaine and count of Poitou, had given her two sons, Peter and Geoffrey. Both sons would become counts of Poitou as William VII and William VIII.[61] When Duke William died Agnes promptly married Geoffrey Martel, Fulk Nerra's son and heir, on 1 January 1032.[62] It is possible that Robert the Burgundian was actually raised by Agnes in the Poitevin court.[63] It was already a widespread custom for sons to spend their teen-age years training in the household of a more powerful family.[64] Close ties between Robert's family and the Poitevins is indicated by Robert's own son Robert Vestrol being sent to serve with the court of Poitou.[65]

In fact, the whole Angevin idea of "empire" revolved around "a flexible and multifaceted network of family connections."[66] Precisely such connections with the house of Nevers were an important thread to Geoffrey's ambitions. As a simple matter of biological descent, Robert the Burgundian personified virtually all of these considerations. In one body he was nephew of the king of France, grandnephew of Geoffrey's

---

60. *Livre des serfs de Marmoutier,* ed. André Salmon (Tours: Ladavèze, 1864), no. 9, where Guy is styled "count." Cf. Halphen, 309, and Guillot, 1: 293.

61. In fact all four sons of William the Great would successively become counts of Poitou. See Alfred Richard, *Histoire des comtes de Poitou,* 2 vols. (Paris: A. Picard, 1903), 1: 220.

62. "Obituaire de Saint-Serge," in *Recueil d'annales angevines et vendômoises,* ed. Louis Halphen (Paris: A. Picard, 1903), 107; Guillot, *Comte d'Anjou,* 1: 45; Halphen, *Comté d'Anjou,* 56–57; Ménage, *Histoire de Sablé,* 68–69.

63. Angot, *Généalogies féodales,* 720. Ménage, *Histoire de Sablé,* 70, believed the same, although there is no evidence for it.

64. Van Luyn, "Milites dans la France," 194.

65. Richard, *Comtes de Poitou,* 1: 379.

66. Bernard S. Bachrach, "The Idea of the Angevin Empire," *Albion* 10 (1978): 298.

wife, nephew of Geoffrey's brother-in-law Bodo, and cousin of the heirs to the countships of Vendôme and Poitou and the duchy of Aquitaine. Such credentials would be sure to attract Geoffrey's attention since it was an Angevin technique of long standing to recruit supporters from relatively distant regions where the count had interests or ambitions.[67] Robert's entry into Geoffrey's entourage must be considered in this light. His birth would provide an entry to the count's service, it would be up to Robert's own innate abilities to prove he was worthy of more.

With these family connections Robert, a landless younger son from Nevers, along with his younger brothers Henry and Guy, were ensured a warm welcome within Geoffrey Martel's entourage.[68]

67. Geoffrey Greymantle (960–87), for instance, made effective use of such a technique. Bernard S. Bachrach, "Geoffrey Greymantle, Count of the Angevins, 960–987: A Study in French Politics," *Studies in Medieval and Renaissance History* 7 (new series, 1985): 8.

68. Henry and Guy do not appear until after 14 January 1056 and then only in the train of their more successful older brother. See *Cartulaire de l'abbaye de St-Aubin d'Angers*, ed. Arthur Bertrand de Broussillon, 3 vols. (Paris: A. Picard, 1903) 2: 171–74, no. 677. Henry plays no further role although it has been assumed that he was lord of Lion-d'Angers and father of Geoffrey of Vendôme. Guy would be an important figure in Fulk Rechin's entourage but by 11 January 1081 was a monk of Chaise-Dieu, *Chartes de Cluny* 4: 715–16, no. 3580.

CHAPTER TWO

Service Under Geoffrey Martel

Robert the Burgundian came to Anjou as a result of his great-aunt's marriage to Geoffrey Martel in 1032. At what point in his life he joined Agnes's entourage is unknown, but he was undoubtedly still a very young man, possibly even a child when he first met the future count of Anjou. If he had been raised at his father's court, he spoke the *langue d'oïl* of northern France with a distinctive Burgundian accent.[1] He would always be known in Anjou as "the Burgundian." Once ensconced in Anjou Robert found it a place of splendid opportunity for a man of military prowess and prudent judgement. Under the formidable Fulk Nerra, Angevin control had expanded over Vendôme, the Gâtinais, Maine and was steadily advancing on Tours. The viscount of Thouars and the count of Maine were both within the count's patronage while his own daughter was the countess of Vendôme. From a small territory dominated by others during the late Carolingian period, Anjou had become by Robert's arrival a vast territorial principality capable of projecting its power into Normandy in the north, Blois in the east, Brittany in the west, and Poitou in the south.[2]

While it is tempting to assume that Robert entered Geoffrey's entourage at the time Geoffrey married Agnes in 1032 or shortly thereafter, the first sure evidence for Robert's presence in Anjou comes in an

---

1. In the eleventh century the spoken dialects of northern France had not diverged as much as they later would. The dialect of Burgundy would not have differed markedly from that of Anjou although peculiarities of pronunciation and vocabulary would have been noted. Peter Rickard, *A History of the French Language*, 2d ed. (London: Routledge, 1989), 39.

2. Dunbabin, *France in the Making*, 186.

act dated between 21 June 1040 and 1 April 1046 in which he is called *Allobros Robertus,* using a more learned word for "Burgundian."[3] A woman of obvious rank and property named Hadoisa made a donation to the nunnery of Ronceray in the presence of "the noble prince Geoffrey, then ruling the city of Angers with his most excellent mother and his celebrated wife Agnes."[4] Of the four witnesses Robert is listed second, after Fulk of Bouère but before two provosts in Angers. This is a relatively restricted witness list, of whom two were merely comital officials of the city. The highest ranking member of the group, Fulk of Bouère, was neither a *dominus* nor a castellan at this time. The relatively low rank of the witnesses suggest that they were members of the count's household. If so it is significant that Robert appears among them. Fulk of Bouère and his son were to appear later in a number of Robert's own acts. Even so early Robert was apparently part of the count's household, forging ties with men who were to play important roles in Angevin affairs for years to come.

Robert then was in Geoffrey's service probably by the time Fulk Nerra died on 21 June 1040, leaving Geoffrey as the count of Anjou.[5] At the time of Fulk's death Robert would have been about 17 years of age at the most, a young, inexperienced, and landless member of the count's household. It was probably at Geoffrey's side that Robert received the training that would make him a *miles,* a soldier, or as we would say, a knight, in the entourage of a count famous for his military skill. Any soldier of Count Geoffrey Martel would have found rich opportunities to impress his lord in the two decades following 1040. So grueling was Angevin service that a priest of the cathedral at Angers complained of being "exhausted by the many affairs of war and labor" under Fulk and Geoffrey, "those most warlike princes."[6] Unfortunately this

3. *Cartulaire de l'abbaye du Ronceray d'Angers (1028–1184),* ed. Paul Marchegay (Paris: A. Picard, 1900), no. 237. For these terms as Robert's nicknames see Jessee, "Family of Robert the Burgundian," 36.

4. "[A]nte nobilis principis Gaufridi, tunc cum sua excellentissima matre ac inclita conjuge Agnete Andegavinam urbem regentis." *Cartul. du Ronceray,* no. 237.

5. Halphen, *Comté d'Anjou,* no. 10, n. 1.

6. "Ego Burchardus . . . sub iisdem bellicossimis principibus multis defatigatus bellorum et laborum negotiis." Burchard the treasurer of St-Maurice d'Angers in a document dated 21 June 1040–1046 before March. See Yves Chauvin, ed., *Premier et second libres des cartulaires de*

chapter of Robert's life is completely closed to us. Despite a disputed chronology the course of Geoffrey's military campaigns can be traced at least in outline, but Robert's role is hidden. The Burgundian's subsequent success in being rewarded by Geoffrey, however, indicates that he was a conspicuous participant in Geoffrey Martel's military affairs.

Robert very likely was present when Geoffrey crowned the decades long drive into the Touraine by capturing Count Tetbald of Blois on 24 August 1044.[7] At one blow the Angevins gained Tours and the remaining castles in the Touraine of Ile-Bouchard, Château-Renault, and Saint-Aignon, all of which required new garrisons and commanders.[8] The count's special care to control all the castles within the Angevin state afforded Robert an opportunity that requires some explanation.

In his drive to protect and expand his nascent state, Fulk Nerra had skillfully utilized an interlocking system of fortifications as a base for offensive and defensive warfare. This network of castles was to ensure the security of Anjou throughout the eleventh century.[9] While the advantages of such a policy were great, it required putting the newly created or acquired castles in the hands of experienced commanders, which of necessity conferred great power and responsibility upon the garrison commanders.[10] The count would therefore need a large pool of trained, competent officers who would be, above all, loyal to the count. Without such men all of the Angevin military engineering would have been useless. Geoffrey even more than his father seems to have understood that his castellans could usurp control of the castles and weaken comital control. He was extremely circumspect about the amount of freedom given to his officers in command of castles.[11]

---

l'abbaye Saint-Serge et Saint-Bach d'Angers, 2 vols. (Angers: Presses de l'Université d'Angers, 1997) 1: 67, no 51.

7. Halphen, *Comté d'Anjou,* 47–48; Guillot, *Comte d'Anjou,* 1: 63 n. 280.

8. Guillot, *Comte d'Anjou,* 1: 63 n. 281.

9. Dunbabin, *France in the Making,* 186–87. The best explanation of Fulk's castle building strategy is Bachrach, "Angevin Strategy of Castle Building," 533–60. A broader discussion of castles is Gabriel Fournier, *Le Château dans la France médiévale: essai de sociologie monumentale* (Paris: Aubier Montaigne, 1978), 100–148.

10. Guillot, *Comte d'Anjou,* 1: 297, discusses this danger. Guillot stressed the role of the growing power and independence of the castle commanders in the later decline of comital power.

11. Bachrach, "Castle Building," 537.

Unlike the Angevins' perennial enemies, the house of Blois, who allowed their subordinates considerable independence, it was always Geoffrey's policy to keep strict control of his castellans so that they could provide military and political support to comital plans. This was perhaps the advantage that explains Geoffrey's victory, and the conqueror was determined to install equally loyal commanders in the Touraine.[12] This led to the replacement of the Blésois commanders with men loyal to Geoffrey in an eviction so complete as to strike contemporaries as remarkable.[13] It was a process that would continue elsewhere in the Angevin state whenever Geoffrey distrusted a commander.

Raoul Glaber recorded a contemporary opinion for a more spiritual explanation for the Angevin success: Geoffrey had carried into battle the banner of Saint Martin, a powerful saint peculiarly associated with Tours, his final resting place. His troops won a bloodless victory when Tetbald's soldiers, their vision distorted by divine influence, saw the Angevin forces gleaming in supernatural white and fled in terror.[14] If the story reflects an attitude among the Angevins ascribing their victory to Saint Martin, it must have had a notable impact on young Robert, who later in life would show a marked regard for the saint's "Greater Monastery," the *Majus monasterium* or simply Marmoutier.

In 1044 Robert would have found at Tours a remarkable series of communities devoted to the cult of Saint Martin strung along the banks of the Loire. Within the walls of Tours itself was the cathedral with its archbishop. One mile west of the cathedral was the basilica of Saint Martin behind the walls of Châteauneuf, the "New Castle." Across the river on the north bank of the Loire and two miles east lay the great Benedictine abbey of Marmoutier, one of the most powerful monasteries in western *Francia*.[15] While Count Tetbald kept some control of the abbey Angevin influence there, established years earlier,

---

12. Guillot, *Comte d'Anjou*, 1: 313. Guillot suggested that tight control over his garrison commanders was the crucial advantage Geoffrey had over the Count of Blois.

13. Jacques Boussard, "L'éviction des tenants de Thibaut de Blois par Geoffrey Martel, comte d'Anjou, en 1044," *Le Moyen Age* 69 (1963): 141–49.

14. Raoul Glaber, 129–30.

15. Sharon Farmer, *Communities of Saint Martin: Legend and Ritual in Medieval Tours* (Ithaca: Cornell University Press, 1991), 17–19.

would continue to grow.[16] Marmoutier would henceforth be the premier monastery within the Angevin state, while the archbishop of Tours would be the most important ecclesiastical leader. Robert the Burgundian's religious life would be an expression of the symbiotic relationship between the religious centers of Tours and the counts of Anjou.[17]

That Robert played a role in the new regime in the Touraine is evident in an act in which he participated at the castle of Château-Renault, involving Rainald, the newly installed Angevin commander of the castle.[18] Some time between the capture of Tours and 15 August 1052 a judgement was made by Count Geoffrey and Countess Agnes concerning Rainald's right to the tolls of Saint-Laurent-en-Gâtines. Of the nine witnesses, Robert is listed sixth after castellans and officials of the Vendômois, and just before a forester, the provost of Angers, and a chaplain.[19] Whatever deeds he may have performed while serving the count during the fighting for the Touraine, Robert was not yet preeminent among the count's followers.

At roughly the same time as the preceding act Robert appeared in a donation of Countess Agnes in favor of the monastery of the Trinity of Vendôme, where he is expressly called "the countess's nephew" and appears as the first witness after the participants of the act. His higher ranking here appears to be directly related to his kinship with the donor. Thus in all three of his first appearances in Anjou Robert is present with his great-aunt, underscoring the importance of this relative to Robert's career.

Yet these three juridical acts, with their carefully noted and formalized relationships among the participants, illuminate one fact of crucial importance to Robert's life. He was accustomed to being in the count's

16. For early Angevin ties, see Steven Fanning, *A Bishop and his World before the Gregorian Reform: Hubert of Angers, 1006–1047* (Philadelphia: American Philosophical Society, 1988), 59–60.

17. Farmer, *Communities,* 71, on this relationship.

18. Château-Renault had been confiscated from its former commander, Wircherius, and given to Rainald of Château-Gontier. See Boussard, "Éviction," 144.

19. *Cartul. Trinité de Vendôme,* I: 146–47, no. 77. The witnesses preceding Robert were Salomon of Lavardin, Geoffrey of Preuilly, Nihard of Montoire, Odo Rufus, and Matheus of Montoire. Most of these men were castellans associated with the Vendômois and can be found in Johnson, *Prayers,* 20, and passim.

presence and the count was accustomed to seeing him there. He was familiar with the count's business and had the opportunity to meet the important figures who surrounded the count. In a world where personal contact counted for so much, the significance of this can hardly be overstated. More pointedly, since Robert was a knight, there can be no doubt that his military role mirrored his juridical role as a witness to comital acts. He was a soldier who campaigned with his count and had ample opportunity to distinguish himself before the count's eyes.

Robert and the Angevin soldiers had hardly adjusted to their brilliant success in the Touraine when they were called upon to reassert their lord's control over the county of Maine. This long-standing claim involved the overlordship of the count of Maine and some control over the appointment of the bishop of Le Mans.[20] Angevin dominance was clearly evident under Count Fulk Nerra when Count Herbert Wake-Dog of Maine served the Angevin count faithfully at the battle of Pontlevoy in 1016.[21] When Herbert later proved an obstacle to Nerra's plans, the Angevin simply imprisoned him in 1025 and took over the government of Maine for two years.[22] This coup was facilitated by Fulk's acquiring the allegiance of the viscount of Le Mans, the bishop of Le Mans, and the *domini* of Craon, Château-Gontier, Sablé, Le Lude, Château-du-Loir, and Bellême, the first three of which would have great importance in Robert's life.[23]

Count Fulk consolidated his domination over Maine by peeling away its southwestern territories and integrating them into the northwestern salient of his own elaborate system of fortifications. The western anchor of this salient was the fortress of Craon, roughly ninety kilometers west-southwest of Le Mans. The lords of Craon may have been attached to the Angevin cause as early as 965. The eastern anchor was the castle of Sablé less than forty-five kilometers southwest of Le

---

20. Bachrach, *Fulk Nerra*, 143. According to Bachrach, Count Hugh of Maine submitted to Fulk before 1014.

21. Latouche, *Maine*, 54.

22. Fulk Rechin would later write of Fulk Nerra, "Ipse enim acquisivit Cenomannicum." "Fragmentum historiae Andegavensis," in *Chroniques des comtes d'Anjou et des seigneurs d'Amboise*, ed. Louis Halphen and René Poupardin (Paris: A. Picard, 1913), 276, hereafter "Fragmentum historiae."

23. Bachrach, *Fulk Nerra*, 173–76.

Mans. This castle also fell under Fulk's control. In order to connect the two into an interlocking system, Fulk constructed a castle named Château-Gontier between them on the Mayenne river, twenty kilometers east of Craon and thirty kilometers west of Sablé. An attack on one of these fortresses would be met by an attack from one or more Angevin castles located an easy day's ride from each other. This comprised the northwestern shield, vital to the defense of Angevin territory, with Sablé on one wing pointing towards Le Mans (see map). When Fulk gained the loyalty of the lord of Bazougers he had an advanced outpost a days ride north of Sablé, flanking Le Mans on the route towards Mayenne.[24] Maine was virtually in a state of subjugation to the count of Anjou.[25]

A final element to domination of Maine was the powerful Bellême family. From strongholds in the nearly inaccessible hill country on the border between Maine and Normandy this family was generally able to maintain its independence from more powerful neighbors.[26] In the period before 1040, the family had succeeded in extending their control so that they held Bellême itself from the king of France, Alençon from the duke of Normandy, and Domfront from the count of Maine, which effectively meant from the count of Anjou.[27] The Bellême therefore controlled what was the northern analogue in Maine of the southern Angevin line of Craon, Château-Gontier, and Sablé. As long as Angevin commanders held the southern line, no one could completely push the Angevins out of Maine, but while the Bellême remained independent, Angevin control of Maine would be incomplete.

By 1035 the head of the family was Ivo, lord of Bellême and bishop of Sées.[28] In the 1030s though it appears that this pivotal local power was maintaining its independence from both Normans and Angevins by

24. Bachrach, "Angevin Castle Building," 554. The early history of Craon and Sablé will be treated in more detail below.

25. "Un état de vassalité," Latouche, *Maine*, 54. See also Bachrach, "Angevin Castle Building," 555.

26. Kathleen Thompson, "Robert of Bellême Reconsidered," *Anglo-Norman Studies*, ed. Marjorie Chibnell, 12: 277; Jacques Boussard, "La seigneurie de Bellême aux Xe et XIe siècle," in *Mélanges d'histoire du moyen âge dédiés à la mémoire de Louis Halphen* (Paris: Presses universitaires de France, 1951), 52–53.

27. Douglas, *William the Conqueror*, 58.

28. Bates, *Normandy*, 69–70; Douglas, *William the Conqueror*, 58.

stressing its allegiance with the king of France.[29] So powerful were they that Angevin control of Maine was dependent on the support of the Bellême as much as on the viscounts of Le Mans.[30] This support was weakened, however, when a cousin of these two influential families, Gervasius of Château-du-Loir, became bishop of Le Mans in December 1035. Geoffrey, who was temporarily in control of the Angevin state while his father completed his third pilgrimage to Jerusalem, was obdurately opposed to Gervasius because he was a staunch partisan of the house of Blois. The situation was further complicated by the death of Count Herbert at almost the same time, leaving his minor son Hugh IV as count of Maine. A struggle for the guardianship of the young count ensued between the boy's great-uncle Herbert Bacon on behalf of Anjou and Bishop Gervasius on behalf of Blois. The resulting war with Gervasius upset the alliances with the viscounts of Le Mans and the Bellême as Gervasius's kinsmen, and lost the key fortresses of Château-du-Loir and Malicorne, which were held by Gervasius.[31] Fulk was furious when he returned, refused to support his son's effort in Maine and, by mid-November 1037, Gervasius triumphantly entered Le Mans.[32]

Angevin control over Maine was seriously weakened, although Count Geoffrey managed to keep control over the northwestern shield of Craon, Château-Gontier, and Sablé. Fulk's death on 21 June 1040 allowed Geoffrey to pursue his own policy in Maine. Forging a close alliance with King Henry against Blésois interests he was able to have the king grant him control of the bishopric of Le Mans, probably in 1041.[33] While this power had no immediate use, it would give legitimacy to whatever moves Geoffrey might take against Bishop Gervasius. All this would affect Robert's future career.

29. Guillot, *Comte d'Anjou*, 1: 82–84, noted the loyalty of the house of Bellême to the king until 1060.

30. Bachrach, *Fulk Nerra*, 229–30.

31. Bachrach, *Fulk Nerra*, 231–32. Malicorne was held from Gervasius as *dominus* of Château-du-Loir by Waldin I.

32. *Actus pontificum Cenomannis in urbe degentium*, eds. Gustave Busson and Ambroise Ledru, Archives historique du Maine, vol. 2 (Le Mans: Société de la Société, 1902), 364–65. See Bernard S. Bachrach, "Henry II and the Angevin Tradition of Family Hostility," *Albion* 16 (1984): 125 n. 80 and *Fulk Nerra*, 229–35, for the best analysis of the complex political maneuvering due to the split between Fulk and Geoffrey. See also Halphen, *Comté d'Anjou*, 69–70, and Latouche, *Maine*, 27.

33. Guillot, *Comte d'Anjou*, 1: 58–60 and 64.

Robert would have been a witness to Geoffrey's next move since it once again involved his family. On 24 November 1043 Robert's first cousin once removed, Agnes the daughter of Countess Agnes and William V of Aquitaine, married Henry III king of Rome, soon to be crowned Emperor.[34] By this marriage Geoffrey ended his alliance with the king and signaled his support for the emperor. With a power base in Anjou, marriage ties to the Aquitaine, Burgundy, Nevers, and now the Empire, Robert's lord became a most dangerous enemy for King Henry.[35] When war finally broke out in Maine the king would therefore be expected to intervene against the Angevins.

Although King Henry had earlier given control of the bishopric of Le Mans to Count Geoffrey, the latter could not actually control the man who was already bishop. When Bishop Gervasius arranged the marriage of Count Hugh IV of Maine to Bertha, daughter of Geoffrey's archenemy Odo of Blois and widow of Alan III count of Brittany, Angevin patience reached the breaking point. The marriage took place between 1045 and 1047, perhaps while Count Geoffrey was absent in Rome for Christmas 1046.[36] By now Robert and the Angevins were fit and ready for another campaign.

Count Geoffrey launched his troops directly against the bishop's stronghold of Château-du-Loir. Although, according to Gervasius, the Angevins "devastated all the property along the circuit of the castle with iron and fire" and burnt at least part of the castle, they were not able to take the fortress itself.[37] Despite this failure, the Angevins soon managed to capture the bishop himself and imprison him. This was ei-

---

34. "Obituaire de Saint-Serge," *Recueil d'annales angevines,* 107.

35. Guillot, *Comte d'Anjou,* 1: 60–63; J. Dhondt, "Henri Ier, l'Empire et l'Anjou (1043–1056)," *Revue belge de philologie et d'histoire* 25 (1946–1947): 88. Guillot critiques Dhondt's analysis but accepts the central thesis that the marriage represented a break with the king.

36. Guillot, *Comte d'Anjou,* 1: 66.

37. The quote is taken from a charter in Gervasius's own words describing damage done to the church at Château-du-Loir. "Orto autem bello inter comitem Gaisfredum et dominum illius castelli, cum idem comes cuncta per circuitum castelli ferro et flamma disperderet res quoque hujus quam dicimus ecclesie ipsas rapere ac vastare sicut et coetera minime formidavit, ita ut plerique de canonicis, inopia coacti, diffugerent et ecclesiam cui deserviebant desererent," *Cartulaire de Château-du-Loir,* ed. Eugène Valée, Archives historiques du Maine, vol. 6 (Le Mans: Société des archives historiques du Maine, 1905): 15, no. 27. The *Actus pontificum,* 365, says simply that the fortress was burnt, "castellum Lir igne cremavit."

ther late 1047 or early 1048.[38] Although Gervasius would later obtain his freedom, his imprisonment marked the end of the first phase of fighting in Maine.

Robert must have watched with some trepidation as the outlines of a new opposing coalition emerged. While the Angevins had been occupied with putting down the bishop of Le Mans, King Henry had used considerable diplomatic skill to detach the emperor from his alliance with Count Geoffrey. This move was completed by October 1048, when the king and emperor met at Ivois.[39] At about the same time Duke William of Normandy realized that with control of Maine the Angevins were now a threat to his duchy. William would show himself to be the Angevins' most dangerous opponent in the eleventh century. Once the duke was allied with King Henry it was clear that the coming war for Maine would test warriors like Robert to the limit. It would involve a coalition of the Angevins' most implacable enemies and result in a full scale invasion of Angevin territory. Robert, his antipathy towards the Normans perhaps heightened by the memory of Norman depredations against his grandfather in 1003,[40] would certainly have expected that the rewards would be great for Angevin knights who fought well for their count and survived. Although what little is known of this campaign is uncertain and disputed, it marks a pivotal change in Robert's life.[41]

It is a measure of Geoffrey Martel's audacity and the aggressiveness of his followers that the Angevins struck the first blow. Pushing deep into Maine, Angevin forces took Domfront, dependent from the house

38. *Actus pontificum*, 365; Halphen, *Comté d'Anjou*, 71.

39. Guillot, *Comté d'Anjou*, 1: 68. For details of King Henry's diplomacy see Dhondt, "Henri Ier, l'Empire et l'Anjou," 91–97.

40. Raoul Glaber, *Historia*, 78–81, 2.viii, 15, tells how Norman troops spearheaded the king's attack on Auxerre. They were stopped from burning down the monastery of St. Germain only by divine intervention.

41. The exact dates and sequence of events in this war are in dispute. The reconstruction here follows Guillot, *Comté d'Anjou*, 1: 69–75. For others see Latouche, *Maine*, 28–30; Halphen, *Comté d'Anjou*, 71–76, and above all Douglas, *William the Conqueror*, 59–60 and 383–90. Bates, *Normandy*, 255–57, has attempted to pick out the merits of both Guillot's and Douglas's chronology, placing the Mouliherne campaign in late 1049 and the Domfront/Alençon campaign in 1051–1052. He finally concluded, however, that the material is too flimsy for categorical assertions.

of Bellême and the count of Maine. Next they captured Alençon, held by Bellême from the duke of Normandy.[42] Since King Henry was now closely allied with the duke and bitterly opposed to Count Geoffrey, these victories at the expense of the Bellême family were interpreted as rebellion against the king when the news reached the royal court in mid-September 1049.

In October the king raised an exceptionally large force and launched a general campaign against the Angevins. This force included a large contingent led by Count Tetbald of Blois while Duke William attacked the Angevins at Domfront. Learning of the king's attack, Geoffrey hurriedly abandoned Domfront and Alençon to the Normans and moved south to face the royal forces. The fighting then centered around the fortress of Mouliherne which was taken by the king.[43] It was probably in the wake of this defeat that Geoffrey attacked a royalist garrison at Sainte-Maure, some sixty kilometers southeast of Mouliherne. A notice from Marmoutier says that "a knight named Hugh the Burgundian was killed at the castle of Sainte-Maure when the king held it and Count Geoffrey besieged it."[44]

Hugh the Burgundian almost certainly was fighting for the Angevin cause and possibly was connected to Robert's family.[45] His brothers were Drogo and Matheus, both of Montoire, a castle in the Vendômois. Presumably Burgundians like their brother, they both appear in the entourage of the Angevin counts.[46] Matheus, in fact, was with Robert the

42. William of Poitiers, *The "Gesta Gvillelmi" of William of Poiters*, ed. and trans. by R. H. C. Davis and Marjorie Chibnall (Oxford: Clarendon Press, 1998), 23; Guillot, *Comte d'Anjou*, 1: 70, believed that Geoffrey took these strongholds from the Bellême family, faithful to King Henry.

43. Halphen, *Comté d'Anjou*, 72 n. 1, placed the taking of Mouliherne in autumn of 1048 rather than late 1049 or early 1050 as Guillot does. He did, however, place the taking of Domfront by the Normans during the winter in late 1049. William of Poitiers, 25, specifically mentions the rigors of a winter campaign. The few details seem to fit Guillot's reconstruction better. Guillot, *Comte d'Anjou*, 1: 72–73, n. 320. Bates, *Normandy*, 255, agrees with Guillot.

44. Bib. nat. ms. lat. 12878, fol. 187 r°v°, Dom Housseau, 12², no. 6740, published in *Cartulaire de l'abbaye de Noyers*, ed. C. Chevealier, Mémoires de la Société archéologique de Touraine, vol. 22 (Tours: Guilland-Verger, Georget-Joubert, 1872), no. 479. "Quidem miles nomine Hugo Burgundio praenominatus apud castellum Sanctae Maure cum a rege teneretur et a Gaufrido comite odsideretur interfectus est."

45. It may be significant that in later years the author of the *Chronique de Parcé* would confuse Robert the Burgundian with a Hugh the Burgundian and Hugh the Breton Eater.

46. *Cartul. Trinité de Vendôme*, 1: 146–47, no. 77; 271–73, no. 157; 273–76, no. 158; *Recueil des actes de Philippe Ier*, ed. Maurice Prou (Paris: Imprimerie nationale, 1908), 396, no. 158.

Burgundian at Château-Renault where they both witnessed a judgement of Count Geoffrey and Countess Agnes after the conquest of Tours.[47] In addition Hugh was said to hold an alod at *Chassagnia*, three miles from Le Nouâtre. Although originally an Angevin fortress in the Touraine, Le Nouâtre pertained to the counts of Vendôme and would later be held by Robert's brother Guy when Guy was acting count of Vendôme.[48] It is likely that the Montoire family were Burgundians established in the Vendômois when Robert's uncle Bodo the Burgundian married the countess of Vendôme. They may then also have been relatives of Robert the Burgundian.[49] Whoever he was, Hugh represents only one of the casualties in a war that swept from Domfront in the north to Sainte-Maure in the southeast.

Fighting of such intensity could not last for long given the limited resources of this era. The struggle soon ended with the Angevins holding their own. Then on 26 March 1051 Count Hugh IV of Maine died.[50] A popular uprising in Le Mans expelled Hugh's widow and welcomed the Angevins into the city.[51] The imprisoned Bishop Gervasius recognized that the Angevin party in Maine was too strong. Giving up Château-du-Loir in return for his freedom, he retired to the Norman court to foment trouble for the Angevins. Château-du-Loir and Malicorne were back within the Angevin defensive web, correcting Geoffrey's misstep of 1036. King Henry, now having more to fear from the growing power of his erstwhile ally Duke William, concluded a rapprochement with Count Geoffrey before 15 August 1052.[52]

47. *Cartul Trinité de Vendôme*, 1: 146–47, no. 77 dated 24 August 1044–15 August 1052. Matheus was listed just before Robert the Burgundian. Among the other witnesses was Nihard of Montoire, probably the father or uncle of Matheus, Drogo, and Hugh.

48. "Guido Nevernensis, dominus Nugastri," *Chartes vendômoises*, ed. Charles Métais (Vendôme: Société archéologique, scientific et littéraire du Vendômois, 1905), no. 53 and *Cartul. de Noyers*, no. 118. Also Guillot, *Comte d'Anjou*, 1: 22 and 460, n. 20, and 2: C 309, published in *Cartul. de Noyers*, no. 50. For Angevin control during Fulk Nerra's time, see Bachrach, "Castle Building," 539.

49. Guillot, *Comte d'Anjou*, 1: 72–73, argues that Hugh the Burgundian was a partisan of the Bellême family fighting with the royal forces because his lord for the alod of *Chassagnia* was Hugh the son of Seinfred bishop of Le Mans, a relative of the Bellêmes. This seems too tenuous a connection to negate the demonstrated ties of the Montoire family, ensconced in the Vendômois and Touraine, to the house of Anjou. At this time Count Geoffrey held Vendôme despite the claim of Fulk l'Oison.

50. Halphen, *Comté d'Anjou*, 75 n.1; Latouche, *Maine*, 29 n. 1.

51. *Actus pontificum*, 366.

52. At this date Geoffrey Martel and his new wife Grace appear before the king at Or-

The outcome of this war dramatically altered Robert's fortunes and was to define the theater of operations for the remainder of his life. The most immediate and important change for Robert was an enormous increase in his power and prestige within Geoffrey Martel's entourage. Around 1050, but certainly before 26 March 1053, Geoffrey Martel gave Robert the castle of Craon, the western anchor of the northwestern shield.[53] Robert was not yet thirty when his fortunes were thus completely changed. No longer a mere household retainer, a simple knight in the service of the count, Robert was now the castellan of a major castle, with all the power, influence, and wealth that went along with the rank and represented his honor. Robert's service to the count must have been considerable to warrant such a reward, his loyalty and skill unquestioned to be entrusted with such a responsibility. Although Countess Agnes likely had a hand in the decision to grant Craon to her nephew (she is known to have advised her husband on the disposition of a church there), family connections and influence do not entirely explain it.[54] It is impossible to believe that the pragmatic and competent Geoffrey Martel would have entrusted an unproven and inexperienced knight, even one so well connected as Robert, with the guard of a stronghold as important as Craon. A brief examination of the fortress and its strategic position within the broader Angevin strategy will indicate why.

Craon was located at the apex of the Angevin line of defense as it pointed into the juncture of Brittany, Maine, and Normandy (see map).[55] Its territory, in fact, was once Breton and had only later been acquired by the Angevins. In the ninth century Craon was merely a small village within the territory of the Breton city of Nantes. It belonged to the nunnery of Saint-Clement of Nantes whose abbess was the sister of

---

leans. Halphen, *Comté d'Anjou*, no. 111; Guillot *Comte d'Anjou* 2:C 141. Bates, *Normandy*, 77 surmises that it was only Henry's fear of William that induced him to come to terms with Geoffrey Martel.

53. *Cartul. Trinité de Vendôme*, 1: 175–77, no. 96.

54. She urged Geoffrey to give the church of Saint-Clement at Craon to the monastery of the Trinity of Vendôme at nearly the same time that Robert received the castle. *Cartul. Trinité de Vendôme*, 179–82, no. 98.

55. Bachrach, "Castle Building," 554, and Tonnerre, *Naissance de la Bretagne*, 298–99.

Count Lambert of Nantes.[56] In 851 Lambert was expelled from the city by Duke Erispoé of Brittany and fled to Craon[57] where he built a strong fortress on the banks of the Oudon River.

Today the site has been turned into a church parking lot looking down on a quiet little park along the river, difficult to imagine as a strong defensive position. Yet while the ridge upon which the fortress was located is low, it dominates the undulating countryside and overlooks a narrow part of the river that would later be bridged. The surrounding countryside was covered then in forests and sparsely populated, a suitable lair for an outlaw count.[58] Until its demolition in 1604, the castle of Craon was able to pose a serious threat to the Angevin region during the wars of religion.[59] From this stronghold Lambert was able to raid the surrounding territory in Anjou as far as the confluence of the Mayenne and the Loir.[60] Lambert was assassinated by Count Gauzbert of Maine on 1 May 852, and by August of that year Craon and its territory were ceded by Charles the Bald to Duke Erispoé.[61]

The Bretons were not able to hold on to this territory in the confusion and civil wars that followed the death of their Duke Alan Twisted Beard in 952.[62] By the death of Geoffrey Greymantle the Angevins completely dominated the counts of Nantes and consequently the castle of Craon. Craon's lord, Suhard the Old, first appears in the entourage of the Angevin count as early as 965.[63] Suhard may have been a Breton lord

56. "Credo . . . tunc temporis Namnetici territorii vicum, jure Sancti Clementis civitatis Namneticiae monasterio pertinentem, cui abbatissa, hujus Lamberti soror, nomine Doda, praesidebat," in the *Chronique de Nantes (570 environ–1049),* ed. René Merlot (Paris: A. Picard, 1869), 29.

57. *Chroniques de Nantes,* 27–28. The chronicle's text gives the name of the Breton duke as Nominoé, but this is corrected by the editor Merlet to Erispoé, his son.

58. Personal observation and Bodard de la Jacopière, *Chroniques craon,* 2–3.

59. André Joubert, "La demolition des château de Craon et de Château-Gontier d'après les documents inédits (1592–1657)," *Revue historique et archéologique du Maine* 17 (1885): 66–100.

60. *Chroniques de Nantes,* 30, "castrum super ripam Uldonis composuit, et occipiens inde in dominatu suo Andegavense territorium, sicut Meduana in Ligerim descendit."

61. See *Chroniques de Nantes,* 30 n. 3, for Lambert's death.

62. *Chroniques de Nantes,* 106 n. 1.

63. Bachrach, "Castle Building," 554 n. 71. Cf. *Cartul. Saint-Aubin,* 1: nos. 20, 34, 38, 48, 132, 281, 281, and *Cartulaire noir de la cathédrale d'Angers,* ed. Charles Urseau (Angers: Germain and Grassin, 1908), no. 18. For early Angevin relations with the counts of Nantes, see Bachrach, "Geoffrey Greymantle," 6–7 and 10–11.

who had entered the entourage of Geoffrey Greymantle or an Angevin whom Greymantle installed at Craon to ensure its control. Whichever is the case, for the next hundred years the counts of Rennes in claiming the whole of Brittany would remember that Craon had once been Breton. Its chief defensive function therefore was to block Breton aggression from the west and to provide support for other Angevin strongholds nearby.

Suhard the Old held Craon until the first decades of the eleventh century.[64] He was succeeded by his son Warin who in turn was succeeded by his younger brother Suhard.[65] With Suhard the Younger the family lost Craon for reasons that are obscure. All that is known is that between 21 June 1040 and 26 March 1053 Geoffrey Martel confiscated the *honor dominicum* of Craon and held it in his own hands.[66]

The exact cause of this confiscation has been obscured by the rejection of later legends, not redacted until the fifteenth century, that claimed Warin lost the honor of Craon when he swore fealty to Count Conan II of Rennes, portrayed as an implacable foe to the Angevins.[67] Angot, for example, believed to see the cause of the confiscation in the succession of Suhard, the younger brother, to his brother Warin, leaving Warin's daughter Bertha out of the inheritance. For Angot this would be a violation of feudal inheritance.[68] This is, however, a classic case of interpreting eleventh century events by nineteenth century conceptions of feudalism.

In fact, there is evidence to support the legendary account. The

----

64. *Cartul. Trinité de Vendôme*, I: 175–77, no. 96 (14 October 1006–29 July 1027), in which Suhard the Old grants the church of Saint-Clement de Craon to the monastery of Saint-Aubin. This church would become the subject of an extended dispute between Saint-Aubin and the Trinity of Vendôme.

65. *Cart. Trinité de Vendôme*, I: 175–77, no. 96, where Warin as lord of Craon reclaims Saint-Clement from Saint-Aubin. In *Cartul. de Saint-Aubin* I: 185–87, no. 160, an act is authorized by the *domini* of Craon, "first Warin and then Suhard." This seems to mean that Warin was lord first and after his death Suhard succeeded him rather than that they were lords at the same time and merely authorized the act one after the other. Cf. Bertrand de Broussillon, *Craon* I: 19.

66. *Cart. Trinité de Vendôme*, I: 175–77, no. 96, "honorem Credonis in manu mea dominicum habui." Geoffrey gave Saint-Clement to the monastery of the Trinity of Vendôme in this period before 15 August 1052.

67. These accounts are discussed more fully in the next chapter.

68. Angot, *Généalogies féodales*, 723.

chronicle of the abbey of Sainte-Croix de Quimperlé clearly reads that in 1048 "Credonenses Conanum recipiunt" or "the people of Craon received Conan."[69] Therefore it seems quite likely that in 1048 Suhard did turn his allegiance to a hostile count of the Bretons who was "received" at Craon. There already existed at least one point of contention between the castellan of Craon and the count of Anjou. At some earlier period Warin rendered himself suspect to the Angevins when he took the church of Saint-Clement at Craon away from Saint-Aubin d'Angers, and this dispute may have continued under Suhard.[70] Whatever the reason, the reception of Conan at Craon in 1048 can be seen as the proximate cause of Geoffrey Martel's confiscation, exactly as the legends assert. It is certain that, for whatever reason, Geoffrey Martel felt he could not trust such an important post to the Suhard-Warin clan and replaced them with a more reliable commander, Robert the Burgundian.[71] Robert was always aware that he held Craon by the authority of Count Geoffrey's word alone, not by hereditary right. As long as mem-

69. "Cartulaire de l'abbaye de Quimperlé," British Museum, ms. Egerton 2802, fol. 41v. Angot and other nineteenth century historians seem to be unaware of this since they relied on a published edition of the cartulary where the editors amended the line without comment to read "MXLVIII, Redonenses Conanum recipiunt," *Cartulaire de l'abbaye de Sainte-Croix de Quimperlé*, eds. Léon Maitre and Paul de Berthou, 2d ed. (Paris: H. Champion, n.d.), 103. I am assured by Prof. Christopher Lewis of the University of Leeds that the manuscript is quite clear. See also Hubert Guillotel, "La place de Châteaubriant dans l'essor des châtellanies bretonnes (XIe–XIIe siècles)," *Mémoires de la Société d'Histoire et d'Archéologie de Bretagne* 66: 20–21 n. 58.

70. *Cartul. Trinité de Vendôme*, 1: 175–77, no. 96, 175–77, "Warinus . . . sibi illam [ecclesiam] resumpserat, et ad clericorum redactam in manu sua tenuerat." Cf. Bertrand de Broussillon, *Craon*, 1: no. 6. Later documents, however, seem to contradict this, claiming that Warin actually wanted to enhance his father's gift of Saint-Clement to Saint-Aubin but was prevented from doing so by Fulk Nerra; see Archives Maine-et-Loire, H360 fol. 2. Either way, St-Clement's appears to be a locus of dispute between the lords of Craon and the Angevin counts.

71. There may have been no more suitable male heirs when Suhard the Younger died. Suhard the Elder had one other son, a bastard named Warin, who became a monk at Marmoutier, *Cartul. de St-Aubin*, no. 737. A Lisoius, son of Suhard, appears in the time of Duke Alan of Rennes, but nothing else is known of him. See P. Hyacinthe Morice, *Histoire ecclésiastique et civile de Bretagne* (Guingamp: Benjamin Jollivet, 1835), 369. There was a Hamelinus, son of Suhard, who would later authorize a donation of Robert's son and consequently must have had some claim to Craon, Archives Sarthe, H 359. Despite Hamelinus, Warin's daughter Bertha was generally regarded as the next in line to inherit. Since she was married to Robert of Vitré, a Breton lord, any devolution of Craon to her would have been unacceptable to Geoffrey Martel. See Bertrand de Broussillon, *Craon* 1: 21.

bers of the Suhard-Warin clan lived, Robert's claim to Craon could therefore be contested.

So great was Robert's loyalty to Geoffrey now that it withstood the shock of Geoffrey Martel's divorce of Agnes sometime between 6 January 1049 and 15 August 1052. Geoffrey seems to have taken this step because Agnes had failed to produce any children for him. While this alone would have justified the divorce, it can also be seen as a necessary first step in a reconciliation of Geoffrey with King Henry. To do this cost the count his tie with the emperor through his stepdaughter and most of his influence over the Aquitaine. Yet there were advantages Geoffrey reaped from his new association with the king that were well worth the price.[72] The king's enmity had nearly caused a disaster in 1052; his friendship was now necessary to successfully confront the Normans.

Whatever the cost for Geoffrey, the repudiation of Agnes had the potential for destroying all that Robert had achieved in his years of service to his great-aunt's husband. Instead it seems to have enhanced his fortunes. Both Agnes and Geoffrey had their own entourages, which had in many ways merged over nearly two decades of union. Robert for one had entered Angevin service due to his connection with Agnes. As Agnes and Geoffrey pulled apart, so too did their respective entourages, many of whom must have felt divided loyalties. Agnes returned to Poitiers and by 1053 relations between Geoffrey and Agnes's eldest son, William Aigret, had almost degenerated into open warfare.[73] If Robert was to follow his family loyalty, he could very well end up fighting his benefactor and therefore losing Craon.

With this fact evidently in mind, Robert remained firmly in the Angevin camp while other Poitevin *fideles,* such as Aimeric of Rancon and William of Parthenay, remained equally loyal to Agnes and her sons.[74] It appears that William, at least, received a tangible inducement for his faithfulness since he gained possession of a fortress at Germond

---

72. Guillot, *Comte d'Anjou,* 1: 77–78, goes so far as to suggest the king was the "inspirateur" of the divorce.

73. Richard, *Comtes de Poitou,* 1: 258–9; Halphen, *Comté d'Anjou,* 61.

74. Guillot, *Comte d'Anjou,* 1: 90 n. 402.

to strengthen his control of the Gâtine.[75] There were, however, other men of Poitevin background such as John of Chinon and his brother Barthelemy who stayed loyal to Geoffrey Martel. Barthelemy was castellan of Mirebeau and provost of Saint-Pierre de Poitiers.[76] Between 14 November 1052 and 13 November 1053 he became archbishop of Tours with Geoffrey Martel's approval. Guillot sees this as a means for Geoffrey "to consolidate the position of an important vassal of Poitevin origin who had remained loyal to him and had not followed, like so many others, his former wife."[77]

For Robert to have done other than John and Barthelemy would have made no sense, even considering the strength and importance of family alliances in the eleventh century. Robert held an honor, a complex of rights, properties, followers, and obligations, from the count. To alienate himself from this man would have destroyed all that he had achieved. Situated on Anjou's northwestern border far from Agnes's major supporters in Poitou, his only alternative would have been to turn to the Normans and their Manceaux supporters. After years of struggle against Norman interests in Maine it is doubtful that Robert considered such an option.

Robert's continued devotion to Geoffrey Martel was splendidly rewarded with the gift of Sablé. This fortress, so crucial to Angevin defense on the northwestern march, came into Robert's possession when he married the castle's heiress, Advisa, called *Blanca*, "the White."[78] This was probably done around 1052, but certainly before 29 December 1059. It is of course not provable that the marriage was an effort to shore up or reward Robert's loyalty, but the timing is certainly suggestive.

Once Robert became *dominus* of Sablé, he took care to learn the his-

---

75. Beech, *Rural Society*, 48, 130–31, observes that the house of Parthenay was usually loyal to Anjou and may have come from the Touraine or Anjou.

76. Guillot, *Comte d'Anjou*, 1: 89–90.

77. Guillot, *Comte d'Anjou*, 1: 90. "Pour Geoffrey Martel, le choix d'un tel archevêque de Tours avait l'avantage évident, au lendemain de sa séparation d'avec la comtesse Agnès, de consolider la position d'un important vassal d'origine poitevine qui lui était resté fidèle et n'avait pas suivi, comme tant d'autres, son ancienne épouse."

78. *Cartul. de Saint-Aubin*, 1: 436–37, no. 376 and *Cartul. manceau*, 2: 69–76, no. 5.

tory of the place, as well as details of his rights, from those he called the *seniores et antiquiores,* the "lords and elders," of the region. He found that the fortress at Sablé, the *castellum* as it was called in Latin, was built some time before 1015 by Count Hugh III of Maine.[79] The site of the new fortress was well chosen. Located on a steep promontory rising over the confluence of the Erve, Vaige, and Sarthe rivers, it was a natural defensive position. Even today the eastern bluff overlooking the Sarthe is a forbidding, steep drop. Construction of the present day château in the eighteenth century smoothed out the western side into a pleasant park sloping gradually down to the Vaige, but local tradition has it that it was once as steep as the other.[80] A gate, remains of a deep fosse, and one tower, supposedly marking the spot of the original castle, still remain.[81] Although the Sarthe was navigable at this point, an island splitting the Sarthe into two smaller channels made it easier to control traffic and to bridge. In addition the confluence of the Vaige and the Sarthe at the foot of the castle made an ideal location for mills, an important source for a lord's income and an economic magnet to attract the local population to Sablé.[82]

Before 15 October 1015 the count of Maine gave Sablé to Geoffrey, brother of Radulf viscount of Le Mans.[83] When he had grown old,

79. Robert's accounts, referred to here as "Testimony" and "Judgement," are discussed in Chapter 5. There is no reason to assume, as Ménage, *Histoire de Sablé,* 18, did, that the construction was done by the viscount rather than the count.

80. "Promenade pittoresque et archéologique dans la vallée de la Sarthe a travers le canton de Sablé," *Le Journal de Sablé* (15 September 1907).

81. For an illustration of the fortifications as they appeared before they were demolished, see Paul Cordonnier, "L'ancien château de Sablé d'après un ancien plan," *Revue historique et archéologique du Maine,* 2d series 46 (1966): 61–66. A seal impression showing the fortress in the thirteenth century shows a high donjon towering over a crenelated outer wall. See Archives Maine-et-Loire, G 562, fol. 6.

82. In *Cartul. manceau,* 2: 78, no. 7, Robert gives such a mill to Marmoutier. It was located on a small channel, probably man made, connecting the Sarthe and the Vaige.

83. "Testimony" and "Judgement." For this family see Latouche, *Maine,* 128–29. Ménage, *Histoire de Sablé,* 3–6 and 15–18, claimed there was an earlier family holding Sablé who used the names Hugh and Salomon. Angot, *Généalogies féodales,* 715–17, demonstrated that Ménage had created this family out of a misunderstanding of the texts. There was a family of Hugh-Salomon from Sablé, but they only appear during Robert's own lifetime. See *Cartul. manceau,* 2: 59–63, no. 2; *Cartul. Trinité de Vendôme,* 1: 428–29, no. 276; Archives Maine-et-Loire, H 110, no. 113; *Cartul. manceau,* 2: 81–85, no. 2, also published in *Cartulaire de l'abbayes de Saint-Pierre de la Couture et de Saint-Pierre de Solesmes,* ed. by the Benedictines of Solesmes (Le Mans: Monnoyer, 1881), 40, no. 30. Nothing ties this family to the original tenth century lords of Sablé.

Geoffrey acquired the *villa* of Solesmes, a few miles upriver, from his brother the viscount. After establishing a monastery there he donated it and other properties to Saint-Pierre de la Couture in Le Mans.[84] By this time the population of the castle had grown, or rather died off, at such a rate that the cemetery within the walls became too crowded. To alleviate this problem Geoffrey ordered that the bodies of the castle garrison be buried at the new monastery.[85]

In some unexplained fashion Robert's wife Advisa came to be the only surviving heir to Sablé. Her father Geoffrey and his wife Adeleis had several sons, the eldest of whom, Drogo, authorized the donation of Solesmes. Two other brothers, Burchard and Lisiard, were with Drogo to witness the count of Maine's confirmation of the donation.[86] Robert and Advisa later made a major donation for the soul of her brother Geoffrey.[87] Aside from this last son Geoffrey, whom Angot identifies as a monk of Marmoutier, it is not known what became of the male heirs of Sablé.[88] Considering the heavy fighting in Maine in the late 1040s and early 1050s it is quite possible that Drogo fell in combat.[89] It is certain, however, that when Robert married Advisa he became the uncontested *dominus* of Sablé by virtue of his wife's hereditary claim.

The two acquisitions of Craon and Sablé and all the territory pertaining to them marked a significant change in Robert's status. He was now a powerful and important figure on the northwestern march of Anjou. His position was such that his support and counsel would mean much to whoever would be count of Anjou. This enhanced respect is evident in the earliest surviving act of Robert after his acquisition of Craon. Far from being merely one witness among many, he is a major participant acting in concert with the main figures of Angevin authori-

---

84. "Testimony" and "Judgement," between 13 June 1006 and 25 October 1015. For the charter of this gift, published in *Cartul. de la Couture*, no. 8, see Stephen Fanning, *A Bishop and his World*, 100–101, no. 3.

85. "Testimony."

86. Fanning, *A Bishop and his World*, 100–101, no. 3; *Cartul. de la Couture*, no. 8 (the donation) and no. 9 (the confirmation).

87. *Cartul. manceau*, 2: 63–66, no. 3.

88. Angot, *Généalogies féodales*, 719.

89. Less dramatically, the heirs could have as likely fallen to disease or injury. Bib. nat., ms. lat. 5446, pp. 280–81, for example, speaks of Hugh of Ballon being killed by accident, "as is common among knights" ("sicut mos est militum"), and the father of one of Robert's wards was killed by a fall from a horse; see Chauvin, *Cartul. de St-Serge*, 1: 8–10, no. 7.

ty: Count Geoffrey Martel himself and Bishop Eusebius of Angers. His new position is literally spelled out: *Robertus, dominus castri Credo,* "Robert, lord of the castle of Craon."[90] His power is evident, in that along with the count and the bishop he gives his official authorization to a donation of a church pertaining to the castle of Craon.[91] In return he is paid 30 pounds of *denarii*. Robert now commanded considerable resources of his own, and was no longer a dependent of the count's household.

For the length of his life Robert was to remember who was responsible for this success. He would describe Count Geoffrey simply as the man "who gave me my honor."[92] Robert also named one of his sons after the count and continually made donations on behalf of Geoffrey's soul.[93] This sense of indebtedness is the only indication of how he felt about the origins of his success. In the more than one hundred extant documents in which Robert appears, there is no evidence of Robert possessing any property or rights before his acquisition of Craon and Sablé. Despite his high birth, Robert owed everything to the personal gift of his count, Geoffrey Martel.

Now that Robert was one of the major Angevin commanders on the border with Maine, his major concern would be the continuing Norman threat from the north. In this respect Robert's position as a marcher lord facing the Normans was greatly enhanced now that Count Geoffrey had been reconciled to King Henry. In the warfare that soon broke out Robert was part of a strong Angevin-Capetian coalition.[94] His command of the key Angevin fortresses on the northwestern border with Maine dictated that he be heavily involved in the succeeding events.[95]

90. *Cart. de St-Aubin* 1: 185–87, no. 160, dated 14 January 1056–26 December 1059.

91. The church is Saint-Martin of Vertou in Lion-d'Angers, given to Saint-Aubin by Alberic the son of Guy the Treasurer of Saint-Maurice, a powerful individual in his own right. *Cart. de St-Aubin* 1: 185–87, no. 160.

92. *Cartul. de St-Aubin* 2: 353, no. 880.

93. Robert's son Geoffrey is mentioned in *Cartul. manceau,* 2: 63–66, no. 3 and 78, no. 7; the donations for Geoffrey's soul in no. 3; *Cartul. de St-Aubin* 2: 353, no. 880; Bertrand de Broussillon, *Maison de Craon,* no. 89.

94. See Douglas, *William the Conqueror,* 62–65, for the Norman point of view.

95. Mayenne was actually the northernmost Angevin stronghold, yet it was too far advanced to be adequately supported by the system of fortifications built up by Fulk Nerra and

At the beginning of February 1054 the Angevins invaded Normandy in conjunction with a larger Capetian force. Robert may have accompanied the Angevin expedition or else stayed in the region south of Le Mans to "encourage" the Manceaux in their loyalty. From his fortress at Craon he or his lieutenants would also be expected to prevent any incursions from the Bretons. Sablé would not have been used as a staging base for the invasion of Normandy since the Angevin forces operating with the king assembled at Mantes and advanced from the west into the Norman county of Évreux. In any case, Angevin participation was relatively slight.[96] A second Capetian contingent invaded eastern Normandy further north by way of Neufchâtel-en-Brey. This force was caught by surprise and decisively defeated at Mortemer. The southern force in Évreux, including the Angevins, was forced to withdraw when the king learned of the disaster, apparently without significant losses. According to Norman sources William was able to conclude an agreement with the king who promised to permit the duke to keep whatever lands he could win from the count of Anjou. While reference to such a treaty is likely a piece of Norman propaganda, William was able to make a counterstroke into Maine and constructed a fortress at Ambrières.[97]

It was precisely to defend Angevin territory from such operations that Robert had been given so much power on the northwestern shield. Sablé and its commander should have played a major role in the Angevin response to the Norman intrusion into Maine at Ambrières. Any forces rushed to the northern border would have to pass through the northwestern shield at Sablé and Château-Gontier. Robert was therefore very likely a participant when Count Geoffrey attacked Ambrières with the aid of Count Odo of Brittany and Robert's kinsman Count William of Poitiers. He certainly took part in an important act of Count Odo, possibly around the date of this expedition.

his son. It is perhaps for this very reason that its *dominus*, Geoffrey of Mayenne, seems to pursue a political strategy independent of the Angevins.

96. Douglas, *William the Conqueror*, 67, "it would seem that there were also men from Anjou perhaps with Count Geoffrey at their head."

97. William of Poitiers, 50–51. Cf. Halphen, *Comté d'Anjou*, 77 n. 4, who doubts William's assertion. Guillot, *Comté d'Anjou*, 1: 82 and 92, pictures a strengthening of the alliance between Geoffrey Martel and the king which would make William's account even more unlikely. In 1055, for example, King Henry cooperated in solving Geoffrey's problem with Bishop Gervasius by having him promoted to the see of Reims.

Odo was the second son of Geoffrey I, count of Rennes, and claimed the countship of Brittany from his nephew Conan II.[98] Geoffrey Martel supported Odo's claim and ensured his loyalty with gifts such as the land of Bazouges.[99] Some time after 14 January 1056 Odo appeared before the assembled knights of Geoffrey's full court, probably at Angers, to give up the land at Bazouges in favor of Saint-Aubin.[100] It is clear from the witness list, which included Odo, his wife and four sons, the bishop of Rennes, and a large number of others, several with distinctly Breton names, that Odo had brought at least a good part of his entourage. In fact they outnumber the Angevins listed. This ceremony apparently had special significance for Robert since he and both his brothers, Henry and Guy, are named in the Angevin witness list immediately after Count Geoffrey, Countess Grace, and Geoffrey's two young nephews, Geoffrey the Bearded and Fulk Rechin. If the attack on Ambrières came as late as 1056, then this ceremony may have occurred right before or after the expedition against Ambrières with the help of Odo's supporters and military household.[101] Robert's prominence as a witness would reflect his prominence in the campaign.

Despite the presence of three counts, the expedition was probably no more than a quick raid launched from the Angevin bases of Château-Gontier and Sablé with the goal of discouraging further Norman penetration of Maine. The failure to take Ambrières would have been less important to Robert and the other Angevins in the northwestern march than the fact that the Norman advance was stopped. The Norman chronicler William of Poitiers describes the failure as a serious check to the Angevins, especially since an important Angevin supporter, Geoffrey of Mayenne, was captured and forced to swear allegiance to Duke William before being released.[102] It is doubtful, though, that such a coerced allegiance could have remained very firm once Geoffrey

---

98. Arthur le Moyne de la Borderie, *Histoire de Bretagne,* 3 vols (Paris: A. Picard, 1897) 3: 14–16; Halphen, *Comté d'Anjou,* 78.

99. *Cartul. de St-Aubin* 2: 171–74, no. 677, an act dated 21 June 1040–25 December 1059.

100. *Cartul. de St-Aubin* 2: 171–74, no. 677, an act dated 14 January 1056–26 December 1059.

101. The date for the expedition is uncertain. William of Poitiers makes it clear that it was after the pact concluded with King Henry, which Guillot dates as 1055 if it actually took place. It would have been before the Angevin-Capetian attack of August 1057. Cf. Douglas, *William the Conqueror,* 70–71.

102. William of Poitiers, 52–57.

was released by the Normans. Robert's holdings to the south were never in serious jeopardy.

Robert's position, in fact, was strengthened by the general health of Angevin control of Maine beyond Sablé. On 15 October 1055 Bishop Gervasius was promoted to the archbishopric of Reims. With his old antagonist out of the way, Geoffrey Martel was able to install Vulgrin of Vendôme, a former knight completely loyal to the Angevin count, as bishop of Le Mans on 31 July 1056.[103] Geoffrey was also able to exert his authority over the house of Bellême through his alliance with King Henry. During most of the 1050s Bishop Ivo, the head of the family, appeared frequently in the company of Geoffrey Martel as his ally.[104] With this powerful family acting as a plug between Maine and Normandy, the northern border of Maine was secure, protecting Robert's position in southern Maine.[105] In addition, Geoffrey Martel still was able to control the young count of Maine, Herbert II, at least until 1056, and probably until Geoffrey's death.[106]

Despite the claims of Norman chroniclers of William's success, the Angevins lost control only of Ambrières, barely seven miles south of the Norman frontier. As a modern historian of the Norman duchy has admitted, "a glance at the map shows how little William actually achieved."[107] As long as this was so, and Angevin control over Le Mans itself remained strong, Robert's strongholds to the south along with their sister fortress of Château-Gontier served not so much as a march as a second line of defense, totally Angevin, dominating the southern part of Maine and offering support for Manceaux lords such as Geoffrey of Mayenne, who were facing the Normans in a more exposed position.

---

103. *Actus pontificum*, 373; Guillot, *Comte d'Anjou*, I: 92, 94. The date is given in Guillot 2:C 161. For Vulgrin's career see Stephen Fanning, "From *Miles* to *Episcopus:* The Influence of the Family on the Career of Vulgrinus of Vendôme," *Medieval Prosopography* 4 (1983): 9–30.

104. Bates, *Normandy*, 79. Bates explicitly states that the evidence for Bishop Ivo's pro-Angevin stance is even stronger than in Guillot, *Comte d'Anjou* I: 84.

105. Guillot, *Comte d'Anjou*, I: 82–85; Bates, *Normandy*, 78–79.

106. Guillot, *Comte d'Anjou*, I: 85–87. The *Actus pontificum*, 366, says that the Angevins controlled Maine for ten years after the death of Count Hugh IV. Latouche, *Maine*, 32, n. 5, thinks that Herbert II switched his allegiance to Duke William only after the battle of Varaville in late 1057.

107. Bates, *Normandy*, 78.

Robert must have taken part in one more attempt by the Angevin-Capetian alliance to invade Normandy itself. In August 1057 the alliance sent a force into the Hiémois heading northwards towards Bayeux and Caen.[108] The Angevin-Capetian forces entered Normandy through the Bellême's district of Sées,[109] which would indicate that they had passed through Maine. Perhaps Le Mans itself was used as a staging area, but it is certain that Robert would have been expected to supply provisions and manpower from Sablé and even Craon. In all likelihood he personally took part in the expedition. While crossing the Dive River near Varaville, part of the invading force was attacked and soundly defeated. Although Norman accounts exaggerated enemy losses, the remainder of the Angevin-Capetian force retreated safely.[110]

Robert could take small comfort from the fact that the Normans failed to follow up this purely defensive victory. Although still secure in Sablé, he must have been aware of a slight but discernible loosening of the Angevin grip on Maine following Geoffrey's retreat. There appears to have been a gradual Norman penetration of Sées at the expense of Angevin ties with the Bellême clan. Eventually Count Herbert was to attempt to escape Angevin control by signing a pact with the duke of Normandy. Still, Angevins such as Robert at Sablé, the castellan at Château-Gontier, and Bishop Vulgrin at Le Mans were able to maintain Angevin control over the county until the day Geoffrey Martel died.[111]

Although Robert obviously was a major player in these events his exact role is obscure. For definite information about Robert during the 1050s, one must turn to the evidence of the charters. These documents, however, were redacted for legal and administrative purposes on matters of interest to the monasteries and churches of the area. Their intent was not to describe military exploits or political maneuvering.

---

108. Dhondt, "Henri Ier, l'Empire et Anjou," 87–109, established the correct date, which Halphen, *Comté d'Anjou*, 79, supposed was 1058.

109. Bates, *Normandy*, 79. Sées, a stronghold of the Bellême family, was allied to Geoffrey Martel at this time.

110. Douglas, *William the Conqueror*, 72; Halphen, *Comté d'Anjou*, 79.

111. For the Bellême shift, see Bates, *Normandy*, 78–81; for Herbert's pact, see Douglas, *William the Conqueror*, 73; for the assertion that Angevin control remained strong, see Guillot, *Comté d'Anjou*, 1: 86.

Consequently, the light they throw on Robert fails to reveal much about his role as military commander involved with a relentless struggle against Duke William. They do, however, reveal details of Robert's role as a *dominus* of unusual power and influence.

This has considerable value, for although Robert was closely involved in the intermittent warfare against the Normans, much of his time would have been occupied with the administration of Craon, Sablé, and the large territory dependent on these two strongholds. It is likely that Robert held a more or less formal inquest into the state of his new holdings implied in his later remark that he learned about the history of Sablé from the "lords and elders" of the area.[112] As *dominus* he was expected to know the details of the history and administration of his honor: Robert now had power over lands and men who depended on his judgement.

In his new role Robert was himself a leader of the soldiers responsible for Angevin military success. In one document he authorizes the donation of a church at Brion to Saint-Aubin by two knights of Sablé, Rannulf and William. Robert is surrounded by what amounts to his own court at Sablé. This includes the two knights, a priest (presumably from Robert's own chapel), Robert's *vicarius* and "many others."[113] This is a fairly complex administrative organization that may even, in the person of the priest Arnulf, have been able to produce the written document that Robert validated with a cross.[114] It also had its enforcers, the knights, and an administrator, the *vicarius*.

Robert, then, was more than a mere soldier of the count; he was even more than a garrison commander. He had full seigneurial rights over both Craon and Sablé. During the decade of hard fighting in Maine and Normandy Robert had been able to secure his position and grow into the role of the leading Angevin lord on the Maine border and

---

112. "Seniores et antiquiores" in *Cartul. manceau*, 2: 69–76, no. 5.

113. *Cartul. de St-Aubin* 1: 436–37, no. 376.

114. The act is performed at Sablé to authorize an act previously performed at Angers for Saint-Aubin. There is no sign of any personnel from Saint-Aubin being present at Sablé. If the document had been produced earlier at Angers as part of *Cartul. de St-Aubin*, 1: 436–37, no. 376, then someone at Sablé was at least able to read it. Later Robert would have access to the talents of monks from Marmoutier dwelling at Sablé.

one of the most influential *domini* in the Angevin court. While Robert could not have been blind to the weakening of Angevin control over Maine after the battle of Varaville in 1057, he must have assumed that following Geoffrey Martel's renewed alliance with King Henry I this would soon be set right. Robert had every reason to expect years of forceful and energetic leadership from his lord Geoffrey Martel. This would be the one thing denied him.

CHAPTER THREE

The Angevin Civil War

In the fall of 1060 Robert the Burgundian and his brother Guy hurried to Angers to attend their ailing count at the monastery of Saint-Nicolas.[1] Geoffrey was dying, and knew it. Fearing for his soul he sought to make amends for his sins by wholesale grants to the great monasteries of his realm.[2] Judging from the number of acts given while Geoffrey was near death it was a protracted and well attended vigil. He was nursed until the final moment by a monk from Marmoutier.[3] On 14 November 1060 Robert's great benefactor finally died.[4] One of Geoffrey's knights, Buhard, probably reflected Robert's own feelings when he described "the pain which struck me at the death of my *dominus* Geoffrey Martel."[5] Thirty-two years later Robert would still be able to testify to the details of one of Geoffrey's deathbed acts.[6]

Beyond their sense of personal loss, Robert and the other Angevin fighting men had good reason to ache at Geoffrey's passing. The count

---

1. Archives Maine-et-Loire, H 1840, no. 13.

2. Ibid.; *Cartul. Trinité de Vendôme,* 1: 271–73, no. 157; Livre noir de St-Florent, Bib. nat., n.a. lat. 1930, fol. 96r–v and fol. 58r–59v; Guillot, *Comte d'Anjou,* C 220; Halphen, *Comté d'Anjou,* no. 157.

3. Farmer, *Communities of Saint Martin,* 71.

4. In Fulk Rechin, "Fragmentum historiae," 379, a witness like Robert, wrote, "In eodem porro anno (MLX) rex Ainricus obiit in nativitate sancti Johannis et meus avunculus Gosfridus tertio die post festivitatem beati Martini bono fine quievit." For other citations see Halphen, *Comté d'Anjou,* 12, n. 1.

5. "Cum Ego Buhardus Brito, dolori meo qui mihi de obitu Domini mei Gauffredi Martelli Andegavorum comitis acciderat," Laurent Le Pelletier, *Rerum scitu dignissimarum a prima fundatione monasterii S. Nicolai Andegavensis . . . , Epitome* (Angers: Mayger, 1635), 19, hereafter cited as *Epitome.* Cf. Guillot, *Comte d'Anjou,* 2: C221, and Halphen, *Comté d'Anjou,* no. 158.

6. Archives Maine-et-Loire, H 1840, no. 13, 17 February 1092.

had left no direct heir of his body to the countship. His attempt to recti-fy this by naming his nephew Geoffrey the Bearded as count was weak-ened by his apparent fondness for this nephew's younger brother, Fulk Rechin.[7] Geoffrey, who already held the countship of the Gâtinais, now became count of Anjou and Touraine. Fulk for his part, although only seventeen, received the Saintonge as an appanage and later the castle of Vihiers to hold from his brother.[8] This division of the Angevin inheri-tance virtually guaranteed the creation of tensions between the two brothers.[9] Robert could not fail to be disturbed by this when he consid-ered his exposed position at Sablé facing the Normans and at Craon fac-ing the Bretons.

Initially, however, it must have seemed as if Robert and his brother Guy would continue to prosper under Geoffrey the Bearded as they had under his predecessor.[10] By 23 May 1061 Count Geoffrey gave the honor of Aimeric of Faye at *Grizaicus* to Guy, presumably as a mark of special favor.[11] Robert himself continued to enjoy a paramount spot within the count's entourage. At a major comital act regulating the affairs of the fortress of Saint-Florent in 1061 Robert once again stood at the forefront of those present with the count. Aside from the count and his brother Fulk, only the bishop of Angers preceded Robert among the witnesses. Immediately following Robert was his close associate on the northwestern march, Rainald castellan of Château-Gontier.[12] Robert always occupied this high position in the numerous comital acts he witnessed throughout the first two years of Geoffrey's countship.[13] During the same period in the count's court at Baugé, Robert and Guy

7. Halphen, *Comté d'Anjou*, 132. Geoffrey and Fulk were sons of Geoffrey's sister Ermen-gard and Geoffrey count of Gâtinais. For a reassessment of Fulk's career as well as an expla-nation of his nickname see Bradbury, "Fulk le Réchin," 27–41.

8. Halphen, *Comté d'Anjou*, 134–35; Guillot, *Comte d'Anjou*, 1: 102–3.

9. Guillot, *Comte d'Anjou*, 1: 103, sees Geoffrey's arrangements as a "modest" sign of a spe-cial regard for Fulk. Fulk often pointed out that he was raised by his uncle, Geoffrey Martel.

10. Robert's brother Henry appears only once in Anjou, *Cartul. St-Aubin*, 2: 171–74, no. 677 (1056–1059).

11. Bib. de Poitiers, coll. Dom Fonteneau, vol. 71, pp. 81–82, published in *Cartul. Noyers*, no. 20. Cf. Guillot, *Comte d'Anjou*, C 222.

12. "Livre noir de St-Florent," Bib. nat., n.a. lat. 1930, fol. 57r–58r.

13. *Cartul. Trinité de Vendôme*, 1: 271–73, no. 157 (22 February 1062); 273–76, no. 158 (24 Febru-ary 1062); Prou, *Recueil des actes de Philippe Ier*, 396, no. 158 (13 April 1062); "Livre noir de St-Flo-rent," Bib. nat., n.a. lat. 1930, fol. 96r–v (14 November 1060–28 December 1062).

both participated as judges for a lawsuit involving a dispute over a land purchase.[14]

No amount of endowments or authority from the count, however, could disguise the fact from the Burgundian brothers that Geoffrey the Bearded was simply not as competent as his predecessor. A century later William of Malmesbury claimed that Geoffrey Martel was unable to pass on his worldly industry to his successor, who "was a simple-hearted young man, more used to praying in church than to handling weapons, and he aroused contempt among the men of that region."[15] With enemies on all sides watching to take advantage of the slightest slackening of vigilance, this was to prove disastrous for the Angevin state. Robert watched with a mounting sense of frustration and anger as his own holdings were increasingly threatened from Brittany and Normandy by the steady erosion of Angevin power.

The first loss was the Saintonge, the bulk of Fulk's appanage. Here again the new count's first efforts were promising. In 1061 Count Guy-Geoffrey of Poitou reclaimed the Saintonge and attacked Saintes. Count Geoffrey came to his brother's aid and on 21 March defeated the Poitevins at Chef-Boutonne in a wind so intense the victors sought shelter behind the corpses of the vanquished.[16] This success was completely negated the following year when Guy-Geoffrey took Saintes after a short siege.[17] Robert's aunt Agnes had retired to her monastery of Notre-Dame de Saintes and was undoubtedly a witness to the Angevin defeat. In fact, she had met with her son Guy-Geoffrey on 11 May 1061

14. *Cartul. de St-Aubin* 1: 306–7, no. 265 (14 November 1060–1062).

15. William of Malmesbury, *Gesta regum Anglorum: The History of the English Kings*, trans. R. A. B. Mynors, completed by R. M. Thomson and M. Winterbottom (Oxford: Clarendon Press, 1998), 438–39, iii, 235, "Is moriens Gaufredo, sororis filio, hereditatem suam contradidit, sed industriam seculi transfundere non potuit: nam ille, simplicium morum juvenis, magis in ecclesiis orare quam arma tractare consuetus, homines regionis illius . . . in contemptum sui excitavit." Bachrach, "Henry II and the Angevin Tradition," 125, concludes flatly that Geoffrey was "manifestly incompetent and probably mentally ill." For Geoffrey's madness at the end of his life, see *Cartulaire du chapitre de Saint-Laud d'Angers*, ed. A. Planchenault (Angers: Germain and Grassin, 1903), no. 16.

16. "Gesta consulum Andegavorum," in *Chroniques des comtes d'Anjou*, 130. Richard, *Comtes de Poitou*, 1: 284, accepts the details here as accurate for Chef-Boutonne, although the chronicle ascribes them to the time of Geoffrey Martel by confusing it with the battle of Saint-Jouin-de-Marnes in 1033. See also "Chronicon de Sainti Maxentii," in *Chroniques des églises d'Anjou*, eds. Paul Marchegay and Émile Mabille (Paris: Jules Renouard, 1869), 402.

17. "Chron. de St Maxentii," 403.

at Saint-Maixent and may well have known of his plans for another attack.[18] Yet Geoffrey the Bearded made no effort to come to his brother's aid nor did he compensate Fulk for the loss. The resulting split between the two brothers was never fully repaired and would seriously weaken Geoffrey.[19] A bitter and hostile Fulk would thereafter provide a rallying point for discontented knights, castellans, and *domini*.

Robert's worst fears were soon realized when Count Herbert II of Maine died on 9 March 1062.[20] Duke William of Normandy simply declared his son Robert Curthose the rightful heir on the basis of an alleged agreement made with Count Herbert after William's victory at Varaville in 1057.[21] This was unacceptable to the Manceaux, who within a year were in full revolt against the Normans. Their resistance was clearly an Angevin initiative and Robert, if not an actual participant, must have followed its course with intense interest. The leader of the revolt was Geoffrey of Mayenne, a somewhat erratic *fidelis* of the count of Anjou and a man well known to Robert.[22] Under Geoffrey's leadership the Manceaux proclaimed as count of Maine a candidate favorable to the Angevins, Walter of Mantes. Geoffrey the Bearded even prepared an expedition to aid the Manceaux against the Normans.[23] Geoffrey, however, had difficulty getting the troops underway and Manceaux resistance collapsed. William of Poitiers makes it clear that the people of Maine could not face the Normans in battle because they received no aid from Geoffrey.[24] After a prolonged struggle Le Mans submitted to

18. Richard, *Comtes de Poitou* 1: 283 and 285. Richard suggests that when Agnes met with her son she actually helped him plan the counterattack.

19. Guillot, *Comte d'Anjou*, 1: 105; Halphen, *Comté d'Anjou*, 137. In 1063 Geoffrey and Fulk faced each other in a lawsuit and henceforth Fulk disappears from Geoffrey's acts.

20. Latouche, *Maine*, 33 n. 3.

21. William of Poitiers, 88, is the only source that mentions the provision. See also Orderic 2: 117 and 305. The provision is most unlikely; see Bates, *William the Conqueror*, 39–40.

22. *Cartul. Trinité de Vendôme*, no. 216. *Cartul. du Ronceray*, no. 93; Bib. nat. Dom Housseau, III, no. 829. For Geoffrey of Mayenne see Halphen, *Comté d'Anjou*, 179.

23. Bib. nat., Dom Housseau, II₂, no. 667; Guillot, *Comte d'Anjou*, C 246, 14 March 1063. Marmoutier challenged Geoffrey's right to call up the abbey's men to serve in the campaign. Cf. Halphen, *Comté d'Anjou*, 137 n. 5. The expedition was prepared; there is no mention of it actually getting under way. There is also a problem with the date. Because Marmoutier habitually used the Paschal year, 14 March 1063 could well mean 14 March 1064, new style. If so it would clearly be a case of too little too late.

24. William of Poitiers, 60–61, "Having repeatedly sent for Geoffrey, whom their ruler Walter had set up as their lord and protector, they often threatened to give battle, but never dared to do so."

William and his forces.[25] The would-be count Walter and his wife were captured, imprisoned, and poisoned. A Norman garrison was installed in the newly strengthened fortifications of the city.[26] William followed up his victory with the sack of the castle of Mayenne, exposed outside the Angevin defensive web. While Robert's territory in southern Maine was not touched by the Normans, by the end of 1063 the Norman conquest of Le Mans was complete.

The Norman triumph was a disaster for Robert, leaving his entire honor centered at Sablé directly exposed to Norman pressure from Le Mans, a mere forty-five kilometers away. Robert's lord, Geoffrey the Bearded, had played no effective role in combating the relentless Norman advance. All that was left was a face-saving ceremony to allow the Angevins to maintain the legal fiction that their count still controlled Maine. Traveling to the Norman stronghold of Alençon, Count Geoffrey received an oath of homage from William's son Robert as count of Maine.[27] While Robert would ultimately use this to his advantage, in 1063 it represented the utter failure of his count to protect his northern border. Robert was not to forget it.

For the moment, though, Robert and his ally, Rainald of Château-Gontier, had other problems to face on the northwestern frontier, problems that may explain why they were so ineffective in Maine. The only details come from a document written by the monks of Marmoutier dated sometime before 26 February 1064. The monks state that Rainald of Château-Gontier was no longer able to usurp their rights, "since he was finally captured anyway in a war waged with the Bretons."[28] These Bretons most likely were followers of Conan II count of Rennes, who claimed Craon and Château-Gontier as part of Brittany.

Though the cause of this "war" *(bellum),* and even its location, are unknown, the war itself caused Rainald considerable trouble. Leaving

25. Latouche, *Maine,* 34; Halphen, *Comté d'Anjou,* 179.

26. Latouche, *Maine,* 34; Halphen, *Comté d'Anjou,* 179. For a description and drawings of the remains of these fortifications, see Gabriel Fleury, "Les fortifications du Maine: la Tour Orbindelle et le Mont-Barbet," *Revue historique et archéologique du Maine* 29 (1891): 136–54 and 279–303.

27. Orderic 2: 304–5. Halphen, *Comté d'Anjou,* 180; Latouche, *Maine,* 54.

28. "Ut quequo in quodam bello cum Britonibus habito captus aliquando fuit," *Cartulaire blésois de Marmoutier,* ed. Charles Métais (Blois: E. Moreau, 1891), no. 42. The following discussion refers to this document.

two sons, Rainald and Guicher, as hostages, he was forced to write to the monks of Marmoutier for money to pay the ransom his captors were demanding. He and his wife then traveled to Tours, received the money, and on 26 February renounced his claim on customs from land in Touraine belonging to Marmoutier.[29] By 1 April, Rainald was back at Château-Gontier to oversee his daughter Milesendis's approval of his renunciation of the customs. Robert met his unfortunate friend at Angers two days later. In an elaborate ceremony before the Angevin court Rainald's two sons, now returned from captivity, formally approved his grant to Marmoutier. While all this frantic activity represents a family crisis of major proportions, to Robert it had more disturbing implications. First, it was a military action on the Angevin border with an enemy who had claims on the whole Craonais. Second, the affair, however small, had ended badly for Robert's ally and neighbor. Third, and most significant, Count Geoffrey played no role in the entire affair beyond serving as Rainald's *fidejussor*, that is, his warrantor. Since this required that if Rainald or his sons ever reneged on their deal with Marmoutier Geoffrey would force them to pay a stiff fine equal to the ransom of ten pounds, it is unlikely that as Rainald's ally Robert took much comfort from it. Thus, while the lords of the northwestern shield were beset by enemies, Count Geoffrey remained passive.

Robert may have had a hand in the protracted negotiations between Rainald and Marmoutier such an elaborate series of ceremonies represented. In the early 1060s, if not before, Robert had established close ties to the abbey of Marmoutier that were essential to Robert's personal and political life. Since the conquest of Tours in 1044, a triumph in which Robert probably participated, the ecclesiastical centers at Tours dedicated to Saint Martin had played an important role in Angevin affairs. His own relationship with the monastery began between 1055 and 1063 when he and his wife Advisa travelled to Marmoutier to pray and to receive the *societas* of the abbey of Marmoutier. This term *societas* represents one of an abbey's coveted privileges, one that conferred

---

29. Ibid. Rainald travelled with a large entourage that included his illegitimate brother Hubert and Burchard, the *sartor* of Château-Renault. It was at Château-Renault that Robert first witnessed an act of Rainald some fifteen years earlier.

a confraternity on Robert and Advisa by which they would be closely associated with Marmoutier's cycle of prayers and ritual.[30]

This *societas* was tied to the special relationship the couple had already developed with the monk Wanilo. In the charter commemorating the visit Wanilo is specifically mentioned as the monk who convinced them to donate to the abbey an exemption on all the tolls and customs placed on the monks' goods transported through any land where Robert held authority *(potestas)*. Abbot Alberic himself was pleased to preside over the ceremony in the abbey chapter house. Robert and Advisa, in turn, were accompanied by a number of Robert's own men, including his provost Ulric, the official who would oversee the collection of all fees due his lord Robert. As a public testament of their generosity the couple together placed a wooden token on the altar of Saint Martin.[31] This was clearly an act of great significance not only to Marmoutier, but to Robert, his family, and his clients.

After this donation, but probably before disenchantment with Count Geoffrey had reached a peak, Robert and Advisa gave Marmoutier the church of Saint-Malo at Sablé along with all the other churches of the castle at the advice of Archbishop Barthelemy of Tours.[32] By transferring the churches of Sablé to Marmoutier at the advice of the archbishop of Tours, Robert was deliberately tying the ecclesiastical foundations of Sablé to the Touraine rather than to the Norman dominated Le Mans.[33] Yet Robert's concern for Marmoutier should not be seen as a cynical political ploy. Most if not all of Robert's class believed sincerely in their faith and were greatly concerned with the fate of the souls of themselves and their families. As Susan Reynolds has pointed out, "the military ethos was a Christian military

30. Stephen D. White, *Custom, Kinship, and Gifts to Saints: The "Laudatio Parentum" in Western France, 1050–1250* (Chapel Hill: University of North Carolina Press, 1988), 26. This is only one of many monastic privileges for favored patrons that White identifies.

31. *Cartul. manceau*, 1: 1–13, no. 1. 1055–1063. Robert's act at Marmoutier was witnessed by his provost and several of his men *(homines)*.

32. *Cartul. manceau*, 2: 69–76, no. 5, 14 November 1052–7 August 1067.

33. There are two versions of this act, *Cartul. manceau* 2: 59–66, nos. 2 and 3. It was an extensive gift, involving not only the churches of the castle, but also the dues on meadowlands and the woods of Bouère and land to construct a burg outside the castle. The customs due to Robert from markets in the burg are specified in the document. The gift also included the church of Angliers and vineyards in Loudun.

ethos"; there was no mental fire-wall separating the ideas of the clergy from the laity.[34] Throughout his life Robert richly endowed several monasteries, was rarely involved in disputes over church property, and eventually died going on crusade for his beliefs. His relationship with the Church, and Marmoutier above all, must be seen in light of our new appreciation of the genuine beliefs of the nobility. Recent research has shown that the great reform movement of the eleventh century was only possible with the active participation of the nobility.[35] Robert was one who would participate, picturing his donation as an attempt to reform the churches of Sablé.

His explanation indicates his sympathy for the deep changes stirring within the Church and marking the prelude to the great Reform movement of the second half of the eleventh century. Geoffrey the Bearded was not capable of seeing the change, or grasping its significance. As religious houses all across France sought to pull away from too close an entanglement with lay powers, the count could no longer control the abbots of his realm. His ability to use the monasteries to sustain comital authority was seriously impaired.[36]

An ominous example was Geoffrey's proposed expedition against the Normans in 1063. Marmoutier challenged Geoffrey's right to call up the abbey's men.[37] From a military standpoint this reform threatened to remove a major resource from the count's control. This forced him to depend more exclusively on the *domini* of Anjou for his military strength. It is also possible that *domini* such as Robert came to the conclusion that if the count could no longer depend on the support of the abbots, they themselves would have to draw closer to the monastic establishment. Their own pious convictions, not to mention their close ties of kinship with the leaders of the Church, would have led them to the same conclusion.[38]

34. Susan Reynolds, *Kingdoms and Communities in Western Europe, 900–1300*, (Oxford: Clarendon Press, 1984), 6–7.

35. Bouchard, *Sword*, 86, 90–169; John Howe, "The Nobility's Reform of the Medieval Church," *American Historical Review* 92 (1988): 317–39. Both document the extent and value of this participation. See also Peneolope Johnson, *Prayers*, 172–75.

36. Olivier Guillot, "A Reform of Investiture before the Investiture Struggle in Anjou, Normandy, and England," *Haskins Society Journal* 3 (1991): 81–100.

37. Bib. nat. Dom Housseau 2, no. 667.

38. For kinship, Bouchard, *Sword*, 46; for lay religious feeling in the second half of the

Robert's carefully considered policy of close cooperation with the ecclesiastical establishment of Tours was now abruptly threatened by Geoffrey's inability to negotiate these changes. The count committed a series of blunders that were to alienate the archbishop of Tours, the abbot and monks of Marmoutier, the bishop of Angers, and eventually the pope. When Abbot Alberic of Marmoutier died on 20 May 1064, Geoffrey insisted that his successor receive his investiture from the count's own hands.[39] Since Marmoutier had never been under the direct control of the Angevin counts, this demand was steadfastly refused by the monks. According to the *Gesta consulum Andegavorum*, Geoffrey became so angry that he threatened to destroy the monastery and the monks in it and followed up the threat by seizing the property of the monks and their men. "The persecution raged and increased so much that even secular men marvelled at the count's intemperance and, cursing the count, prayed to God for the monks."[40] Finally the monks called for the intervention of the highly respected Abbot Hugh of Cluny, but this merely provoked Geoffrey into a fresh outburst of rage. The author of the life of Saint Hugh says that at the interview with Abbot Hugh Geoffrey boasted that he would reduce Marmoutier to "the obedience of an ass." As Hugh tried to halt him by grabbing a piece of his cloak, the count tore out the fibula that held it and abruptly left without further response.[41]

Geoffrey now proceeded to make the situation worse by attempting to dictate to Archbishop Barthelemy regarding his choice for bishop of Le Mans. Bishop Vulgrin, always attentive to Angevin interests, died on 10 May 1065, giving Duke William the opportunity to install his own partisan, Arnold.[42] Desperately seeking to prevent this, Geoffrey threat-

---

century see Marcus Bull, *Knightly Piety and the Lay Response to the First Crusade: The Limousin and Gascony, c. 970–c. 1130* (Oxford: Clarendon Press, 1993).

39. "Gesta consulum," 134.

40. "Gesta consulum," 136. ". . . in tantumque desaeviit persecutio et excrevit ut etiam saeculares homines comitis intemperantium mirarentur et, imprecantes comiti, Deum pro monachis precarentur."

41. "Vita Sancti Hugonis," in *Patrologia Latina* 159: 881 section 33. "Ut diceret se B. Martini conventum, ad obsequium unius asini redacturum." Cf. Guillot, *Comte d'Anjou*, 1: 106, and Halphen, *Comté d'Anjou*, 139–40. Guillot emphasizes how maladroit this action was at a time of increasing monastic independence.

42. *Actus pontificum*, 374–75.

ened Barthelemy so violently that the archbishop complained bitterly by letter to Pope Alexander II. Barthelemy protested that "this new Nero," as he called Geoffrey, "has sacked all my goods and those of my church, tearing down my dwelling and those of my canons." In return, "I have denounced his audacity to the French bishops when the count himself was present at the king's court in Orleans."[43] This is, of course, a highly partisan version of the controversy. Geoffrey could claim that he was only demanding legitimate support in a time of grave danger for the Angevin state from an institution that had always provided such support. There can be no doubt, however, about the result of this position. When all efforts at compromise failed, Archbishop Barthelemy excommunicated the count. The pope eventually responded by dispatching his legate Steven to Anjou to settle matters.[44]

Robert's sympathies on this last controversy are likely to have been divided. He can have had little enthusiasm for a Norman candidate in the see of Le Mans. Geoffrey's brutal treatment of the archbishop, however, may have offended his religious sensibilities and certainly threatened his own vital ties with the Church. The treatment of the archbishop coupled with the discontent of Marmoutier aggravated Robert's existing discomfort at Geoffrey's ineffectualness on the northwest frontier. Slowly Robert found himself drawn into the growing number of *domini* hostile to Count Geoffrey who were now coalescing around two dangerous nodes of discontent: Archbishop Barthelemy and Fulk Rechin.[45]

For Robert the final impetus to revolt was an invasion of his territory in 1066 by Duke Conan II of Brittany. Our best source is Orderic Vitalis's continuation of William of Jumièges, although his story does not fully make sense. As Duke William was distracted by his preparations to invade England, Conan supposedly claimed Normandy and threatened William with war. William ignored the threat. Conan promptly raised an army and inexplicably attacked Anjou, the only other power

43. C. Erdmann and N. Fickermann, *Briefsammlungen der Zeit Heinrichs IV* (Weimar: Hermann Böhlaus Nachfolger, 1950), 156, no. 90; Guillot, *Comte d'Anjou*, 1: 106–7; Halphen, *Comté d'Anjou*, 142.

44. Halphen, *Comté d'Anjou*, 142, citing a letter of Bishop Eusebius of Angers who stated that Steven was sent expressly to curb Count Geoffrey, "that angel of Satan."

45. Guillot, *Comte d'Anjou*, 1: 108.

strong enough to endanger William's enterprise. In return for clearing the Norman's southern flank, William allegedly induced Conan's chamberlain to poison Conan when "the count of the Bretons was laying siege to Château-Gontier in the county of Anjou, and after the soldiers within the stronghold had surrendered he entered the place with his own army."[46] The Bretons retreated with their stricken count, who soon died.

Aside from Orderic's account in William of Jumièges, there is virtually no reliable information concerning this episode in any of the histories, annals, or chronicles of this period. There is, however, a body of material nearly four centuries after the event by Pierre Le Baud and Jehan de Bourdigné, containing stories about Robert the Burgundian leading the defense against an invasion led by Conan. This would exactly fit the situation in 1066 since Robert would be expected to play just such a role. Anyone laying siege to Château-Gontier would lay himself open to attack from Craon and Sablé, both within an easy day's ride from Château-Gontier.

These late fifteenth and early sixteenth century accounts are too distant in time to be used with assurance but there is a still earlier account of Conan's invasion. This is found in the *Chronique de Parcé* written by Gregory, curé of Saint-Martin de Parcé, probably in the mid-thirteenth century, about 200 years earlier than Le Baud and de Bourdigné and about 200 years after the event. In this version, when King Robert II of France had gone to Orleans, Conan the duke of Brittany attempted to seize Angers "by force and by treachery." This time it is Count Fulk who was the victim of Breton aggression. Robert the Burgundian, with his brothers Henry and Hugh, immediately came to Fulk's aid, catching the enemy outside the walls of the city and slaughtering them. To commemorate the bloodletting, Robert was henceforth called *Trucida Britonem*, "the Breton Slaughterer," and Hugh, *Manduca Britonem*, "the

---

46. "Tunc idem comes Britonum in Andegavensi comitatu castellum Guntherii obsederat, et oppidanis militibus sese illi dedentibus suos intromittebat. Interea Chuningus chirotecas suas incaute induit, tactisque habenis, manum ad os levavit. Cujus tactu veneno infectus est et paulo post omnibus suis lugentibus defunctus est." William of Jumièges, *The "Gesta Normannorum ducem" of William of Jumièges, Orderic Vitalis, and Robert of Torigni*, ed. and trans. Elisabeth M. C. van Houts (Oxford: Clarendon Press, 1992), 163–65, repeated in Orderic, 5: 259–60.

Breton Eater." Hugh had earned his nickname because his horse had strangled one of Conan's nobles with its teeth. Later, when Fulk's son Geoffrey Martel became count, he gave Craon to Robert and other castles to Henry and Hugh.[47]

There are major problems with the Parcé account. First, the genuine invasion by Conan II in 1066 that resulted in the siege of Château-Gontier is confused with a legendary invasion by the sons of Conan I le Tort, count of Rennes, supposedly foiled by Fulk Nerra around 991.[48] In making use of this earlier legend the author of the *Chronique de Parcé* makes two errors: he places the invasion in the time of Fulk Nerra, and the climax of the attack comes before the walls of Angers itself, not at Château-Gontier.

Still, there is much to be said of the chronicle's version of events. The invasion of 1066 is a fact, attested by William of Jumièges. If 200 years later the author used a legendary account of an earlier invasion, connected to another Conan, as a model, that does not mean that everything be rejected as untrue. Keeping in mind the location of Craon and Sablé in relation to Château-Gontier, and the defensive purpose of this line of fortifications, nothing is more likely than the picture of Robert the Burgundian and his brothers riding to the rescue, catching the enemy before the walls, not of Angers, but of Château-Gontier. The fact that William of Jumièges and Orderic are both silent on this counterattack, however, indicates that if the attack took place it was not nearly as successful as the later Parcé account would have it.

On the other hand, the historical Robert *did* have two brothers, Henry and Guy, who served with him under the counts of Anjou. Hugh the Breton Eater is also a real person and a contemporary of Robert's although not, as far as we know, a relative. He is found serving with Robert as a judge or witness in at least three formal acts.[49] The chronicler evidently knew of the Hugh the Burgundian killed years before at the siege of Sainte-Maure, conflated the two Hugh's into one person, and assumed that his creation was a brother of Robert the Burgundian.

47. *Chronique de Parcé*, 3–4.

48. Halphen, *Comté d'Anjou*, 25, n. 3, and La Borderie, *Histoire de Bretagne* 2: 432.

49. *Recueil des actes de Philippe Ier*, 396, no. 158; Livre noir de St-Florent, Bib. nat., 1930, fol. 96r–v; *Cartul. de St-Aubin* 1: 306–7, no. 265.

This is perhaps the origin of the confusion of Robert and Hugh the Burgundian in the later versions of Le Baud and Bourdigné. The Parcé chronicle is also correct in naming the lord of Château-Gontier as Rainald. One further fact should be noted: there is no connection here between Conan's attack and Warin lord of Craon. The winning of Craon by Robert is clearly separated from the events of Conan's invasion.

This is not so in the later versions of Le Baud and de Bourdigné. There the events relating to the confiscation of Craon are thoroughly mixed with those of 1066. Warin, lord of Craon, is said to have given his daughter Bertha in marriage to Robert de Vitré, a follower of Duke Conan, which resulted in the confiscation of Craon, the invasion of Conan, and Conan's death.[50] As has been shown in the previous chapter, however, Craon was confiscated not from Warin, but from his younger brother Suhard, and Robert the Burgundian had received the lordship of Craon by 1053 at the latest.[51] Therefore the whole affair of Warin of Craon and his son-in-law Robert de Vitré must be separated from the events of 1066.

Yet the fact that Robert de Vitré is associated with the 1066 attack is both suggestive and plausible. De Vitré was an historical character who did, indeed, marry Warin's daughter.[52] This is significant for it gave him a claim to Craon when Suhard died. He was also a staunch supporter of Conan II who likewise could claim Craon.[53] In 1066, a family member, probably Robert's son Andrew, is reported to have been with Duke William's forces at the invasion of England.[54] If Conan had been encouraged by Duke William to invade Angevin territory, Robert de Vitré is the most appropriate intermediary.[55] Aside from being allied to both

50. Halphen, *Comté d'Anjou*, 143, n. 2.
51. *Cartul. Trinité de Vendôme*, 175–77, no. 96.
52. *Cartul. Trinité de Vendôme*, 1: no. 217. Ménage, *Histoire de Sablé*, 125.
53. La Borderie, *Histoire de Bretagne* 3: 15 n. 4; Le Baud, *Chronique de Vitré*, 9–10.
54. The only evidence for this is Wace, *The Conquest of England from Wace's Poem of the Roman de Rou*, trans. by Alexander Malet (London: Bell and Daldy, 1860), 196–97 and 210–11. Wace only gives the name of "de Vitré" which Elisabeth van Houts, "Wace as Historian," in *Family Trees and the Roots of Politics*, 132, assumes is Andrew of Vitré.
55. Geoffrey of Mayenne is also a possibility. At this time he was supposedly loyal to Duke William whose forces dominated northern Maine. In 1065 Geoffrey appears at Marmoutier as an important member of Conan's entourage, among "these my barons." See Morice, *Histoire de Bretagne, preuves*, 1: 408–9.

men, de Vitré had a personal interest in seeing the Craonais in friendlier hands. If Conan had won Château-Gontier, detaching Craon from the Angevin defensive line, Robert de Vitré or one of his sons doubtlessly would have been installed as the new Breton *dominus*.

At their core the accounts of Le Baud and de Bourdigné tell of a Breton invasion at the time of Conan's death inspired by the lord of Vitré that caught the count of Anjou by surprise while he was at Brissac. After initial success, the attack was defeated by Angevin forces at a battle in which Robert the Burgundian played a major role. Considering the accounts of William of Jumièges and Orderic Vitalis, the earlier legend from Parcé, and the location of Robert's fortresses of Craon and Sablé in relation to Château-Gontier, all of this is not only possible, but probable. It is clearly a version of events that the Angevins, Robert above all, would have wished it to have been.

The attack was the gravest military threat that Robert ever faced. The aim of Conan's campaign was clearly to penetrate the Angevin lines at Pouancé and Segré, swing north behind Craon, and isolate it by taking Château-Gontier.[56] If Conan had not died at the moment of his success, Robert would have lost all of the Craonais at one blow. Every indication is that Robert and Rainald faced this threat on their own, with no help from Geoffrey the Bearded. In the accounts of Le Baud and de Bourdigné the Angevin count is taken by surprise while busy at Brissac, about twenty kilometers southeast of Angers. In the *Chronique de Parcé* the counterattack against the Bretons was led by the Burgundian brothers, not the count. William of Jumièges and Orderic Vitalis, our most reliable sources, do not even mention the count of Anjou. Le Baud, in fact, only mentions Geoffrey as the source of discontent at Pouancé and Segré, the two strongholds surrendered to the Bretons. William of Malmesbury's claim that under Geoffrey the Bearded all of Anjou was "left a prey to marauders" is vividly affirmed.[57] In this case the exposed land was that of Robert and his ally Rainald of Château-Gontier.

Shortly after Conan's invasion, if not before, Robert joined the party

---

56. Le Baud supplies the name of these two strongholds, and on this detail he is followed by nearly all modern scholars.

57. "Tota terra praedonibus exposita," William of Malmesbury, *Gesta regum Anglorum*, 439.

in opposition to Geoffrey the Bearded that looked to Fulk Rechin as their leader. Far from being the action of an overpowerful castellan pursuing his own selfish and narrow interests to the detriment of a central power, Robert's rebellion was forced upon him by Geoffrey's weakness and bad judgement. In six years Robert had watched "an almost catastrophic decline" in Angevin fortunes.[58] His own position had been rendered untenable by Geoffrey's utter lack of military ability.[59] The Norman enemy was now barely two days ride to the north behind the strengthened fortifications of Le Mans where a Norman bishop presided. In the west the Bretons had very nearly succeeded in taking Craon and Château-Gontier. In the Angevin heartland to the south the count of Anjou, Robert's lord and protector, seemed incapable of any action other than threatening those very churchmen with whom Robert was allied. Late in his life Geoffrey was observed to be obviously mad. There is much in his actions to suggest that by 1067 he was already losing his emotional grip. While there is no indication that Fulk Rechin had displayed any great ability, Robert, like many Angevin nobles, must have decided that an unknown quality was preferable to a proven incompetent.

Robert's motives were not, to be sure, altruistic. Sometime during 1067 Fulk gave Robert the manor of Brion near Baugé.[60] At about the same time he also gave Robert the land of Genneteil in Angliers, the angle of land south of Angers formed by the Maine and Loire Rivers, now called l'Onglee. Nearly forty years later, when Robert was dead, Fulk would return the land to the church of Saint-Laud, explaining, "I had unjustly taken it away . . . and had given it to Robert the Burgundian since he claimed it was in his *fevum,* which it was not." Fulk then admits, "I gave it to him along with other gifts so that he would support me against my brother who violently took my honor away from me."[61]

---

58. "Un déclin quasi catastrophique," Guillot, *Comte d'Anjou,* 1: 105.

59. At least part of this failure may have been due to Geoffrey's inability to raise troops rather than his personal leadership. In the expedition of 1063 or 1064 Marmoutier refused to provide support demanded of it and several of Geoffrey's acts concern problems with raising either troops or supplies.

60. *Cartul. de St-Aubin,* 1: 440–41, no. 381, 11 March–7 August 1067.

61. *Cartul. de St-Laud,* no. 55. "Ego illam et injuste abstuleram et dederam eam Roberto Allobrogi, dicenti eam esse de fevo suo, quod non erat, sed ego illam ei cum aliis muneribus

With the receipt of these gifts Robert was now firmly ranked with the disaffected nobles collecting around Fulk Rechin and Archbishop Barthelemy. There is some slight indication that he may have been in Angers with Count Geoffrey right before the coup d'etat.[62] If so he abandoned the count, left Angers, and joined Fulk in open revolt.

On 25 February 1067 the castle of Saumur went over to Fulk, who immediately made it his headquarters.[63] For a few weeks the anti-Geoffrey movement gathered its strength at this fortress. Robert and his brother Guy were definitely there by 11 March, when they witnessed an act of Fulk's. Judging by the witness list they were the highest ranking lay members of the rebel entourage. Among the others were Guy of Laval, John of Chinon (the archbishop's brother and perhaps the earliest of the conspirators), Jocelin Rotundator, Robert of Moncontour, and Durand provost of Saumur.[64] If this represents a complete, or nearly complete, list of the major rebels, it can be seen that Fulk's forces were relatively small and consequently Robert and Guy together represented a major part of the rebels' military strength. As one of the most powerful of the Angevin lords, Robert's presence may have tipped the scales in Fulk's favor.

By this point Robert was aware that Fulk possessed overt support from the Church. Pope Alexander's reply to Archbishop Barthelemy's appeal arrived at Saumur in the person of his legate Cardinal Steven. For Robert, like most of the conspirators, Steven's role was crucial, for it provided him with a religious rationale justifying his rebellion. Repudiating the chosen successor of his benefactor must have cost Robert considerable anguish as it was. As far as the rebels were concerned,

---

ideo dederam, ut adjuraveret me contra fratrem meum qui mihi honorem meum violenter auferebat."

62. *Cartul. de St-Aubin* 1: 189, no. 164 and 208–9, no. 179, both 14 November 1060–4 April 1067 and both having the same witnesses. Robert and two of his knights, Waldin of Malicorne and Marcoard of Daumery, and a third, Artald, who is possibly also one of Robert's men, are present, along with two of the participants of Geoffrey's final betrayal. While this proves nothing, it is suggestive.

63. "Chron. St Maxentii" in *Chron. des églises d'Anjou*, 403. "Eodem anno (MLXVII) tradito Salmuri castri facta est Fulconi, fratri Gaufredi comitis Andegavorum, prima dominica die quadrigesime, V kalendas marcii."

64. Archives Maine-et-Loire, H 1840, no. 9, 11 March 1067 at Saumur. John of Chinon's role as an intermediary between his brother Barthelemy and Fulk dated back to 1063. Guillot, *Comte d'Anjou*, 1: 108, n. 480 and 2: C 267.

Geoffrey had demonstrated his unfitness to rule by his inability to defend the realm. Robert in particular would have been susceptible to this logic after the loss of Maine and his narrow escape from Conan's invasion. In speaking for the papacy Cardinal Steven delivered the divine judgement, in effect, that Geoffrey was indeed unfit to rule. He indicated this judgement by signing the written act of the judicial meeting *(placitum)* held at Saumur on 11 March in which Fulk is styled *comes,* that is, "Count."[65] By implication Geoffrey no longer was to be considered the legitimate count of the Angevins.[66] Robert would have noted the impressive array of ecclesiastical dignitaries present to add their names to the same document. They included Archbishop Barthelemy, Bishop Warech of Nantes, Bishop Mengisus of Vannes, and five abbots. Robert's friend from the monastery of Marmoutier, the monk Wanilo, was acting as the head of Steven's secretariat.[67]

Robert and the rebels now had the explicit approval of the Church, without which the conspirators probably could not have proceeded. While the exact course of events is confused, it seems that Geoffrey remained in Angers awaiting developments while surrounded by those of his nobles and knights who remained loyal. One of these was Rainald of Château-Gontier, who was presumably in contact with the rebel camp. On 4 April 1067, Rainald joined with other members of Geoffrey's entourage in revolt, betrayed Geoffrey, and handed him over to the forces of Fulk Rechin.[68]

At the moment of their triumph the warriors and ecclesiastics Robert had joined were checked by a force they had completely misjudged—the townspeople of Angers itself. The day after Geoffrey's betrayal the city erupted with a vicious assault on the rebels. Rainald of

65. Archives Maine-et-Loire, H 1840, no. 9.

66. Guillot, *Comte d'Anjou*, 1: 108–9, highlights the "sanction étonnamment vigoureuse" of the cardinal against Geoffrey. Halphen, *Comté d'Anjou*, 145, doubts that Steven actually deposed Geoffrey at this time. It is difficult, however, to believe that Steven could have assumed that there could be two legitimate counts for one realm. A later papal legate stated that Steven excommunicated Geoffrey and gave the *principatus* of Anjou to Fulk. See *Cartul. de St-Laud*, no. 16, analyzed by Guillot, *Comte d'Anjou*, 1: 109 n. 483 and 2: 356, "erratum."

67. Archives Maine-et-Loire, H 1840, no. 9. Wanilo dictates the act to another monk to write down.

68. "Annales de Vendôme" and "Annales de Renaud" in *Recueil d'annales angevines*, 64, 87. "Gaufidus comes junior . . . tradito est a suis Fulconi fratri suo et civitas Andecavis pridie nonas aprilis, IV feria ebdomade qui dicitur penosa, inter duo Pascha."

Château-Gontier, Geoffrey of Preuilly, and Gerard of Montreuil-Bellay were killed in the fighting. Robert the provost of Angers was captured and soon "slaughtered with stones and clubs,"[69] while another of Fulk's men, Adelard Ticio, was burned to death.[70] Such losses imply a concert-ed, planned action, not the "mob disordered by a malicious spirit," de-scribed by an eyewitness sympathetic to Fulk.[71] Fifty years later a Nor-man writer would claim that the common people *(plebs)* of Angers organized a *conspiratio* (presumably during the night of 4 April) to avenge their count's "evil betrayal," and this might well be closer to the truth.[72] The townspeople of Angers were accustomed to serving in the city militia and the better off merchants among them would have pro-vided a natural, and well armed, leadership loyal to the legitimate count.

Even a veteran soldier like Robert must have been shocked at the heavy losses. His closest ally on the northwestern border was dead, as well as at least two other members of the Angevin nobility and the highest ranking comital official. Except for the most intense and bitter fighting, eleventh century warfare produced relatively few casualties among the armored elite. The main objective was not to kill, but to capture top ranking enemies to hold for ransom, exactly as Rainald had been captured by the Bretons. Duke Conan's death at Château-Gontier was so unusual as to invite stories of assassination. The number and

69. "Annales de Vendôme" and "Annales de Renaud" in *Recueil d'annales angevines*, 64, 87. "Nam die crastina dominice scilicet cene anniversaria, ab Andecavina turba maligno spiritu turbata, miserabili nece peremptis tribus maximus auctoribus illius traditionis, Gaufrido videlicet de Prulliaco, Rainaldo de Castro Gunterii, Giraldo de Monasteriolo quartoque capto ac non multo post simili modo mortus, Rotberto scilicet ipsius Andecavis preposito, pluribus plures proinde, ut existimatio dedit, tribulati sunt ac mortui," and "Tempore quo Robertus prepositus adhuc vivebat qui et lapidus atque fustibus postea mactatus expiravit," *Cartul. du Ronceray*, no. 242.

70. Hugh of Fleury, "Modernorum regum Francorum liber," in *Recueil des historiens des Gauls et de Francs*, vol. 12, ed. Léopold Delisle (Paris: V. Palmé, 1877), 792.

71. "Annales de Renaud," 87. "Turba maligno spiritu turbata."

72. Hugh of Fleury, "Modernorum regum Francorum liber," 797. For the role of the townspeople, see W. Scott Jessee "Urban Violence and the Coup d'État of Fulk le Réchin in Anjou," *Haskins Society Journal* 7 (1997): 75–82. For a discussion of this event in the broader context of Angevin urban development see Hironori Miyamatsu, "A-t-il existé une com-munne à Angers au XIIe siècle?" *Journal of Medieval History* 21 (1995): 117–52. For the wealth of certain townspeople at this time, see Miyamatsu's "Les premiers bourgeois d'Angers aux XIe et XII siècles," *Annales de Bretagne et des Pays de L'Ouest* 97 (1990): 1–11.

rank of the slain was a severe blow to Robert's cause. Rainald was castellan of a major link in the northwestern shield. Geoffrey was *dominus* of Preuilly, a castle as old as Sablé, as well as treasurer of Saint-Martin of Tours with control over Saint-Martin's castle of Châteauneuf.[73] Girard was castellan, if not *dominus,* of Montreuil-Bellay and from an important Tourangeau family allied to the king. He was also Geoffrey Martel's stepson by his second marriage.[74] The provost on the other hand was of humble origins but had risen to be the count's highest official, not merely of the city but of the whole county of Anjou.[75] Robert the Burgundian, of course, knew all these men quite well.[76] However shaken, though, Robert now withdrew with the captive Count Geoffrey to the security of his formidable fortress at Sablé.[77] It was imperative that Geoffrey be kept imprisoned safely away from his supporters in the capital.

This action was too late to save the conspirators' plans. Nearly a week after the coup the monks of Marmoutier had to seek justice before the count of Poitiers because "there was not then at Angers a count to whom one could go for justice."[78] If a monastery that had openly sided with Fulk was unwilling or unable to hail Fulk as count, the coup was in serious difficulty. Within a relatively short time Robert and the rebels, including Fulk, were forced to release Geoffrey and to re-acknowledge him as count.[79] Despite papal approval, everyone, in-

73. Guillot, *Comte d'Anjou,* 1: 90–91, 456, and 468.

74. Girard's brother and immediate successor, Rainald, was styled "dominus de Castro Mosteriolo." See Liv. noir de St-Florent, Bib. nat., n.a.lat. 1930, fol. 107. For the family tie to the king, see Guillot, *Comte d'Anjou,* 1: 113–14.

75. See Guillot, *Comte d'Anjou,* 1: 410 and 413–14 for the extent of his powers.

76. Rainald of Château-Gontier has already been discussed. For Robert's appearance with Geoffrey of Preuilly, see *Cartul. Trinité de Vendôme,* 1: 273–76, no. 158 and *Livre des serfs,* nos. 16 and 19; for Girard of Montreuil-Bellay, see *Cartul. Trinité de Vendôme,* 1: 175–77, no. 96. For Robert the provost, see *Cartul. du Ronceray,* nos. 237 and 242; *Cartul. de St-Laud,* no. 25; *Cartul. Trinité de Vendôme,* 1: 271–76, nos. 157 and 158; and *Cartul. de St-Aubin,* 1: 189 and 208–9, nos. 164 and 179.

77. *Cartul. du Ronceray,* no. 176. "Quando erat comes Gaufridus Junior in prisione apud Sablolium." This is Geoffrey's first imprisonment since the act was confirmed when Geoffrey was temporarily freed. Halphen, *Comté d'Anjou,* 146, n.2.

78. Bib. nat., Dom Housseau, II$_2$, no. 708, 10 or 11 April 1067. "Nec erat tunc in Andecavo comes quem idem deduci ad justiciam posset."

79. Guillot, *Comte d'Anjou,* 1: 110, and Halphen, *Comté d'Anjou,* 146–47.

cluding Robert, was beginning to have second thoughts about deposing a count, even one as feckless as Geoffrey.

Robert may have been one of the first of the rebels to push for a reconciliation with the count. Perhaps serving as Geoffrey's jailor had given Robert an opportunity to reflect and to be persuaded by the count himself. On 16 July 1067, Robert presided over his full court at Craon and specifically dated the event as "the seventh year of Count Geoffrey."[80] With these words Robert signified that he was recognizing Geoffrey as the sole legitimate count of Anjou.[81] A month later he was the center of an even more significant act. King Philip joined Robert, his cousin, along with Count Geoffrey and Fulk Rechin at the siege of Chaumont-sur-Loire.[82] There on 7 August 1067 the king confirmed a donation that Robert and his wife Advisa had made earlier of all of the churches of Sablé and other properties to the monks of Marmoutier. Among the others who confirmed the gift were Count Geoffrey, his wife Juliette, and his brother Fulk.[83] This act was filled with political implications. Most striking is the marked honor shown Robert, no doubt due to the key role he had played, at the king's instigation, in Geoffrey's restoration.[84] Since Geoffrey and his wife confirmed the donation, Robert was clearly reconciled to the count and forgiven his part in the revolt. Fulk's presence was needed to complete the confirmation, indicating some quasi-official role in comital affairs, but he no longer bore the title of count. Finally, Robert was taking the churches of Sablé away from the control of the bishop of Le Mans, now firmly under Norman control, and placing them under the control of the abbey of Marmoutier.[85]

80. *Cartul. de Trinité de Vendôme*, 1: 316–19, no. 184. "Actum est hoc . . . anno MLXVII ab Incarnatione Domini . . . anno quoque Gosfredi comitis VIIo." Guillot, *Comte d'Anjou*, 1: 110, discusses this document's relevance to Geoffrey's countship. The wording is, of course, that of the scribe who wrote the document, probably a monk of the Trinity of Vendôme. On such an important and delicate turn of phrase relating to a formal meeting of Robert's own court, the scribe would have written only what was in accord with Robert's own political stance.

81. Guillot, *Comte d'Anjou*, 1: 110 n. 487. Unfortunately, no document gives us even a hint of events between 5 April and 16 July to explain the turn around.

82. The lord of Chaumont was Sulpicius of Amboise who tried to remain neutral. Supporting neither he made enemies of both. Halphen, *Comté d'Anjou*, 147.

83. *Cartul. manceau*, 2: 59–66, nos. 2 and 3, 7 August 1067, Chaumont-sur-Loire.

84. Guillot, *Comte d'Anjou*, 1: 113 n. 501.

85. Guillot, *Comte d'Anjou*, 1: 110, finds the king's approval of this "amusing." It was, of course, a sly way of taking a slap at Duke William.

There is a hint as to why Robert may have exerted his considerable influence to effect a rapprochement between the two brothers. Robert had turned against Geoffrey the Bearded for at least two reasons: Geoffrey's mistreatment of Marmoutier and the Breton threat to Craon. The problem of Marmoutier was at least partially addressed by the nature of the act at Chaumont. All of Robert's arrangements regarding the transfer of the churches of Sablé to the abbey were confirmed. Not only did Geoffrey the Bearded publicly acknowledge the gift to the monks he had so excessively attacked, his confirmation was backed by Fulk Rechin and the king of France.

As for the threat to Craon, it must be remembered that Robert had no hereditary claim to Craon, so that he held it only at the count's pleasure. Worse yet, there was a legitimate heiress, the daughter of Warin of Craon, married to a Breton lord, Robert de Vitré. Sometime between the act of 16 July 1067 and the royal confirmation of 7 August 1067 a major change in this situation occurred. In the first act Robert acts as lord of Craon presiding over the court of Craon. In the second document, the donation confirmed by King Philip, Robert's son Rainald appears at Craon, approving the donation made by his parents as if he were in command of Craon, as, in fact, he was from that point on.[86] Rainald eventually married the legitimate heiress of Craon, Ennoguena, the granddaughter of Warin of Craon.[87] Her father, Robert de Vitré, was present at this act, Rainald's first at Craon. Robert's price for his support for Geoffrey's restoration may have been the betrothal of his eldest son to the heiress of Craon and his installation at Craon as *dominus*. If the marriage had not already taken place, de Vitré's presence certainly indicates amicable relations with the Burgundian family at Craon. In either case, a major concern of Robert's at Chaumont would have been to get the king's signature on the document of donation for the churches of Sablé, because the written document contained a notice of Rainald's act at Craon. In effect King Philip was also confirming Rainald's status as *dominus* of Craon. This and the

---

86. *Cartul. manceau,* 2: 63–66, no. 3, shortly before 7 August 1067.

87. *Cartul. Trinité de Vendôme,* 1: no. 217, where Rainald speaks of "uxor mea Eunoguena, filia Roberti de Vitreio, nata de ipsius legali conjuge, filia videlicet Warini, naturalis haeredis et domini Credonensis honoris."

presence of Robert de Vitré at Craon indicate that Robert's political skill had succeeded in diffusing the Breton threat. Having satisfied himself on his concerns for Marmoutier and Craon, Robert was willing to see a restoration of Geoffrey the Bearded.

However important this was to Robert and his son, not everyone was reconciled to the count at Chaumont. While Robert was clearly in the forefront of the reconciliation movement, Fulk and an unknown number of the former rebels were not ready to accept Geoffrey as count. Resentment and fear must have been just below the surface on both sides. The result of Robert's peacemaking lasted less than a year. Robert is not mentioned in any extant document as having taken part in the renewed fighting. He may have been so effected by the events of the preceding year that he deliberately stayed in the background, but an argument *ex silentio* is unconvincing. Since he retained all the gifts Fulk had given him and remained preeminent in the reinstalled Fulk's entourage it is more likely that he again played an active and decisive role and that it is only our impoverished sources that prevent us from seeing him.[88]

It is known only that Fulk once again recruited supporters and seized the fortress of Brissac around April 1068.[89] Fulk would later describe the resulting struggle:

My brother once again attacked me, besieging my castle which is called Brissac. I rode against him there with those nobles whom God's clemency allowed me, and fought with him in open battle in which by the grace of God I vanquished him. And he was captured and returned to me, and a thousand of his townspeople with him.[90]

Militarily inept to the end, Geoffrey disappeared into a dungeon at Chinon, not to reappear for over twenty-eight years. "And Fulk was re-

---

88. *Cartul Trinité de Vendôme*, I: no 216, two acts, 6 April 1069, Angers and 20 April 1069, Baugé, where Robert and Guy head the witness lists.

89. For the date, Halphen, *Comté d'Anjou*, 147 n.4.

90. Fulk Rechin, "Fragmentum historiae," 379. "... invasit iterum idem frater, ponens obsidionem circa quoddam castrum meum, quod vocabatur Brachesac: ubi equitavi contra illum cum illis proceribus quos Dei clementia mihi permiserat, et pugnavi cum eo campestri praelio, in quo eum, Dei gratia, superavi; et fuit ipse captus et mihi redditus, et mille de civibus suis cum eo." Here the term *cives* clearly means the townspeople of Angers, probably the urban militia.

ceived back into the countship by the Angevins, whether they wished it or not," the Angevin chronicles say.[91] Now it remained for Robert to count up his losses, consolidate whatever he may have gained from the new count, and face the Norman power on his northern border.

91. ". . . ac Fulco in comitatum ab Andecavinis, vellent nolent, receptus," in "Annales de Vendôme," "Annales de Renaud," and "Annales de St-Aubin," all in *Rec. d'annales angevines*, 5, 65, and 87 respectively.

CHAPTER FOUR

Robert and Fulk Rechin

On 9 November 1068 Robert's aunt Agnes, countess of Poitou, duchess of Aquitaine, countess of Anjou, died at the abbey she had founded of Notre-Dame de Saintes. She had retired there to find peace after an eventful life.[1] "After a husband of this world, she had coupled with God, a better husband, while living in the world. Dead, she would triumph more auspiciously after death," her obituary from Notre-Dame de Vendôme would say.[2] Save for Geoffrey Martel, she was the person most responsible for Robert's acquisition of wealth, power, and rank. If Robert took notice of her death, it must have seemed like the passing of the last link with the great days of Geoffrey Martel, the man who had once called Agnes "my dearest wife uniquely beloved by me."[3]

Robert could have had little time for nostalgia in any event, for affairs in Anjou were still too unsettled. The period that had ended only a few months before with the final capture of Geoffrey the Bearded was aptly described by Fulk Rechin as "a tribulation which [my brother and I] dragged out for eight years, often making war and occasionally having truces."[4] Such an extended period of civil conflict had called into

---

1. Richard, *Comtes de Poitou* 1: 305–6.

2. "Post saecularem maritum Deo marito meliori copulata, vivens mundo, mortua post mortem felicius victura," in Jean Besly, *Histoire des comtes de Poictou et des ducs de Guyenne, contenant ce qui s'est passé de plus mémorable en France depuis l'an 811 jusques au Roy Louis le Jeune* (Paris: R. Bertault, 1647) 349bis of "Preuves."

3. "Agnes, unico mihi amore dilectissima uxor," *Cartul. Trinité de Vendôme* 1: 165–66, no. 92, 6 January 1049.

4. "Fragmentum historiae," 379. "Quam tribulationem cum per annos octo protendissemus, guerram saepe facientes et interdum inducias habentes."

question the most basic assumptions of loyalty to the count of Anjou. This in turn had a detrimental effect on the relationship of trust and mutual dependence between the count and his *fideles*, the fundamental basis of the Angevin state.

Robert would have been preoccupied with preserving the security of his own honor while Angevin comital power was seriously weakened and in danger from external attacks and internal disorders. He was a major participant at the siege of Chaumont, the one certain thing on which Geoffrey the Bearded and his brother Fulk could cooperate during Geoffrey's brief restoration. When the castellan of Chaumont, Sulpicius of Amboise, apparently tried to use the confusion of the civil war to escape his obligations to the count of Anjou, he found himself besieged by the forces of both claimants to the comital title as well as of the king of France and the count of Flanders in August 1067.[5] Robert clearly agreed with the two brothers that whatever their differences, comital control over the key fortresses of the state must be preserved. Once Fulk had seized power for a second and final time, he had to find some way to assert his authority and reforge the ties that bound the Angevin *fideles* to the count.

At the castle of Trèves, Fulk demonstrated that one way to do this was by brute force. Like Robert, Harduin the castellan of Trèves first supported the rebel cause. He was not as skilled as Robert, however, in negotiating the rapid change of fortune from Fulk to Geoffrey and then back to Fulk. With Fulk's final victory Harduin was left supporting Geoffrey as count. Fulk promptly marched on Trèves, destroyed the castle, and blinded the unfortunate Harduin in June of 1068.[6] Count Guy-Geoffrey of Poitou took this opportunity to intervene on behalf of Geoffrey the Bearded and his supporters at Trèves by attacking and burning Saumur on 27 June 1068.[7] Two documents have survived of

---

5. *Cartul. manceau*, 2: 59–63, no. 2, August 1067. Cf. Halphen, *Comté d'Anjou*, 147.

6. "Redeunte comite a castro de Treviensis et ea die destructo," Bib. de Poitiers, coll. Dom Fonteneau, 13, fol. 283, dated Thursday, 19 June 1068. Harduin's punishment is in Bib. nat., Dom Houss., II$_2$, no. 735. See Guillot, *Comte d'Anjou*, C 292 and C 293 respectively. Harduin was deprived of his paternal heritage and became a monk of Saint-Nicolas. Nearly 30 years later Robert took part in a judgement when Harduin's family tried to reclaim a portion of this in Bib. nat., Dom Housseau, 3, no. 1001.

7. "Chron. St. Maxentii," Bib. nat., lat. 4892, pub. in Halphen, 150, n. 5. "Anno MLXVIII . . . castrum Salmuram horribili incendio combustum est a Guidone comite Pictavorum cum ec-

acts of Fulk at Trèves at this time, but Robert is not listed among the witnesses.[8] Probably he was staying in the north with his own forces to keep watch on the Normans in Le Mans with other border castellans. Whatever Robert's role, it is important to notice that enough *domini* followed their count to allow him to project his power dramatically and ruthlessly.

The fate of Sulpicius of Amboise at Chaumont and Harduin at Trèves also highlights the extreme skill Robert had displayed during the Angevin crisis. In a volatile situation where the slightest misstep could have led to a disaster, Robert emerged with a position in the new count's entourage not inferior to that which he had held in the old, while at the same time his actual holdings were increased. Fulk Rechin had felt compelled to give Robert Brion, Genneteil, and other gifts for his support. Robert was then able to make use of the king's interest in a reconciliation between the two counts to secure what amounted to a royal confirmation of his son Rainald's command at Craon.

When the civil war broke out again in 1068, Robert returned to his support of Fulk without any apparent bitterness on the new count's part. This is certain because his position is still preeminent in charters of Count Fulk. In two acts from 1069, for example, Robert and his brother Guy are listed first after the count himself.[9] In 1070 Robert and his son Rainald continued to take precedence over such early supporters of Fulk as John of Chinon and Hugh of Montreuil-Bellay.[10] In the same year Robert accompanied Fulk Rechin to Tours with those called the count's "barons" and again is listed first.[11] All of this evidence together indicates that Robert was the leading *fideles* in the new regime.

Robert's brother Guy also prospered under Count Fulk Rechin. Count Fulk l'Oison of Vendôme died 21 November 1066, leaving a mi-

---

clesia Sancti Florentii . . . V kalendas julii." It is imperfectly reproduced in *Chron. des églises d'Anjou*, 404.

8. Cited in n. 6 above.

9. Two acts in *Cartul. Trinité de Vendôme*, 1: no. 216, 6 April 1069, Angers, and 20 April 1069, Baugé.

10. "Livre noir de St-Florent," Bib. nat., n.a. lat. 1930, fol. 105v, 24 May 1070.

11. *Cartulaire de Cormery*, ed. J. Bourassé (Tours, Paris: Guilland-Verger, Dumoulin, 1861), no. 41, 28 August 1070, Tours. *Barones* was a relatively new term for the nobles of the region. It filled the need for a specific title to separate the increasingly powerful *domini* from other nobles and knights.

nor son named Burchard to inherit the countship. Guy received the
guardianship of the county of Vendôme during the minority of Count
Burchard. Along with the boy's mother, Petronilla, Guy served as regent, and in some documents is even styled "count."[12] In conjunction
with this he was granted the castle of Le Nouâtre that pertained to the
counts of Vendôme, although originally an Angevin stronghold.[13] This
charge almost certainly came to Guy after Fulk took over the countship
of Anjou. By November of 1066 Guy and Robert were probably already
estranged from Geoffrey the Bearded. If Guy had received the ward-
ship of young Burchard from Geoffrey at that time, it seems unlikely
that he would have been among the rebels at Saumur in March 1067. If
he were acting count of Vendôme at Saumur, one would expect that
the document produced there by the rebels would have noted the fact,
and it does not.[14] Fulk Rechin, then, was the donor of this gift to Guy,
probably in an effort to reward him for service against Geoffrey and to
maintain his loyalty just as he had his brother.

At first glance it appears that Guy was raised even higher than
Robert, but the "countship" of Vendôme was seen as a temporary gift,
lasting only until the legitimate heir to Fulk l'Oison came of age. This,
in fact, happened on 14 January 1075.[15] In the meantime Guy appears to
have been immersed in Vendômois affairs, playing a more restricted
role in Fulk's entourage than Robert. Still, Robert and Guy were close,
cooperating on numerous occasions and, no matter how temporary,
this honor bestowed on his brother enhanced Robert's own position.[16]
Guy apparently shared his brother's respect for the Church—his rule

12. *Cartululaire de Marmoutier pour la vendômois*, ed. Trémault (Vendôme: Clovis Ripé,
1893), no. 12, dated 1066–1075; *Livre des serfs de Marm.*, no. 9. Cf. Halphen, *Comté d'Anjou*, 309,
and Guillot, *Comté d'Anjou*, 1: 293. See also *Cartul. Trinité de Vendôme* 1: no. 188, where Guy
holds a court, and no. 247. Cf. Johnson, *Prayer*, 78. Johnson, following Métais, misidentifies
Guy as the youngest son of Robert's uncle Bodo.

13. Guillot, *Comté d'Anjou*, 1: 460, no. 21 and 2: C 309 published in *Cartul. de Noyers*, no. 50.
For Le Nouâtre, see Bachrach, "Castle Building," 539.

14. "Livre noir de St-Florent," Bib. nat. n.a. lat. 1930, fol. 58r–59v, 11 March 1067 at Saumur.

15. Halphen, *Comté d'Anjou*, 309.

16. For Robert and Guy working together, *Cartul. de St-Aubin* 1: 306–7, no. 265; Livre noir
de St-Florent, Bib. nat., n.a. lat., 1930, fol. 137v; *Livre des serfs de Marmoutier*, no. 116; Archives
Maine-et-Loire, H 1840, no. 13; *Cartul. de St-Aubin*, 2: 353, no. 880. The overall impression is
that Guy cooperated closely with Robert in a slightly subordinate role since Robert is invariably listed first.

was unusually free of conflict with the abbey of the Trinity of Ven-dôme.[17]

Robert's own position in relation both to the count and to his own subordinates is dramatically portrayed in a document that seems to rep-resent one of the operations Fulk, in this case explicitly with Robert's aid, carried out in order to secure his realm after defeating Geoffrey in 1068.[18] The act concerns the status of the castle of Durtal. Fulk Rechin believed that Fulk Nerra first built a fortification at Durtal,[19] but a no-tice of Saint-Aubin shows that it was constructed by Geoffrey Martel between 1047 and 1060 and given to Hubert the Razor of *Campania.*[20] In any case Durtal became another link in the network of fortresses secur-ing the valley of Le Loir as the Angevin northeastern line of defense. This line ran from the junction of the Sarthe and Le Loir at the castle of Briollay eastward to include the fortresses of Matheflon, Durtal, La Flèche, Le Lude, Château-du-Loir, La Chartre-sur-le-Loir, Lavardin, and finally Vendôme. Like the northwestern shield of Craon, Château-Gontier, and Sablé, each of these strongholds was an average of sixteen kilometers apart from the next so that support from either side was only a days ride away.[21] On its western extremity this line tucked in be-hind the northwestern shield so that fortresses like Durtal and La Flèche could back up Sablé and Malicorne to the north.

As the monks of Saint-Aubin described the event, Count Fulk marched on Durtal with Robert the Burgundian and Marcoard of Daumeray, "ejected" Rainald of Maulévrier, and "returned" the place to both Robert and Marcoard.[22] All three men entered the castle and

17. Johnson, *Prayer,* 84.

18. Angot, *Généalogies féodales,* dates the act ca. 1070 without explanation.

19. "Fragmentum historiae," 377. ". . . in Andegavo aedificavit Baugiacum, Castrum Gun-teriii, Duristallum, et multa alia [castra]."

20. *Cartul. St-Aubin,* no. 306. "Temporibus Gaufridi Martelli . . . comitis cum idem . . . princeps castellum quod dicitur Duristallum construxisset illudque Huberto de Campania cognomento Rasorio dedisset." Cf. Guillot, *Comte d'Anjou,* C 207. Fournier, *Château,* 293–303, details the history of Durtal and provides extracts of the relevant documents translated into French. He renders *Campania* as Champigny although earlier scholars such as Angot, Port, and De Brousillon give Champagne.

21. Bachrach, "Castle Building," 555–56.

22. *Cartul. de St-Aubin* 1: no. 289. ". . . Fulco comes . . . Rainaldum de Maloleprario de Duristallo ejecit et Rotberto Burgundo et Marcoardo de Dalmeriaco Duristallum reddidit." Latin quotes in the following notes refer to this document. How much force involved in the

were met by Abbot Otbrand of Saint-Aubin with some of his monks
and servants. The abbot was concerned about the property his abbey
had already acquired in the honor of Durtal and asked the count what
would be done about this.

When Fulk heard this he turned to Robert and said, "Lord Robert,
you heard what the lord abbot said. What should we do about these
properties which they have legally held until now, as we have heard?"[23]

Robert replied, "How else, lord, other than as is right and as you
wish it? For my part, for love of you who have restored my right I freely
grant that they should hold it as they did, free and secure."[24]

Fulk then asked the same question of Marcoard, but before Marcoard could answer Robert broke in, "Lord Marcoard, let me tell you
what to do. For the love of God and our lord count accept Saint-Aubin's
beneficium for your soul and the souls of your ancestors and willingly
grant the monks their property as they held it in the past."[25]

Marcoard obviously had little choice in the matter but Count Fulk
tactfully suggested that the abbot "give him something so that he will
willingly authorize whatever you seem to hold in your jurisdiction."[26]
The monks agreed to pay Marcoard eight pounds of new *denarii* and
Robert one hundred *solidi* of "old Angevin *denarii*."

The painstaking efforts made by the monastic scribe to record this
remarkable dialogue show that to the monks of Saint-Aubin what was
said between these two men was of the utmost importance.[27] In the
scene as painted by the monk, Fulk's new regime is barely on its feet

---

ejection is unstated. It probably did not involve a siege, which may explain why Rainald did
not suffer the fate of Harduin of Trèves but was soon back in the count's entourage.

23. "Audistis, domine Rotberto, quid dicat dominus abbas. Quomodo erit modo de rebus
suis quas hic, sicut audimus, huc usque auctorabileter tenuerunt?"

24. "Quomodo, domine, nisi sicut rectum est et sicut vultis? De mea parte libenter concedo pro vestro amore, qui michi rectum meum reddidistis, ut quiete et secure teneant sicut
tenuerunt."

25. "Tunc interjecit domnus Rotbertus et ait: 'Domine Marcoarde, dicam vobis quomodo
faciatis. Accipite beneficium loci Sancti Albini animae vestrae et parentum vestrorum, et con-
cedite libenter ut teneant monachi, sicut tenuerunt, pro amore Dei et sancti Albini et domini
nostri comitis.'"

26. "Et adjecit comes: 'Et vos, domine abbas, date ei aliquam rem ut libenter auctorizet
quicquid de suo jure habere videmini.'"

27. For the significance in charters of what look like extraneous details, see Marcus Bull,
"The Diplomatic of the First Crusade," in *The First Crusade: Origins and Impact,* ed. by
Jonathan Philips (Manchester and New York: Manchester University Press, 1997), 35–54.

and everyone is feeling his way, literally negotiating questions of power and property as they speak, and the scribe wants to hold them to it for the benefit of his monastery. Count Fulk cannot simply impose his decision; he defers to the veteran Robert the Burgundian, a man who helped put him in power. He asks Robert what should be done and Robert's courteous reply does not obscure this fact. Yet Robert then turns the decision back to Fulk: he really is the legitimate count and Robert will respect his will. The implication is there, though, that since he is consulted, Robert could advance his own agenda if he wished but he refuses to do so. Robert then exercises a strict authority over his own follower, Marcoard of Daumeray. He does not even let his subordinate reply to the count's question, but bluntly tells him what to do. While Robert must be consulted, he will respect the count's position and his own subordinate will simply obey. The payments to the three men are intended to establish an ongoing and reciprocal relationship between these powerful secular lords and the monastery. There is still order in the Angevin world, Saint-Aubin will continue to have his property rights respected, and relations with the nobility will be restored.

Robert is the key player in the conversation and this underscores the fact that he had been able to call on the count and his authority to restore him and his *fidelis* Marcoard to the honor of Durtal. This operation must have been more than a simple "return" of the castle to a man who had been its rightful *dominus* all along. The monks of Saint-Aubin were uneasy indeed if their abbot was willing to travel with an entourage of monks and servants to this outpost to prevent confiscation of their property. Saint-Aubin was a monastery dear to the townspeople of Angers, the very people who had violently resisted Fulk's takeover attempt in April 1097. Possibly the monks themselves had sided with the rioters.[28] Abbot Otbrand clearly feared that the new rulers might consider the previous donations invalid. He was careful to

---

28. Abbot Otbrand admitted to Fulk that it was not by chance that he had come upon them so suddenly but by deliberate action. ". . . adjecit abbas propter quod non casu, sed ex industria sic repente eos subsecutus erat." For Saint-Aubin's possibly pro-Geoffrey stance in Angers during the fighting that ruined Fulks first coup-d'état, Jessee, "Urban Violence," 80–81.

list the donors by name: Count Geoffrey Martel, the bishop of Angers, Agnes the wife of Hubert of *Campania,* and her sons.[29]

Robert's absence from this list implies that he had not been exercising the rights of the *dominus* of Durtal long enough to have made any donations of his own or to have approved any donations made by anyone else. This is borne out by the evidence of other charters. When Agnes, the widow of the original castellan, donated the parish church at Gouis and the chapel of the castle to Saint-Aubin sometime between 1056 and 1060, she did not secure the authority of Robert the Burgundian as *dominus* of Craon. Instead, she secured the approval of Count Geoffrey Martel and a certain William of Montsoreau, "in whose *casamentum* were the things I bestowed on the monks," as Agnes says.[30] Yet when Agnes's son, Hubert the Younger, confirmed his mother's donation sometime after 1067, he secured the approval of "Rainald, *dominus* of Craon and Sablé, son of Robert the Burgundian."[31]

This suggests that while Robert may have claimed Durtal as part of the honor of Craon from the time before the castle was built, he had not actually exercised any real authority over it until Fulk ejected Rainald of Maulévrier sometime after 1067. By October 1072 Durtal is listed specifically as part of the honor of Robert the Burgundian and Rainald, that is, part of the honor of Craon rather than Sablé. This is the earliest certain evidence of Robert's possession of it. Unfortunately, it is impossible to know exactly how or when Robert acquired Durtal. Port felt that the land on which it was built in the parish of Saints-Gervaise-et-Protais of Gouis was already within the territory of Craon.[32] If this were so, then it seems that Geoffrey took it out of the hands of the lord of Craon and gave it to Hubert the Razor to hold directly from the count.[33] Nowhere does Robert or his son Rainald play any certain role

---

29. ". . . de rebus nostris quas hic per comitem Gaufridum, avunculum vestrum, et episcopum Andecavensum et uxorem Hucberti de Campania, Agnetem, hujus castri tunc dominam, et per filios suos . . . adquisivimus."

30. *Cart. St-Aubin* 1: no. 287; dated in Guillot, *Comte d'Anjou,* 2: C 214.

31. *Cart. St-Aubin* 1: no. 288, in a gloss added by the redactor of the cartulary.

32. Célestin Port, *Dictionnaire historique, géographique et biographique de Maine-et-Loire,* 3 vols (Paris: Dumoulin, 1878), 2: 89.

33. While this is uncertain, there is no doubt that the status of the religious jurisdiction was disrupted by the construction. See Fournier, *Château,* Document A, 303.

in affairs at Durtal until 1072. The hypothesis that Durtal had been taken out of Robert's or his predecessors' control when Geoffrey Martel fortified it would neatly account for Robert seeing it as a "return" of his rightful property. If so, Fulk was paying off heavy political debts to Robert in giving him the fortress of Durtal.

Whatever the earlier status of Durtal, its castellan, Hubert the Razor, died and his widow Agnes married Rainald of Maulévrier.[34] Rainald apparently tried to usurp the lordship of Durtal from his stepson Hubert, or at least to keep it independent from Robert, who claimed it. He may also have supported the wrong side in the civil war. There is no doubt that Robert intended for Marcoard of Daumeray to hold Durtal directly from himself while Hubert was a minor, no matter what arrangements Geoffrey Martel may have made. The most likely time for such confusion would be the period of the civil war when other Angevin lords tried to escape comital authority. Once the war was over Robert was in a position to call in his debts from Count Fulk.

Thanks to Robert's skill in manipulating Fulk's insecure claim to the countship, by the end of 1072 his holdings of Craon and Sablé included Lion-d'Angers, Brion, Durtal, and Malicorne as well as Genneteil in l'Onglée, the forest of Bouère, Brûlon, and Cornillé.[35] At least five of these, Craon, Sablé, Durtal, Malicorne, and Brûlon, were fortified. This represented a formidable array of power across the northern marches of Anjou. Except for Craon, the fortresses formed a diamond shaped block connecting the river routes of the Sarthe and the Loir and covering the southwestern approaches to Le Mans. Fulk's weakness compelled him to grant extraordinary power and independence to the *domini* and castellans of his realm, especially those on an exposed border region as Robert was.

Now Robert was able to bolster his own position as frontier lord even further by arranging the marriage of his daughter Burgundia to

34. Angot, *Généalogies féodales*, 456, no. 16. Agnes and Rainald donated the churches of Gouis, Durtal, and Châtelais to the abbey of Saint-Aubin, Angot, 456, no. 15, 1047–1067, pub. in *Cartul. St-Aubin* 1: no. 287.

35. For Lion-d'Angers, Brion, Durtal, and Malicorne, see Bertrand de Broussillon, *Craon*, no. 34, before October 1072; for Genneteil, see *Cartul. de St-Laud*, no. 20 and no. 55; for Bouère, see *Cartul. manceau*, 2: 59–63, no. 2; Brûlon, *Cartul. de la Couture*, 22–23, no. 15; Cornillé, *Cartul. du Ronceray*, no. 164 and no. 165.

Rainald III of Château-Gontier. Robert's relationship with the family of Château-Gontier had always been close, going back at least to 1052 when he was a witness to an act of Rainald's father at Château-Renault.[36] He had assisted the Rainaldi clan again when his future son-in-law was given up as a hostage to the Bretons.[37] It was probably sometime after the death of the elder Rainald at Angers in 1067 that Robert arranged for his daughter to marry the young heir.[38] The betrothal may have allowed Robert to exercise guardianship over the neighboring castle, at least until Rainald came of age. Robert's authority, experience, and personality must have made a deep impression on the younger man so that as long as they both lived Robert exerted considerable influence over Château-Gontier and its dependencies. These included Segré, the western angle of the Angevin defensive line and the key stronghold that had given way in 1066.[39] This left the major portions of the Angevin defensive web constructed by Fulk Nerra and Geoffrey Martel on the northwestern border in Robert's overall control.

There were various ways in which Robert could exert his control at the personal level over the *domini* and knights within his patronage. When he was face to face with a subordinate, as he was with Marcoard of Daumeray, the force of his personal authority could impose itself. Robert was effective in exerting his will by a combination of authority and persuasion. In 1094, for example, Marcoard's son Rainard gave in "to the counsel of his *dominus* Robert the Burgundian and some of his own men," and dropped his claim against Marmoutier for the woods of

36. *Cartul. Trinité de Vendôme*, 1: 155–56, no. 85, 24 August 1044–15 August 1052.

37. *Cartul. blésois de Marmoutier*, no. 24, 3 April 1064, Angers.

38. Angot, *Généalogies féodales*, 147, mentions earlier writers who held that Alard I (d. 1060–1063) had married Robert's daughter Mathilda, but there is no evidence that Robert had a daughter of this name.

39. Rainald III of Château-Gontier had his hall (*aula*) at the foot of the *mota* of Segré and Witern of Segré witnessed an act there on his behalf. *Cartulaire d'Azé et du Géneteil*, ed. M. du Brossay, Archives historique du Maine, vol. 3 (Le Mans: Société des archives historiques du Maine, 1903), no. 2, 1080–1096. See also Bib. nat., Dom Housseau, 13, no. 9556, "in curia domini Raginaldi de Castro Gunterii ad Segreium," dated 1079–1096. Guillot, *Comte d'Anjou*, 1: 294–95, sees Segré as a comital castle, even though he admits that Rainald held rights amounting to a "seigneurie châtelaine." If he held such rights and held his court at Segré he clearly controlled the castle, whatever its correct legal status. Perhaps Segré was taken away from its castellan after its betrayal in 1066 and given to Château-Gontier as a reward for Rainald's father's support of Fulk Rechin.

Chalonnes-sur-Loire.[40] The unusually large number of people who appear in Robert's entourage on that occasion gives some hint as to the extent of Robert's influence and power.

Robert's most faithful subordinate was his eldest son Rainald, installed as *dominus* of Craon. From 1068 until Robert's departure on Crusade in 1098, Rainald authorized and confirmed every gift and judgement his father made regarding the Craonais without hesitation.[41] On several occasions Rainald gave blanket approvals to acts his father might make, indicating that whatever was in his honor was also in his father's honor. This finds its clearest expression in Rainald's statement that he and his wife Domita "confirm whatever the monks of Saint-Aubin d'Angers have acquired by donation or purchase in the whole honor of my father and myself, that is, at Lion-d'Angers, Brion, Durtal, Malicorne or in any other place in the whole honor."[42] Rainald did virtually the same thing for Marmoutier, where he authorized whatever the monks held "in his honor and his father's honor, which he will hold after his death."[43] The most sweeping of his blanket confirmations was made when Robert went on Crusade in 1098. Rainald granted and authorized in advance any donation that his father might make on his journey.[44] It is clear that Rainald functioned as his father's faithful lieutenant at Craon, even though he was the *dominus* there in his own right by virtue of his marriage to the legitimate heiress.[45]

40. Archives Maine-et-Loire, 40 H1, no. 19, 1094. "Hoc fecit consilio domini sui Rotberti Burgundionis, et quorundum suorum hominum."

41. *Cartul. Trinité de Vendôme*, 1: 316–19, no. 184; *Cartul. manceau*, 2: 59–63, no. 2; "Livre d'argent de Saint-Florent," Archives Maine-et-Loire, H 3714, fol. 63v–64r; *Cartulaire de Saint-Cyprien de Poitiers*, ed. L. Redet (Poitiers, 1874), 201, no. 322; Archives Maine-et-Loire, H 110, no. 113; *Cartul. manceau*, 2: 78, no. 7; Bib. nat., Dom Housseau, 13₁, no. 9632; *Cartul. manceau*, 2: 86–89; *Cartul. manceau*, 2: 89–91, no. 14. For other acts of Rainald not involving his father see Bertrand de Broussillon, *Maison de Craon*, 1: 37–52, and Angot, *Généalogies féodales*, 765–82. Rainald's attitude is in contrast to his brother, Robert Vestrol, who created problems for his father on several occasions; see *Cartulaire de Saint-Vincent du Mans*, ed. S. Menjot d'Elbenne (Le Mans: A. de Saint-Denis, 1888–1913), no. 367, 14 July 1085–24 March 109 and *Cartul. manceau*, 2: 89–91, 1098, before 26 March.

42. Bertrand de Broussillon, *Craon* 1: 40–41, no. 34. ". . . confirmamus quidquid monachi Sancti Albini andegavensis in toto honore patris mei Roberti ac meo, id est apud Legionem, apud Brionem, apud Duristallum, apud Malicornant vel in quibuscumque locis in toto honore . . . dono vel emptione acquisierunt."

43. Ibid., 41–42, no. 38. "Quicquid habebamus in honore suo et in honore patris sui, quem habiturus erat post decessum illius."

44. *Cartul. manceau*, 2: 86–89, 1098, before 25 March.

45. It is not until late in his life that Rainald took a significant step on his own, the founda-

Robert's control over the northwestern rim of the Angevin state was the single most important factor governing his relationship with his own lord, Count Fulk Rechin. Robert's importance in the north as well as his key role in the coup-d'état that had put Fulk in power had altered his personal stance towards the count. Although Robert always remained loyal to the Angevin comital house, the respect and gratitude that he manifested for Geoffrey Martel was absent from his dealings with Fulk. He continued to be an active member of Fulk's entourage but now played a more important and complex role than he or anyone else had in the days of Geoffrey Martel.

This was all the more significant because Fulk relied on the members of his court for increasingly sophisticated judicial functions. As the foremost member of Fulk's court, Robert had a leading role in this regard. Within the territory he exercised direct authority over, his honor, Robert was accustomed to holding his own courts.[46] Now in several instances involving the broader sphere of Angevin justice, Robert was the chief judge (*judex*) after the count himself in large assemblies of nobles. In these assemblies the count appears merely as first among equals.[47] Even in the instance where Count Fulk and Bishop Eusebius of Angers are said to be *in judicium*, it is clearly Robert and the large number of others in attendance who are vital to the legitimacy of the process.[48] Stephen White in his study of the legal system of eleventh century western France has shown that these "courts" were not a formal legal process, with judges seeking to reveal the facts of the case and system-

---

tion of the monastery of La Roë, which involved the gift of substantial lands in the Craonais forest. For the original donation see "Cartularium abbatiae Beatae Mariae de Rota," copy made by Paul Marchegay, Archives Maine-et-Loire, 61H1. Original in Archives de la Mayenne, no. 1 fol. 3r and v, published in *Gallia Christiana in Provincias Ecclesiasticas Distributa* (Paris: Didot Fratres, 1744, 1853), 14: 151, no. 10 of the *Instrumenta*. Robert the Burgundian was not a participant.

46. *Cartul. Trinité de Vendôme*, 1: 316–19, no 184, 16 July 1067. An agreement with Marmoutier from about this time mentions that cases involving a monk shall be referred to Robert, who retains the right to make the monk stand to justice if the monk is not on Marmoutier's property. See *Cartul. manceau*, 2: 59–63, no. 2.

47. Bib. nat., Dom Housseau, 3, no. 829, 6 January 1084, in which a large number of churchmen as judges take precedence over Fulk and Robert. See also *Cartul. du Ronceray*, no. 244, before 9 April 1090; Bib. nat., Dom Housseau, 3, no. 1001, 24 August 1096–14 March 1098; and Archives Maine-et-Loire, H 1840, no. 13, 17 February 1092, where the count and his nobles (*proceres*) are said to judge (*censere*).

48. *Cartul. du Ronceray*, no. 47, 1075–27 August 1081.

atically apply an accepted code of laws, but rather courts of arbitration where a compromise could be reached that left both parties with something. Yet White also admits that in this region, including Anjou, formal judicial processes had not died away, but "could sometimes lead to legal decisions that left one party a winner and the other a loser; and these decisions were sometimes reached through the application of legal rules to the facts of a dispute."[49] In other words, Robert was a central figure in a system where courts and judgement could be important.

Whether Robert played the role of a modern judge with specialized legal knowledge or of a powerful and respected arbitrator looking for a compromise, he held a preeminent position. In one complaint heard in Fulk's court *(curia)*, Robert and the count alone heard the case *(judicare)*, apparently acting with shared and equal authority.[50] The preeminence of Robert's judicial function is made clear in a *judicium* in which Fulk ordered Robert alone to render the judgement, or *sentencia*, which was then ratified by the count and his barons.[51] Robert exercised the same function, rendering a judgement by himself, "with the rest consenting," before Bishop Geoffrey in the episcopal chamber of Angers.[52] Late in Robert's life Fulk arranged a judicial meeting *(placitum)* for Saint-Aubin and commanded Robert and his son-in-law, Rainald of Château-Gontier, to carry out the order. Robert then functioned as a high judicial official, one who could operate outside his own honor; he was hardly inferior to the count in this respect. A case from August 1092 neatly illustrates Robert's judicial authority within his own honor. In Robert's absence a proposed trial by combat could not be conducted because no suitable judges could be found. When Robert returned, he simply met with those involved in his court at Sablé and settled the

49. Stephen D. White, "Pactum . . . *Legem Vincit et Amor Judicium*, the Settlement of disputes by Compromise in Eleventh-Century Western France," *American Journal of Legal History* 22 (1978): 307–8. In his *Custom, Kinship and Gifts to Saints*, 71–73, he goes further, saying there were nothing like legal arguments and that legal processes "did not involve the direct, systematic application of rules to facts."

50. "Livre blanc de St-Florent," Archives Maine-et-Loire, H 3713, fol. 44r, 30 December 1092.

51. Bib. nat., Dom Housseau, 13₁, no. 9549, 11 March 1067–27 March 1093. Also see *Livre des serfs de Marmoutier*, no. 116, 20 May 1064–11 January 1081, for a case Robert judges with his brother Guy and two others in the count's court.

52. "Livre d'argent de Saint-Florent," Archives Maine-et-Loire, H 3714, fol. 63v–64r, 9 September 1082.

matter on his own authority.[53] While the role of judge is not unique to Robert among the barons, the extent of his authority within Anjou at large was nearly so.[54]

Within his own domain Robert was able to act more independently of Count Fulk than he had under Fulk's predecessors. When he had King Philip confirm his donation of the churches of Sablé to Marmoutier in 1067, Count Geoffrey the Bearded also confirmed the donation specifically because the property was within his *casamentum*.[55] Thereafter Robert made numerous donations to the Church and approved several more made by men within his own *mouvance*.[56] Of these acts of donation or authorization only three were confirmed by a higher authority, and in one of these cases the higher authority was William of Normandy and his son Robert Curthose count of Maine rather than the count of Anjou.[57] Only the remaining two cases were approved by Fulk Rechin. One of these was the donation of a collibert and his family to the abbey of Saint-Florent.[58] Since this occurred in the first year of Fulk's countship, it may represent the special circumstances of Robert's adjusting to a new regime.

Robert's only other act of donation confirmed by Fulk was in 1079 at Angers. Hugh of Sablé granted a waterway on the Loire to the Trinity of Vendôme and had both his lord, Robert the Burgundian, and Count Fulk approve the act. Even though the waterway was said to be in

---

53. Archives Maine-et-Loire, H 110, no. 113, 29 August 1092.

54. Robert also served as a judge in other cases where the count was not involved: *Cartul. du Ronceray*, no. 242, 14 January 1056–4 April 1067; *Cartul. de St-Aubin*, 1: 421–24, no. 364, 1065–24 May 1095 with the viscount of Maine; ibid., 377–79, no. 329, 1075–Easter 1092, wherein a case was appealed to him after it had been heard by Waldin of Malicorne; Bib. nat., Dom Housseau, 13₁, no. 9504, 11 May 1097, in which he renders a judgement carefully based on precedent; and *Cartul. de St-Vincent*, no. 394, 1086–1098.

55. *Cartul. manceau*, 2: 59–63, no.2, 7 August 1067. See also *Cartul. du Ronceray*, no. 164, 14 November 1060–19 June 1068 for a similar case.

56. "Livre noir de St-Florent," Bib. nat., n.a. lat., 1930, fol. 137v, 1067 or 1068; *Cartul. de la Couture*, 22–23, no. 15, 1068; *Cartul. Trinité de Vendôme*, 1: 413–14, no. 264, 30 November 1077; *Cartul. Trinité de Vendôme*, 1: 428–29, no. 276, 13 or 14 March 1079; *Livre des serfs de Marmoutier*, 156, no. 32, before 24 March 1098; *Cartul. manceau*, 2: 78, no. 7; *Cartul. de St-Aubin*, 1: 441–42, no. 382, 10 July 1093–24 March 1098; Bib. nat. Dom Housseau, 13₁, no. 9632, May 1067–24 March 1098 and May 1096–24 March 1098; an extensive series of gifts in 1098, *Cartul. manceau*, 2: 85–89, no. 12 and 13; Ménage, *Histoire de Sablé*, 82.

57. *Cartul. de la Couture*, 22–23, no. 15, 1068.

58. "Livre noir de St-Florent," Bib. nat., n.a. lat., 1930, fol. 137v, 1067 or 1068.

Robert's *feudum* it was located near Angers, between Sainte-Gemme and the island of Chapouin.[59] A site so far from Sablé and Craon and so near Angers was probably judged to have special interest to the count and therefore required his intervention to validate the gift. Except for these few instances, Fulk played no part in Robert's disposition of property granted him by the counts of Anjou.

Robert was able, on the other hand, to influence the direction of Fulk's own donations. As has been shown, Robert had negotiated grants for himself during the struggle against Geoffrey the Bearded. When the civil war was over he induced Fulk to march on Durtal and return it to him and a picked member of his entourage. At Durtal Robert made the decision regarding Saint-Aubin's property at Durtal; in fact, he was asked to do so by Fulk. In 1092 Fulk confirmed the donation Geoffrey Martel had made to the monks of Saint-Nicolas of the fodder right on all their land and added an additional gift of his own. The document recording this act in Fulk's own words adds that "Robert the Burgundian, one of my nobles, kissed my hand on account of this donation."[60] Ostensibly a gracious act of a subordinate's gratitude, Robert's gesture actually signaled a degree of intimacy with the count that allowed him publicly to take credit for suggesting a major donation.[61]

As we have seen, Geoffrey Martel had pursued a policy that resulted in Robert, as a commander of crucial border strongholds, gaining greater power than other Angevin castellans. Indeed, Robert had grown to be the most important of these *domini*. His consolidation of power under Fulk Rechin during the civil war, his close alliance with the castellan of Château-Gontier, and his brother's de facto countship of Vendôme had brilliantly enhanced this position. Without question he was now the most powerful Angevin on the northern march facing the Normans. Fulk, perforce and by policy, gave him wide latitude in running his domain. Yet Robert did not pursue a completely independ-

59. *Cartul. Trinité de Vendôme*, 1: 428–29, no. 276, 13 or 14 March 1079.

60. Le Peletier, *Epitome*, 49–50, 1092 before 27 July. "Robertus etiam Burgundus unus ex meis optimatibus manum meum propter hoc oculatus est."

61. The kiss, as part of a public ritual, has particular significance in demonstrating personal ties. See Geoffrey Koziol, *Begging Pardon and Favor: Ritual and Political Order in Early Medieval France* (Ithaca: Cornell University Press, 1992), 6, 111, and 255.

ent policy of his own. The ties of gratitude, affection, and respect for the house of Anjou that had made a place for him among its soldiers and had advanced him to the highest rank were too great for that. For as long as he lived, no matter how hard pressed he was by the Normans or how enmeshed in Manceaux affairs Robert became, he remained first and foremost an Angevin.

One may rightly point out that Robert had little choice in any case since his only alternative would have been to throw in his lot with the Normans. In fact, this is generally considered as exactly what happened in 1068 while Fulk was preoccupied with the consolidation of his precarious hold on Anjou and Robert was left to face the northern threat alone. Robert took part in an act that gives the initial appearance of more or less acknowledging the overlordship of the Norman house. The act involved Brûlon, a castle within the *mouvance* of Robert as lord of Sablé, whose *dominus,* Geoffrey, donated the church of Brûlon to the monastery of Saint-Pierre de la Couture in Le Mans. La Couture was an abbey that Robert himself generally ignored and that was to cause him considerable trouble, but in this instance he acceded to his *fidelis'* wishes and confirmed the donation. The document recording this act has an interesting passage:

Therefore, approving this gift and the document of the donation, William, the renowned king of the English and his son Robert, the most noble count of Maine, and also my *dominus* Robert the Burgundian, their most faithful one, strengthened and confirmed it.[62]

Robert here seems to acknowledge the overlordship first of Robert Curthose as count of Maine and ultimately of William the Conqueror, at least for the property at Brûlon. Yet the act has not survived in its original charter, but only as a notice incorporated into another act. It is not at all clear that the three men actually appeared together, for King William was supposedly occupied in England throughout 1068.[63]

---

62. *Cartul. de la Couture,* 22–23, no. 15, 1068. "Hoc igitur donum et donationis scriptum annuentes corroborarunt et confirmaverunt inclitus rex Anglorum Wilielmus et ejus filius Robertus comes Cenomanensis nobilissimus, Robertus quoque Burgundus meus dominus illorum fidelissimus."

63. Douglas, *William the Conqueror,* 214–15, 217–18, n. 7. Douglas presents three possibilities. The first is that the clause, if not the whole charter, is simply a confection of the monks of La

The document seems to be simply a notice of previous acts of confirmation done at different times and places by the three participants on Geoffrey of Brûlon's behalf. The notice would have been added to the document commemorating the actual act of donation. This may have made it easier for Robert to bring himself to confirm a donation made by one of his men to an abbey so dominated by the Normans that it in turn would seek to gain the confirmation of their Norman lords.

Robert and his men were hardly cowed by the Normans whose dominance in Maine would be completely reversed in the following year. He was not the only lord in the disputed county who found Norman rule distasteful. The *Actus pontificum* notes that in 1069, "the nobles of Maine together with the people unanimously defected from their fidelity" to King William.[64] Soon, as the Norman historian Orderic Vitalis puts it, "the whole district was thrown into disorder: the Norman power there grew weak and was attacked by all and sundry as a general curse."[65]

The rebels sought to install a descendent of the count of Maine and sent for Azzo lord of Este in Italy and husband of Gersendis, the daughter of Count Herbert Wake-Dog. By 2 April 1069, Azzo and Gersendis had arrived in Maine with their son Hugh, a legitimate claimant to the countship.[66] Soon the Norman garrison at Le Mans was expelled and the king's seneschal killed.[67] Azzo gained control of the whole of Maine after the expulsion of the Normans by a combination of force and bribery. When his money ran out, however, he feared that Manceau loyalty would likewise disappear. Azzo therefore thought it prudent to retire to Italy, leaving his wife and son in the care of

---

Couture trying to prove that the Burgundian had approved the donation and acknowledged the overlordship of the Norman house. The second possibility is that William *was* in Normandy at the end of 1068 and had the opportunity personally to approve the act. Douglas regards this as merely a possibility.

64. "Cenomannensium proceres una cum populo ab ipsum regis fidelitate unanimiter defecerunt," in *Actus pontificum,* 376.

65. Orderic, 2: 306–7. "Deinde regio tota perturbatur, et ibidem Normannica uis offuscatur, ac pene ab omnibus quasi generalis lues passim impugnatur."

66. *Actus pontificum.*, 376–77. For Azzo, see Latouche, *Maine,* 115–16, n.8. Azzo first appears in a charter dated 2 April 1069 as a witness without the comital title, *Cartul. Trinité de Vendôme* 1: no. 216.

67. *Actus pontificum,* 376.

Geoffrey of Mayenne, "a man full of innate cunning."[68] Geoffrey soon became the most powerful leader of the new regime, acting as a guardian for young Hugh and, in the words of the *Actus pontificum,* "like a husband" for Gersendis.[69]

On 6 April 1069, shortly after Azzo's arrival in Maine, Robert was in Angers with his brother Guy to attend a meeting of the count's court. This was a council to develop a policy towards Maine judging from the number of prominent men connected with the Maine border. Robert, for instance, brought two important members of his entourage, Fulk of Bouère and Guy of Malicorne. They were joined by Georffrey of Segré and Rainald of La Suze, a castle very near Le Mans.[70] Two weeks later Robert and Guy moved up to Baugé with the count and his court. There they met Geoffrey of Mayenne himself and another Manceau, Geoffrey of Entrammes. Hugh of Saint-Christopher, a stronghold not far from Château-du-Loir, was also present.[71] This would indicate that Geoffrey of Mayenne had not yet broken with Fulk. The Angevins, including Robert, were deeply involved with the chief figure of the Manceau resistance to the Normans.

Yet Robert and the Angevins kept their distance from Geoffrey's new government after Azzo's departure. Although Geoffrey may have been the "fidèle vassal du comte d'Anjou," as Halphen describes him,[72] he had a history of erratic allegiances. His position at Mayenne was simply too exposed for him to feel strong ties of loyalty to the Angevin.[73] Geoffrey, caught between the two powers of Anjou and Normandy, usually sought a more independent role. After he became Gersendis's lover and guardian of her son, the legitimate count, Geoffrey seems to have envisioned himself as de facto count of an independent Maine. He

68. *Actus pontificum,* 377. ". . . in manu Gaufridi de Meduana, viri nobilis et versuti admodum ingenii."

69. *Actus pontificum,* 377. ". . . hujus igitur Gaufridus de Meduana tutor et quasi maritus effectus."

70. *Cartul. Trinité de Vendôme,* 1: no. 216, 6 April 1069, Angers.

71. Ibid., 20 April 1069, Baugé.

72. Halphen, *Comté d'Anjou,* 179, and n.3.

73. Douglas, *William the Conqueror,* 71, lists his possible overlords: the count of Maine, the count of Anjou, the king of France, or the duke of Normandy. Geoffrey attempted to play one off against the other. He had little choice, since no one of his overlords was powerful enough to protect him from the others.

was probably as intent on expelling Fulk Rechin from Maine as on expelling William the Conqueror.[74]

This, of course, would have been unacceptable to Robert the Burgundian. Aside from his traditional loyalty to the house of Anjou, Robert could never have stood for an independent Maine dominated by a lord of no higher standing than Robert himself, never mind this lord's illicit affair with the true count's mother. However delighted Robert was at the discomfiture of the Normans, the regime of Geoffrey of Mayenne did not gain full Angevin support. After Robert's meeting with Geoffrey and Fulk at Baugé in April 1069, there is no evidence of any further Angevin contact with the new regime. This lack of Angevin support left Geoffrey unable to consolidate his control over the fractious Manceaux.[75] When Geoffrey made himself obnoxious to the citizens of Le Mans with his "unheard-of exactions," a conspiracy arose to form what the citizens called a commune.[76]

The conspirators took an oath to support the commune and forced Geoffrey and other nobles of the region, willing or not, to take the same oath. After a series of brutal executions, the destruction of several nearby castles, and a botched attempt at taking the stronghold of Sillé, Geoffrey retreated to the castle of Le Chartre-sur-le-Loir, ironically a place he held from the count of Anjou. Young Hugh was sent back to his father in Italy. Inexplicably Geoffrey left his lover, Gersendis, at Le Mans. Invariably hostile to Geoffrey and Gersendis, the contemporary *Actus pontificum* of Le Mans primly claims that "because Gersendis could not bear his absence due to the illicit intimacy that had so wickedly sprung up between them, she began to plot how to betray the city to him."[77]

Her opportunity came when her men handed over the keep of Le Mans to Geoffrey and nearly eighty of his knights. From there he began to harass the townspeople once again until in desperation "they sud-

---

74. Guillot, *Comte d'Anjou,* 1: 119.

75. Douglas, *William the Conqueror,* 224.

76. *Actus pontificum,* 377–78. "Facta itaque conspiratione, quam communionem vocabant." Latouche, *Maine,* 37 n. 1, however, doubts that the term "commune" applies to "ce mouvement insurrectionnel."

77. *Actus pontificum,* 379. ". . . propter illicitam familiaritem, que jam inter eos male succreverat, ejus absentiam sustinere non posset, cepit machinari qualiter ei traderet civitatem." The author is extremely hostile to Geoffrey of Mayenne and his party.

denly called together the nobles of the whole region, especially Count Fulk of Anjou."[78] By "nobles of the whole region," the author of the *Actus pontificum* obviously meant the nobles of lower Maine loyal to the count of Anjou, chief of whom was Robert the Burgundian. There can be little doubt that Robert and his followers were part of the Angevin army that Fulk sent into Le Mans in response to the townspeople's plea in 1072.[79] The Angevins could not allow the anarchy and civil war in Le Mans to continue posing a temptation for Norman intervention. In savage street fighting the Angevins forced Geoffrey's men into the keep, which they nearly burnt down. Geoffrey abandoned his besieged garrison and fled in the night. Facing starvation and battered by Angevin siege engines, the men in the keep finally surrendered to Count Fulk.[80] Le Mans was once again in Angevin hands.

The city, however, proved impossible for the Angevins to hold in the face of renewed Norman aggression. William the Conqueror raised a huge army, even transporting large numbers of English troops to the continent in order to crush "invading enemies and disloyal rebels," as Orderic puts it.[81] Before the end of March of 1073, this overwhelming force entered Maine through the valley of the Sarthe and quickly captured the castles of Fresnay, Beaumont, and Sillé.[82] Soon Le Mans itself was completely invested. On 5 March Robert and Guy were with Count Fulk and his entourage judging a complaint of Abbot Barthelemy of Marmoutier. They must have been at Tours since the next day the written document commemorating the act was read in the presence of Archbishop Radulf of Tours.[83] Fulk evidently used the occasion to de-

78. *Actus pontificum*, 379. ". . . cives . . . totius regionis proceres, et precipue Fulconem, Andegavorum comitem, subito convocarunt."

79. For the date, see Latouche, *Maine*, 38 n.1. Halphen, *Comté d'Anjou*, 181, says simply "around 1072."

80. *Actus pontificum*, 380. While the author is vague about who defeated Geoffrey, calling the fighters *nostri*, "our men," he explicitly states that Geoffrey's men "sese et munitionem Fulconi comiti tradiderunt."

81. Orderic 2: 306–7. ". . . ad compescendam hostium inuasionem et proditorum rebellionem." Orderic states that the English and Normans were composed in "multis armatorum legionis," while *Actus pontificum*, 380, describes the force as "innumerabilis exercitus." For an English account of the expedition see *Anglo-Saxon Chronicle*, translated by Dorothy Whitelock (London: Eyre and Spottiswoode, 1961), versions D and E, 155.

82. For the date, see *Anglo-Saxon Chron.*, version E, 155; and Latouche, *Maine*, 38 n. 7.

83. Bib. nat., Dom Housseau, 2₂, nos. 773 and 776, 5 and 6 March 1073.

cide how to meet the Norman invasion of Maine that was probably just getting under way. They could do little: Angevin forces retired before the Normans. Without the protection of an Angevin garrison and with much of the northern part of the county terrorized into submission, the townspeople of Le Mans capitulated. William graciously received the keys of the city from a thoroughly cowed delegation at his newly constructed stronghold of La Mue.[84]

Orderic tells us that Maine was subdued almost without fighting, which is true enough for the city of Le Mans.[85] In the north, though, especially around Fresnay, there was considerable devastation, implying a spirited resistance.[86] The Anglo-Saxon chronicle says of Maine that "the English damaged it severely: they destroyed vineyards and burned down cities and damaged the country severely."[87]

Angevin involvement in this fighting is not mentioned by either the *Actus pontificum* or Orderic, but the latter is often vague when he talks of the local nobility. Sometimes he refers to them as "Angevins" and at others as "men of Maine."[88] Robert was clearly an Angevin, or at least a lord owing his allegiance to the count of Anjou, but Sablé had originally pertained to the count of Maine and some of his men, such as Geoffrey of Brûlon, clearly would be considered as "men of Maine." In effect, "Angevin" denotes political affiliation while "Manceau" denotes geographic location. It is therefore possible that we would see Robert and men of his entourage closest to Le Mans in Orderic's description of events immediately after the surrender of the city.

The remaining men of Maine were now terrified by the invasion of this huge army which was overrunning their whole territory, and the knowledge that their friends and supporters had collapsed at the sight of the renowned war-leader. They too sent ambassadors to ask the conqueror for peace; and when pledges of peace had been given they thankfully joined their standards with the royal banners, and were allowed to return home and live quietly, each man under his vine, as he chose.[89]

---

84. *Actus pontificum*, 380–81.   85. Orderic 2: 308–9.
86. *Actus pontificum*, 380–81.   87. *Anglo-Saxon Chron.*, 155.
88. John of La Flèche, for example, who is called "an Angevin" but revolted against Fulk along with the "men of Maine" on behalf of the Normans. See Orderic 2: 310–11.
89. Orderic 2: 306–7, Chibnall's translation.

So it seemed, at any rate, through Norman eyes. Orderic Vitalis, though a mixed Saxon-Norman who claimed to be impartial in his view of the Normans, could not escape seeing events in Maine through the lens of Norman historical memory. His awareness of these events depended on oral tradition, which he would have heard from individuals with a distinctly Norman experience. No matter what Orderic may have thought, his pool of "collective memory" would have been completely different from that of Robert the Burgundian and his followers.[90]

For them Norman rule in Le Mans might again have been a reality, yet there is no evidence that William exercised any real authority over Robert or Sablé. Between 1068 and 1090 Robert appears neither in the Norman duke's entourage nor in that of the duke's son Robert Curthose.[91] The Normans might have been able to hold Le Mans and the north of Maine but just a few miles to the south Robert continued to conduct himself as a loyal *fidelis* of the count of Anjou, albeit a remarkably powerful and independent one. While the Angevins were not yet strong enough to reassert their claim to Maine, neither were the Normans strong enough to push directly into territory held by a lord so adamantly Angevin. Robert quite possibly saw this as as much of a triumph as Orderic saw William's victory at Le Mans. Both sides, however, were soon to make indirect efforts at securing their claims.

90. See Leah Shopkow, *History and Community: Norman Historical Writing in the Eleventh and Twelfth Centuries* (Washington: The Catholic University of America Press, 1997), 193–94, for this collective memory and how it would differ from the written word.

91. *Cartul. de la Couture*, 22–23, no. 15, 1068; Archives Maine-et-Loire, H 110, no. 113, 1090–29 August 1092, in which Robert is said to be serving Count Robert of Normandy.

CHAPTER FIVE

The Struggle for the Churches of Sablé

On 24 February 1076, Robert the Burgundian rose up in the house of Saint Martin, kept by the monks of Marmoutier within the castle walls of Sablé, to deliver a remarkable statement detailing his understanding of the history of the castle and churches of Sablé as part of a legal inquiry before an audience of high ranking churchmen, monks from several abbeys, and his own loyal supporters from the region. Such testimony was not rare for a man so richly endowed with landed wealth as Robert, but it was such an unusually important case that the monks of Marmoutier carefully recorded Robert's words. Even more unusual, two versions of these transcripts have survived, each purporting to be Robert's own first-person account. One has the appearance of a verbatim transcript of Robert's testimony in the first person. This version may have been redacted from extensive notes taken at the trial.[1] The second version is found in the lengthy document produced by the monks of Marmoutier as the official record of the entire proceeding and its ultimate judgement at a later date.[2] Within this official document is found Robert's testimony, also in the first person, but contain-

---

1. *Cartul. manceau,* 2: 67–69, also published in *Cartul. de la Couture,* 39, no. 29, hereafter cited as "Testimony." In "Livre noir de St-Florent," Bib. nat. n.a. lat. 1930, fol. 58r–59v., Wanilo dictated the details of the act to another monk who wrote it down. Thus he was able to compose an official document in suitable Latin and probably oversaw the preparation of the final document. Doubtlessly he performed the same function at Sablé. Wanilo even had a modest literary career. See Laurain, *Cartul. manceau,* 1: 3 n. 3.

2. Original in Archives d'Indre-et-Loir, H 306, no. 3, published in *Cartul. manceau,* 2: 69–76, no. 5 and in *Cartul. de la Couture,* 23, no. 16. Hereafter referred to as "Judgement."

ing additional information. This expansion may have been done by the monks when the final document was drawn up and may not reflect Robert's actual words. Still, considering that the monks were working rapidly and translating from the vernacular into Latin, the tone is remarkably like the transcript version. It may reflect additions Robert made later in the trial, perhaps while under cross examination. To understand the forces that produced these unusual documents we must examine Robert's relationship with the Church and above all the monastery of Marmoutier, which were so important to him.

It was precisely Robert's preference for the monks of Marmoutier that had precipitated the legal proceedings, called a *judicium* in the documents, of 1076. In his testimony Robert displayed no doubt that as *dominus* of Sablé he controlled the churches of the parish centered on his castle: "I have held these churches firmly and without other claim up until this hour, so I can sell or give both the churches and the prebends to whomever I wish without any opposing claim."[3] While not entirely correct (he had to secure the bishop's approval), this is certainly Robert's own opinion of his rights over the churches.

This does not mean that Robert saw the churches as owned by him in the same fashion as his other property, to be devoted only to his narrow secular interests.[4] Robert was as sincere in his religious devotion and his desire for a well-ordered, spiritually effective church as any of the lords of his era. If a lay lord like Robert felt he controlled his local parish church, it was at least partly because he felt he had an obligation to meet the religious needs of the people under his lordship, needs that

3. "Judgement." "Et ego ita solute et quiete ipsas ecclesias usque ad hanc horam tenui, ut absque ulla calumnia et ecclesias et prebendas dare et vendere cui volui potuerim."

4. At first glance this seems a clear statement of the theory of the *Eigenkirche*, or "proprietary church." The church was supposedly a part of the lord's property and therefore all rights over it belonged to the lord as part of his property rights. See Ulrich Stutz, "The Proprietary Church as an Element of Mediaeval Germanic Ecclesiastical Law," originally given in German as a lecture in 1894, ed. and trans. by Geoffrey Barraclough in *Mediaeval Germany, 911–1250: Essays by German Historians* (Oxford: Blackwell, 1938), 41. See also Gerd Tellenbach, *Church, State and Christian Society at the Time of the Investiture Contest*, trans. by R. F. Bennett (Oxford: Blackwell, 1959). It was assumed that this concept of church as property originated among germanic peoples and then became an essential feature of property law in western France. See Madeleine Dillay, "Le régime de l'église privée du XIe au XIIIe siècle dans l'Anjou, le Maine, la Touraine," *Revue historique de droit français et étranger*, ser. 4, 5 (1925): 253–94. But see the following two notes.

were not always attended to by the Church hierarchy.[5] He did not regard it in the same way as he regarded his ownership of land, but rather
as his peculiar responsibility as secular ruler of a territory comprising
the parish. He was both benefactor and protector of "his" church.[6] Any
attempt by an outside force to exert control over the churches or any
part of the rights and privileges pertaining to them would be seen as a
direct assault on Robert's dominion over Sablé.

Possibly Robert saw such a threat after the death of Bishop Vulgrin
in 1065 from the bishop of Le Mans, thoroughly dominated by the Normans. As described in Chapter Three, he gave the church of Saint-Malo
at Sablé and its subordinate churches to the monastery of Marmoutier
in 1067. Marmoutier was not only in the Touraine, now part of the
Angevin heartland and clearly well disposed to Angevin interests, but as
Robert made clear, Archbishop Barthelemy of Tours personally advised
Robert to take this step.[7] Marmoutier might control the churches, but it
would do so with the complete approval of the archbishop of Tours.[8]
Since Le Mans was within the archiepiscopal province of Tours, this
means that Robert's move can be seen in effect as excluding the bishop
of Le Mans from interfering at Sablé by going directly to his superior,
the archbishop, and at his advice giving the churches to an abbey that
would not be subject to the bishop of Le Mans.[9] This would prevent the
churches at Sablé from being controlled by a power inimical to Robert's
political interests.

This is rationally convincing to the modern mind and no doubt it

5. Susan Reynolds, *Kingdoms and Communities*, 87–90.

6. Susan Reynolds, *Fiefs and Vassals*, 61 and 418–19. Reynolds critiques the "proprietary
church" concept as an "interpolation into a quite different society of a crude form of nineteenth-century ideas of property and power."

7. "Judgement," 14 November 1052–7 August 1067, probably after the death of Geoffrey
Martel in 1060. Barthelemy (1052–1068) had been appointed by Geoffrey Martel from a family
of his supporters. See Guillot, *Comte d'Anjou*, 1: 89–90.

8. This detail is important because relations between the archbishops of Tours and the
monks of Marmoutier were not always harmonious. See Farmer, *Communities of Saint Martin*, 73–75. This does not mean, of course, that the archbishop and the abbey could not see a
common interest as parts of the church of the Touraine.

9. This has an analogy in Fulk Nerra's foundation of the abbey of Beaulieu in 1007–1008.
Fulk put the abbey directly under Pope Sergius to get around Archbishop Hugh of Tours,
with whom he was in conflict. Bernard S. Bachrach, "Pope Sergius IV and the Foundation of
the Monastery at Beaulieu-lès-Loches," *Revue Bénédictine* 95 (1985): 263.

played a major role in Robert's decision. But before the judicial assembly in the house of Saint Martin, Robert told a different story. Saint-Malo had originally been staffed by four canons who had been given prebends for their support by Geoffrey of Sablé. The canons had close ties to the Manceau abbey of Saint-Pierre de da Couture, while the church itself belonged to the diocese of Le Mans. Canons did not live under the same strict rules as monks, and over the years discipline had grown lax.[10] After Robert married Advisa and took possession of Sablé he became dissatisfied with this arrangement. In his own words,

It pained me when I saw that the canons had wickedly mixed with the company of prostitutes. I believed that God and the saints, for whom so much patronage was contained in that church, were offended by this service rather than pleased. Because of this I wished the house of canons to be converted into a house of monks and I called the monks of Marmoutier, whom I had heard were well ordered, and gave them the canonical church of Sablé.[11]

Here Robert presents himself as a reformer, very much in the fashion of the many lay lords who we know did participate with the Church in the Reform movement.[12] The gift also created bonds with both the greatest monastery in the Angevin state and the highest ranking churchman, Archbishop Barthelemy.[13] Marmoutier in particular was associated with reform in the Angevin region, just as Robert says.[14] If Robert were typical of the nobles of his age, he believed that the actions expected of a man of his rank could indeed imperil his soul, and that the prayers of monks were an effective way to help ensure his sal-

10. As a useful example, see the distinction between the canons of Saint Martin and the monks of Saint-Martin at Tours in Farmer, *Communities of Saint Martin*, 189–92.

11. "Judgement." ". . . donec canonicos meretricum male admisceri consortio vidi et dolui, quorum scilicet servitio Deum et sanctos quorum multa in ecclesia illa continentur patrocinia offendi credidi pocius quam placari. Unde et canoniam volui in monachiam converti, vocavique quos bene ordinatos audivi Majoris monasterii monachos, ac dedi eis ecclesiam de Sablolio canonicalem."

12. Johnson, *Prayers*, 173. "Sentiment for religious reform flowed upward from the laity in this period, particularly in west-central France." See also Howe, "Nobility's Reform," 336, and Bouchard, *Sword*, 232–33. Howe admits to secular motives Bouchard dismisses too categorically.

13. Barbara H. Rosenwein, *To Be the Neighbor of Saint Peter: The Social Meaning of Cluny's Property, 909–1049* (Ithaca: Cornell University Press, 1989), 202–3.

14. For a case study of Marmoutier's role in an attempt at reform at about the time Robert became lord of Sablé, see William Ziezulewicz, "Sources of Reform in the Episcopate of Airard of Nantes, 1050–1054," *Ecclesiastical History* 4 (1996): 432–45.

vation. Along with gaining entry to the monastic prayer fellowship, though, Robert could also expect more tangible aid ranging from hospitality at the abbey while traveling to direct aid in time of crisis.[15]

Robert attached great importance to the reform of his churches and devoted all of his considerable diplomatic skill and influence to this end. Possibly as a reward for acting as the main go-between in Fulk Rechin's brief reconciliation with Geoffrey the Bearded, Robert was able to have the transfer confirmed by King Philip, Count Baldwin of Flanders, Geoffrey the Bearded and his wife, and Fulk Rechin.[16] With the support of these major figures Robert even managed to have Bishop Arnold of Le Mans grant his official consent to the donation, called the *auctoramentum* in these documents.[17] Robert went to great lengths to ensure that as churches were brought back under ecclesiastical control in the course of the eleventh century, his churches at Sablé would be administered by a pro-Angevin institution. For the rest of his life he was to make numerous endowments to Marmoutier to assure that it was also "pro-Robert."[18]

Why the attachment to Marmoutier and not some other monastery such as the Trinity of Vendôme, which many of Geoffrey Martel's knights continued to venerate as their count's special foundation?[19] Had he felt as a young knight a spiritual aspect to the Angevin conquest of its site that he surely participated in? People at the time told how Saint Martin himself had intervened to give the Angevins the victory. Was it a special relationship that grew when he saw Geoffrey Martel nursed at his deathbed by a monk of that abbey?[20] Did his wife Advisa lead him to her family's favored monastery, as the wives of nobles often did? Her brother Geoffrey was a monk of Marmoutier and women were known

15. For benefits Robert could expect from his association with a monastery, see Johnson, *Prayer*, 90–96 and 162–164; White, *Custom, Kinship, and Gifts to Saints*, 26–29.

16. *Cartul. manceau*, 2: 59–63, no. 2, 7 August 1067.

17. "Judgement," 1068.

18. For example, *Cartul. manceau*, 1: 1–3 no. 1, 2: 59–66 nos. 2 and 3, 2: 78 no. 7, 2: 79–80, no. 9, 2: 85–91, nos. 12, 13 and 14; *Livre des serfs de Marmoutier*, 156, no. 32. This could simply be that the monks of Marmoutier were more careful in preserving their records from Sablé, but the details they leave indicate both Robert's interest in Marmoutier and the abbey's interest in Sablé.

19. Johnson, *Prayer*, 85–89, suggests a special preference for the Trinity of Vendôme from Geoffrey's knights and officials.

20. Farmer, *Communities of Saint Martin*, 72.

to have influenced their husbands' patronage towards abbeys favored by their families.[21] Robert is quite specific in both versions of his testimony that Advisa was his partner in donating the churches to the abbey. Or was it simply the personal bonds that had grown between him and individual churchmen, so that he listened to their advice? We can never know for sure, though Robert tells us explicitly that he listened to the advice of the monk Wanilo and Archbishop Barthelemy in making donations to Marmoutier. What is certain is that it was a genuine and strong attachment, one that lasted to the last recorded act of his life.

Robert's religious motivations should not be discounted or underestimated; nevertheless, there seems to be more to his gift than simple religious fervor, no matter how sincere. Robert's attachment to the ecclesiastical establishment at Tours was an essential element of his political policy as a member of the Angevin ruling elite because the church at Le Mans had become hostile to Angevin interests. In 1065 Arnold had succeeded Vulgrin as bishop of Le Mans as a result of Duke William of Normandy's intervention. Geoffrey the Bearded's anger at this pro-Norman appointment was so great that he blundered into a violent conflict with the archbishop of Tours over it. The prelate remained an active partisan of Norman interests in Maine. During the revolt of 1069, Arnold fled to England where William received him with honor.[22] He returned to Le Mans where he joined, or was forced to join, the popular *communio,* a sworn association of the citizens of the city attempting to direct their own affairs. Arnold accompanied the army that the leaders of the commune sent against the castle of Sillé and was captured in the ensuing rout. Because of the bishop's rank, his captor, Hugh of Sillé, quickly released him.[23] In March 1071 Arnold set out for Rome, "for the occasion of prayer."[24] While making his return he was captured by Azzo of Este, whose son had laid claim to the countship of Maine. Af-

---

21. Bouchard, *Sword,* 142. "It is noteworthy that in the primarily patriarchal eleventh and twelfth centuries, when office and power were almost always inherited in the male line, women still played an important role in deciding *where* a family would make its pious gifts." Both Robert's wives, Advisa and Bertha, play important roles in his donations to monasteries. For Geoffrey at Marmoutier, see Angot, *Généalogies féodales,* 719.

22. *Actus pontificum,* 377.   23. *Actus pontificum,* 378–79.

24. "Causa orationis," *Cartul. de St-Vincent,* col. 28.

ter being held for seven months, he was released to return to his own see of Le Mans.[25] These trials did nothing to soften Arnold's disposition towards the Angevins.

When Norman rule was finally restored in Maine, Arnold "settled down undisturbed in his see and provided, as far as he was able, for the needs of his church," or so the author of the *Actus pontificum* rather disingenuously reports.[26] Arnold was the appointee of Duke William and was expected to further Norman policy. With Le Mans secure, it remained either to disrupt or co-opt the Angevin controlled march of southwestern Maine, to which Sablé was the key. In this instance Arnold can be seen as acting to advance both the demands of Norman rule and the needs of his own church, for he sought to reassert Cenomanian claims over the churches of Sablé.

Arnold attacked Robert's careful arrangement with Marmoutier obliquely through the abbey of Saint-Pierre de la Couture at Le Mans. This abbey had a cell at Solesmes, a mere two miles up the Sarthe river from Robert's castle. The monks of Solesmes made claims against the church of Saint-Malo of Sablé, specifically for the burial dues, the prebends for each canon of the church for thirty days after the canon's death and the oblation of *denarii* given to the abbot of la Couture or the prior of Solesmes for chanting the mass on the feast day of Saint Malo.[27]

It is clear that Bishop Arnold himself was behind this charge and that he had the support of Duke William. On 30 March 1073, immediately after William had restored Norman rule over Maine, Arnold met with the duke at Bonneville-sur-Touques. His main order of business was to have William confirm all the rights in Maine that la Couture had received from Geoffrey of Sablé. To Arnold, this included rights over the mother church of Sablé. William willingly granted his confirmation.[28]

Fortified with the Conqueror's approval, the monks of la Couture

---

25. Presumably the political situation in Maine was behind Arnold's trip, his capture, and his ultimate release. The *Actus pontificum*, however, claims Azzo released Arnold because "he repented that he had dared to unjustly sadden such a respectable man."

26. *Actus pontificum*, 381.

27. "Judgement," 1068–23 February 1076. Whatever the monetary value of these rights, and it could have been considerable, the chief goal seems to have been the establishment of a legitimate claim over Saint-Malo.

28. *Cartul. la Couture*, no. 9.

went to Robert and demanded that he "stand to justice" for the things they claimed. Robert in response arranged a court date for the suit to be heard before the judgement of Archbishop Radulf of Tours and Bishop Arnold of Le Mans. Robert then immediately informed the monks of Marmoutier that they should be present at the impending judicial process (*placitum*) to argue against the monks of la Couture. The seriousness of the case is indicated by the fact that all the principals involved travelled to Sablé for the *placitum*. This included Archbishop Radulf and Abbot Barthelemy of Marmoutier, who must have been on the road for nearly a week in the middle of February.

The hearing where Robert gave his testimony was held in the house of Saint Martin next to the church of Saint-Malo within the walls of the castle on 24 February 1076. The house was either quite large or extremely crowded since Archbishop Radulf, Bishop Arnold, their staffs, the monks representing Marmoutier with their abbot, Barthelemy, the monks representing la Couture, and Robert the Burgundian along with his son Robert Vestrol and his supporters all attended. Among the monks of Marmoutier was Wanilo, whom Robert and his wife had known at least since 1063.

As the trial began Abbot Barthelemy protested that the monks of la Couture were without an abbot. Bishop Arnold responded that he would act as the abbot of la Couture. With these words Arnold revealed the key role he had played in bringing forth the claims of la Couture. The Manceau abbey was, in fact, under his direction. From this point on Arnold acted as the monks' advocate rather than as a judge.[29] Arnold was so forceful and energetic in this role that there can be no doubt that the monks of la Couture were merely a means for Arnold to press his and his church's own interests.

The monks began their case by reading out the original written charter of Geoffrey of Sablé that listed the things that he had given to their cell at Solesmes over sixty years earlier. Then Bishop Arnold directly addressed Robert the Burgundian, making a point of reminding him that "he was the bishop's parishioner."[30] The surviving documenta-

29. "Judgement."
30. "Judgement." "Cujus [i.e. Arnoldi] parechianus erat."

tion of the case, biased as it is towards Marmoutier, may have reduced a key element of Arnold's case to this one phrase.

Robert's case was fundamentally that the church within the walls of his castle was his responsibility and that he had every right to give it to anyone he wished. Opposed to this was the idea, based on both canon and Roman civil law, that everything within the territorial jurisdiction of the bishopric was subject to the rule of the bishop.[31] By reminding Robert that he was a parishioner of Le Mans, Arnold was stressing that since Sablé was within the territorial boundaries of his see, Robert, and by consequence the churches of Sablé, should look to the bishop of Le Mans as his spiritual leader. Therefore Arnold "ordered Robert on behalf of God and Saint Julian and of the bishop himself, whose parishioner he was, to speak the truth concerning this suit."[32]

Robert simply responded that he would tell the truth and began his testimony. According to the final version of the judgement, Robert began by telling how the original church of Sablé had been built by Saint Julian and dedicated to Saint Mary in the distant past.[33] It subsequently fell into ruin, was restored by unknown Christians and rededicated to Saint Martin with the status of a parish church.[34] The shorter transcript version begins with the construction of Sablé. Robert testified that when the count of Maine built a fortress (castellum) at Sablé he provided the garrison with a church of its own dedicated to Saint-Malo within the newly erected walls.[35] He also established four canons for the

31. Stutz, "Proprietary Church," 39, describes the situation in the late Roman Empire. "[A]ll ecclesiastical wealth was the property of the episcopal church, and a rule expressed in both secular and ecclesiastical legislation hindered or even prevented the alienation of church property, the administration of which was otherwise left to the discretion of the bishop." This was exactly the point made by the advocate of Archbishop Hugh in protesting before a papal court Fulk Nerra's foundation of Beaulieu at about the same time Solesmes was founded. Bachrach, "Sergius IV and Beaulieu," 258–59.

32. "Judgement." ". . . praecepit episcopus Cynomannensis Rotberto ex parte Dei et Sancti Juliani et ex sua, cujus parechianus erat, ut de causa ista veritatem diceret. Ille contestatus veritatem se dicturum respondit."

33. "Judgement," 3rd–4th century. Julian was regarded as the first bishop of Le Mans and is sometimes called the Apostle of Celtic Gaul. See S. Baring-Gould, *The Lives of the Saints*, vol. 1 (Edinburgh: John Grant, 1914), 398.

34. "Judgement," late 10th century. This information is not found in the "Testimony" version and may be an addition added by the monks to fit Sablé into a more "learned" history of the region.

35. "Testimony" and "Judgement," before 25 October 1015. Malo, also known as Machutus

church and gave them land, mills, and half the tolls of Sablé for support. Once Geoffrey of Sablé acquired the castle he took by right all that the count had given the canons of Saint-Malo. To compensate them for their loss he gave them the mother church of the parish, that is, Saint-Martin, and all the revenue from it.[36] From this point on Saint-Malo incorporated the parish of Saint-Martin and acted as the mother church of the parish of Sablé.

This was all well for Saint-Malo and its parish, but according to Robert, when Geoffrey grew old he changed the arrangement significantly. He established a monastery at the hamlet of Solesmes after acquiring it from his brother Radulf viscount of Le Mans. He then gave it along with the parish of Solesmes to the abbey of Saint-Pierre de la Couture at Le Mans. Two miles up river from Sablé, Solesmes was part neither of the *casamentum* nor the parish of Sablé.[37] The original cemetery of Sablé pertaining to Saint-Malo lay within the walls of the castle and had become overly crowded over the years. Geoffrey ordered that henceforth the bodies of deceased members of the garrison, the *castellani*, be carried to Solesmes for burial, "partly because they were barely being given a decent burial at Sablé and partly because he wished to exalt the monastery he himself had built."[38] "I heard, however," Robert testified in the official version, "that the canons always claimed the burial dues and that Geoffrey ought to have given them compensation for it but never did."[39]

Robert went on to refute the specific claims of la Couture. The

---

or Maclou, was a Welsh missionary to the Bretons. He founded a monastery on the site of present day Saint Malo on the Breton coast and died around 621. Baring-Gould, *Saints*, 13: 336–39.

36. The revenue consisted of the tithe (*decima*), the burial dues (*sepultura*), and other unspecified returns (*redites*). See "Testimony," before 25 October 1015. "Judgement," the longer version of the legal process, makes no mention of this act.

37. "Testimony." The foundation of Solesmes is mentioned in both documents and took place 13 June 1006–25 October 1015. A fifteenth century copy of the charter of foundation is found in the Archives de l'abbaye de Solesmes and is published in *Cartul. de la Couture*, no. 8; analyzed in Fanning, *A Bishop and his World*, 100–101, no. 3.

38. "Testimony": ". . . tum quia intra castellum honeste minus tradebantur sepulture, tum quia locum quem ipse edificaverat cupiebat exaltare."

39. "Judgement," 13 June 1006–7 August 1067. "Audivi tamen quod canonici semper illam calumniati fuerint et quod Gaufredus commutationem eis pro illa dare debuerit, sed numquam dederit."

prebends of the canons that the monks claimed should be paid to them for thirty days after the death of each canon was not a right listed in Geoffrey's charter of donation to la Couture. Besides, Robert continued, "I have heard the older canons say that the monks were never accustomed to receive such a prebend unless at the same time as a canon fell ill he was made a monk and then died. Then the canons, upon a communal consultation, gave his prebend to the monks on behalf of his soul for thirty days." Robert then made the point clear. "This was all they received, not from any established due, but simply out of compassion."[40] In other words the monks at Solesmes had no legal right to the prebends; it was simply done at the discretion of the canons as a sign of good will.

As for the oblation that la Couture claimed, Robert admitted that while it was not stipulated in Geoffrey's original charter, the canons had in fact made an agreement of friendship *(amicitia quasi foedus)* that on the feast day of Saint Malo, 15 November, the monks of Solesmes would come to Sablé where the abbot or prior would chant the mass and receive the oblations. Robert was quick to add, however, that the abbot always "returned the money to the canons, never taking it off with himself."[41] Its value, then, was symbolic rather than material.

In the transcript Robert returns to the idea of his absolute right to Saint-Malo as a part of his castle. After stating that although Solesmes had "usurped" the burial dues from Saint-Malo, it had been done in accordance with the will of a *dominus* of Sablé. For this reason, Robert said, "I will defend their right to it however they might hold it." He might not agree with it, but he would uphold the right of his predecessors to dispose of the rights of the church in any way they saw fit. He then adds rather cryptically, "I do not listen to anyone's judgement re-

40. "Judgement." "Audivi ego antiquiores canonicos solere dicere numquam eos ullam habuisse, nisi semel tantum unam cujusdam canonici qui infirmitate pressus factus est apud eos monachus, de qua et mortuus est; canonici autem ex communi consilio dederunt monachis prebendam ejus pro anima illius xxxta diebus. Hanc solam habuerunt, non pro ulla consuetudine sed pro misericordia."

41. "Judgement." ". . . et denarios qui ei offerebantur ipse quidem recipiebat, sed eos tamen canonicis reddebat, nunquam secum exportabat." These details are found only in the official version. Perhaps this was part of a statement added by Robert under specific questioning about the prebends after he completed his statement in "Testimony."

garding this."[42] Evidently, he meant that this was his judgement as *dominus* of Saint-Malo of Sablé and consequently not a matter anyone else had jurisdiction over. He then spells out the status of the canons of Saint-Malo: "The canons of this church held everything intact by legal right except for the burial dues. They had no *dominus* or abbot at any time except only the commander of the castle of Sablé."[43]

Having established the rights and status of Saint-Malo and its canons, Robert describes how he turned the church over to Marmoutier after finding the canons mixing with prostitutes. In this fashion all of the rights that Robert had so carefully delineated before the court were transferred in their entirety to the monks of Marmoutier. In the transcript version Robert concluded his testimony with a challenge to the court in the following manner: "I and my wife and my children did this, without any money being involved, either paid or promised to us, but solely for divine remuneration. Then when it might be so, the monks of la Couture made a malicious claim against my charity to me and those to whom I gave it. Did they do right or not? Let him who knows speak."[44]

Robert's statement in the final judgement ends on an equally testy note. He concluded with his assessment of the rights of la Couture over Saint-Malo. In Robert's view the monks did indeed hold the burial dues from Geoffrey of Sablé's original donation. Beyond that, though, neither Robert nor any of his predecessors had granted anything to the monks of la Couture at Solesmes. "And if they say so," Robert stated, "they cannot prove it either by written document or witnesses."[45]

When Robert had finished his testimony, Archbishop Radulf asked those assembled if they would confirm it. One of the monks of la Cou-

---

42. "Testimony." ". . . et sepulturam quam antecessores mei, castelli istius domini, monachis de Cultura dederunt, hanc utcumque habeant eis defendo. Nec cujusquam super hac judicium ausculto."

43. "Testimony." ". . . sed canonicis ecclesie sue jura omnia ex integro preter sepulturam habentibus nullum isti aut dominum habuere unquam aut abbatem preter solum Sablolii castelli principem."

44. "Testimony." "Feci autem hoc ego et uxor mea et liberi mei, non aliqua interveniente pecunia que aut daretur nobis aut promitteretur, sed sola remuneratione divina. Quod cum ita sit, monachi de Cultura eleemosynam meam mihi et quibus dedi calumpniantur. Quod utrum recte faciant an non? Dicat qui intelligit."

45. "Judgement." "Et si dixerint, nec per scriptum nec per testes probare poterunt."

ture contradicted Robert, saying that he had seen the monks at Solesmes receive the prebends of several deceased canons. He could not, however, remember the names of these canons. His objection was thrown out of court when a monk of Marmoutier testified that he had seen two of the canons, whom he named, die without their prebends going to Solesmes. Once this was cleared up, Robert's testimony went unchallenged. Archbishop Radulf and Bishop Arnold retired apart to consult with their staffs.[46]

When the archbishop finally returned he rendered the judgement which he and Bishop Arnold had worked out. It was judged that Geoffrey's original charter of donation gave the monks of la Couture only the burial dues of Saint-Malo, which Robert had always been prepared to admit. As for everything else pertaining to Saint-Malo, "the *dominus* of this castle retains it in his own hands"[47] and therefore Robert or his heirs could give it to anyone they wished. As a consequence the monks of Marmoutier could hold it without any claim being made on it, as long as they received the consent of the bishop of Le Mans.

For Robert this was the crucial finding since it meant that his attempt to get the churches of Sablé out from under the jurisdiction of Le Mans and into friendlier hands had been a success. Everything that had belonged to the original canons now belonged to the monks of Marmoutier by Robert's will. It might appear, however, that the Robert's triumph was incomplete for the judgement also acknowledged the bishop of Le Mans's authority over the parish. Robert's transfer was good only if he received the bishop's consent *(auctoritas)*. As events would prove, Robert was convinced that he had already received such authority. Arnold seemed equally convinced that he had not.

The archbishop quickly recited the remaining details. As for the prebends and oblations, the monks of la Couture would have to prove with witnesses or documents that they had a right to them before any further action would be taken. When he had finished pronouncing the judgement, Archbishop Radulf said that if anyone disagreed he and Bishop Arnold were prepared to defend this judgement all the way to

---

46. From here on the events are related only in "Judgement."
47. "Judgement." "dominus hujus castelli retinuit in manu sua."

the Pope in Rome: "And when he had fallen silent there was no man who contradicted him."[48]

Having been forced to agree in public with this judgement, Bishop Arnold soon revealed himself as a determined man who was not yet ready to admit defeat. The next day all the participants met again in the archbishop's hospice in the burg of Saint-Martin at Sablé.[49] There Arnold "privately advised"[50] Robert to eject the monks of Marmoutier from Saint-Malo and replace them with canons because he, Arnold, had never given his *auctoramentum,* his offical consent, to Robert's donation of the churches to Marmoutier. The judgement of the previous day had specifically made this a requirement for Marmoutier to possess the churches.

When Abbot Barthelemy and the monks of Marmoutier learned of this they indignantly replied that not only had Arnold given them his *auctoramentum,* they still had the document to prove it. Arnold denied this and continued to deny it even when Archbishop Radulf declared that he himself had been a witness in the chapter house of Marmoutier when Arnold had made his sign on the written charter of this *auctoramentum.* Even in the face of direct contradiction by his superior Arnold refused to admit what he had done "unless the charter itself be shown to him."[51] A *terminus,* or legal deadline, for Marmoutier to present the charter was established by the archbishop and with this the meeting at Sablé seems to have concluded.

On the agreed upon date the monks of Marmoutier showed Bishop Arnold the document in question.[52] By this point it was clear that, no matter what the facts of the case were, Arnold was determined to

---

48. "Judgement." "Cumque tacuisset, nemo fuit qui contradiceret."

49. The fact that the archbishop had a hospice (*hospitium*) set aside for him at Sablé indicates that he may have made other trips to the town, either to consult with the monks of Marmoutier or with Robert in the castle. The presence of a burg developed by Marmoutier at Sablé also indicates the abbey's strong economic presence.

50. "[S]ummonuit." The word means "to advise privately" or "to give a gentle hint."

51. "Judgement." "nisi eadem carta monstraretur sibi."

52. The text of the document has survived and is published in *Cartul. manceau,* 1: 4–7, no. 2. Laurain, the editor, dates it 1068–1071. It is a confirmation by Bishop Arnold of all the property Marmoutier possessed within his diocese including the "locus Sancti Macuti de Sablolio, salva querela monachorum Sancti Petri qui de istis rebus inferunt calumniam jam dictis monachis."

reestablish some type of control over the churches of Sablé. In the words of the exasperated monks of Marmoutier, "he finally acknowledged what he had done, yet still he did not stop demanding that Robert eject the monks and recall the canons."[53] When Robert refused to do this, Arnold put the church of Saint-Malo and the whole castle of Sablé under an interdict. This was the ultimate weapon at Arnold's command and the fact that he resorted to it in spite of his archbishop's ruling shows how important Sablé had become for him.

No less determined, Robert took immediate steps to have the interdict lifted. He sent his own representatives along with monks from Marmoutier to ask the bishop to emend the injustice he had done. Arnold flatly refused even to hear them. Next Robert informed the bishop that since he could not come to Le Mans because of "his war" (*guarra sua*), he would go to the archbishop of Tours for justice.[54] This *guarra*, so briefly mentioned, is obviously the continued state of hostility between Robert and the Norman party headquartered at Le Mans.[55] Robert had no intention of putting himself in the hands of the Normans. Instead he exerted considerable political skill in forcing the decision at Tours, where he would find many supporters. Presumably Arnold labored just as hard though unsuccessfully for the opposite end.

It took Robert some time to marshal his defenses. However well disposed to him the archbishop might be, Robert had to prepare his case with care and to behave correctly. First he sent his representatives to Tours to "complain bitterly" to the archbishop regarding the wrong that had been done to him and to his people. At the same time men were dispatched to meet once more with Bishop Arnold. This accomplished nothing, as Robert must have expected. It did, however, justify Robert's next step. Robert made his complaint in person before Arch-

---

53. "Judgement." "'Tandem recognovit quod fecerat, nec sic tamen desistens exposcere a Rotberto monachos eici, revocari canonicos."

54. "Judgement."

55. Angot, *Généalogies féodales*, 728. We need not assume that this means an actual state of open warfare. There is a difference between the Latin *bellum* and *guerra*. "The former is rightly translated as 'war,' but the latter can mean something more like a vigorous disagreement," states Bachrach in "Henry II and the Angevin Tradition," 121. Cf. Guillot, *Comte d'Anjou*, 1: 384–86. There is no doubt that at this time there was a "a vigorous disagreement" between Robert and the Normans.

bishop Radulf. At the archbishop's advice, "Robert patiently bore this injustice for some time."[56]

Robert waited at Tours during this period and "after several days"[57] his complaint was heard by an impressive assembly of bishops who had gathered for the ordination of Silvester of La Guerche as Bishop of Rennes. Silvester, a former Angevin knight and lord of a territory just to the west of Craon, must have been well known to Robert. Aside from Silvester and Archbishop Radulf there were present Bishop Eusebius of Angers and Bishop Isembert of Poitiers. Robert had had a long association with Bishop Eusebius and could count on a favorable hearing from him. Robert had either skillfully timed his arrival to coincide with this conclave or, more likely, Archbishop Radulf had advised him beforehand to take advantage of it.

Bishop Arnold was also present with a retinue of his clerics to attend the consecration. It is possible that he was ignorant of the hearing and was not expecting to defend himself in this forum when he arrived at Tours. If so, then Radulf's cooperation with Robert was particularly evident and effective. At any rate, Arnold's defense was remarkably inept and it appears as if the tribunal could hardly be expected to be sympathetic to his case. Almost immediately Archbishop Radulf demolished Arnold's case, narrating the events that had already happened and then displaying Arnold's charter of *auctoramentum* with the archbishop's own sign on it as corroboration. This was the very document whose existence Arnold had denied at Sablé. When the charter was read aloud to those present the bishop's case collapsed.[58]

The conclusion of the assembled bishops was that in the document Arnold had admitted that the *querela*, that is, the legal complaint of the monks of la Couture against those of Marmoutier, was *salva*, or "healthy," in the sense of "cured" or "settled."[59] Therefore it followed that Arnold's continued claim on Saint-Malo was by his own opinion rather than by sound legal justification since his earlier act of consent had supposedly ended this complaint. It was the opinion of the bishops

---

56. "Judgement." "ejusque rogatu patienter aliquandiu eamdem injustiam tulit."
57. "Judgement." "Post aliquot dies."
58. "Judgement."
59. This is precisely the wording of Arnold's consent as cited in n. 52 above.

that "the monks of la Couture were not able to reprotest what they thought could be reprotested by themselves."[60] Consequently, all their actions since the original act of consent were invalid. Bishop Eusebius sarcastically noted that "whatever had been done afterwards in such a fashion ought not to be called a legal complaint now but rather, as the common people say, a *jangularia.*"[61] The latter word, difficult to translate, can perhaps be understood to mean "frivolous nonsense."[62]

This being the case, the council ruled that Bishop Arnold had acted unjustly when he had demanded that Robert expel the monks of Marmoutier and recall the canons and even more unjustly when he placed Sablé under an interdict for Robert's failure to do so. They gave Arnold the opportunity to correct his action. If he refused, the archbishop would lift the interdict on his own authority.

At this point Archbishop Radulf rose and spoke directly to the bishop. "Look here! Listen to the judgement of our fellow bishops: See what the decision is for you to do!"[63] Even yet Arnold hesitated to admit defeat. He said that he would heed the archbishop and then retired to consider the matter with Bishop Eusebius and Bishop Silvester, his own clerics, and others. After listening to their advice, Arnold sent the two bishops to go to the archbishop and request a delay so that Arnold might return to Le Mans in order to carry out the judgement with the counsel of the cathedral clerics at Le Mans.

The archbishop at first refused but Eusebius and Silvester convinced him to grant a delay of eight days with the stipulation that if his clerics at Le Mans opposed the bishop's judgement, Arnold would refuse to take their advice. If, however, Arnold did not lift the interdict of Sablé at

---

60. "Judgement." "quominus reclamare possent monachi quod sibi putabant esse relcamandum."

61. "Judgement." "quicquid deinceps tale fiebat, sicut nominatim Andecavensis episcopus ait, non jam debebat dici querela sed, sicut vulgariter dicitur, jangularia."

62. Charles du Fresne du Cange, *Glossarium mediae et infimae Latinitatis,* 10 vols. (Niort: L. Favre, 1883–1887), under "jangularia" gives "garrulitas, nugae"; the *Dictionnaire de la langue Francaise de Seizieme Siècle,* ed. Edmund Huguet, 7 vols. (Paris: H. Champion, 1925–1967), defines *janglerie* as "bavardage" or "médisance." This latter meaning of "slander" or "backbiting" may be the closest to what Eusebius had in mind. Dom Anselm Le Michel in his history of Marmoutier of 1644 (published in *Cartul. manceau,* 2: 452) cited it as an archaic word for "circulatio et praestigiatoria."

63. "Judgement." "Ecce audistis, inquit, judicium coepiscoporum nostrorum; videte quid vobis facere sit placitum."

the end of the eight days, the archbishop's own absolution would go into effect and services could be held again. There is no record whether Arnold took advantage of this face saving device, but his effort had failed.

With this the threat to Robert's control over the churches of Sablé and his arrangement with Marmoutier came to an end. While Arnold continued to obstruct the work of Marmoutier, this amounted to nothing more than harassment.[64] According to recent thinking on the settlement of disputes in western France in this period, this case should have been settled as Robert may have intended: by a compromise that left both sides with something.[65] He sent representatives to Bishop Arnold to seek a settlement and only after the bishop refused to grant him any satisfaction did he go to the archbishop for a formal hearing. At the end of the process at Sablé, there was at first the appearance of a mutually agreed upon compromise when the final judgement was said to be one made as much by Bishop Arnold as by Archbishop Radulf. Arnold's intransigence afterwards and Robert's willingness to appeal directly to Tours rendered this settlement moot. The stakes were high, involving prestige, politics, wealth, and, for all we can know, the inmost feelings of outraged faith on both sides. Both went to extremes to win a clear cut victory. This was a genuine legal hearing, one that involved a finding of fact, the application of the rule of church law, and the imposition of a verdict on a most reluctant Bishop Arnold.

Whether it was an honest hearing is another matter. Arnold's shock at finding his sign on a document he insisted he had never authorized might well be because the document never existed before the monks of Marmoutier produced it for an exceedingly friendly court. There is evidence that the monks of Marmoutier, if not Robert himself, were pre-

---

64. As late as 1080 the monks of Marmoutier were unable to get Arnold's permission to consecrate a new chapel at Sablé. They had to approach the primate of Lyons and the assembled bishops at the Council of Poitiers to force Arnold to relent. Arnold's order to the deacon of Le Mans to go to Sablé for the consecration has survived, Bib. nat., Coll. Baluze, 77, fol. 7bis, published in *Cartul. manceau,* 2: 77, no. 6. The conflict between Marmoutier and la Couture would not be completely solved until 14 January 1095 when Robert hosted a meeting between the two bodies of monks to ratify a settlement. See *Cartul. manceau,* 2: 81–85, no. 2, also published in *Cartul. de la Couture,* 40, no. 30.

65. White, *Custom, Kinship, and Gifts,* 70–73, and *"Pactum . . . Legem Vincit,"* 307–8. Johnson, *Prayer,* 93–94, draws the same conclusion.

pared to create a false version of the charter of Robert's original donation to strengthen their case, although ultimately they declined to use it
for fear of overplaying their hand.[66] Robert, the successful military
commander and soldier, had shown himself capable of skillfully maneuvering in the political and legal arena of the church. With the
monks' connivance he may have been willing to tilt the evidence in his
favor. He was certainly able to exploit the ties he had carefully forged
with the most powerful ecclesiastical personages in the region: the
archbishop of Tours and the abbot of Marmoutier. However it was
done, with their support he was able to defeat Bishop Arnold's persist-
ent attempts to exert his authority over Sablé. Behind Arnold stood his
patron, Duke William of Normandy. With the legal assault from Le
Mans deflected, Robert and William were left to carry on their struggle
by other means.

66. For this remarkable development see Guillot, *Comte d'Anjou*, 2: 170–76, C 264, <Ver-
sion A'>. The alleged original was discovered in 1943, Archives d'Indre-et-Loire, H 1002. The
manuscript tradition is complicated, but Guillot has worked out a plausible scenario. The
point of the forgery was to make it appear that Archbishop Barthelemy had given his consent
to the donation of the churches to Marmoutier. If he had, and there were a written document to prove it, than there would be no need for Bishop Arnold's consent. Guillot offers two
possible explanations of why the monks did not use the false document: it was either not yet
fabricated in 1076, or its error in chronology was so glaring that the monks knew better than
to try to use it. In any case they had already tried to alter King Philip's confirmation of the
original donation by inserting Archbishop Barthelemy's name into it. See Archives d'Indre-et-
Loire, H 306, no. 2. They botched that job also.

CHAPTER SIX

The Struggle for Maine Continues

After the final collapse in March 1076 of Bishop Arnold's case against Robert and Marmoutier for control of Sablé's churches, Robert was free to turn his attention to other matters. Early May found him in the entourage of Count Fulk in the Loire valley travelling towards Angers. Shortly before 15 May, Robert stopped to pray with Count Fulk, Odo of Blaison, and Rainald of Maulévrier at Notre-Dame de Cunault, midway between Angers and Saumur. From Cunault the party pushed on to Angers where the count held his court.[1] By 17 May, Fulk, and presumably Robert, were in Angers.[2]

There can be little doubt as to the major concern of the Angevin court on this occasion. Dissatisfaction among William the Conqueror's Breton followers in England had erupted in a full scale revolt in 1075.[3] The revolt was put down by William's loyal earls but one of the ringleaders, Radulf the Breton, known to English scholars as Earl Ralph of Norfolk, escaped to his holdings in Brittany. There he joined with Geoffrey Granon in revolt against Count Hoel of Brittany. The two rebels established themselves at Geoffrey's stronghold of Dol, which soon became a center of anti-Norman activity on the border. The whole operation was seen as a challenge Duke William could not ig-

---

1. Archives Maine-et-Loire, G 842, fol. 281, several days before 15 May 1078. Guillot, *Comte d'Anjou,* 2: 197–98, C 312.

2. Guillot, *Comte d'Anjou,* 2: C 313, where Count Fulk concedes part of the forest of Échats to Saint-Nicolas d'Angers. Robert is not recorded among the witnesses.

3. For details of this revolt, which had English support, Orderic 2: 310–23; *Anglo-Saxon Chronicle,* D and E, 157. Discussion in Douglas, *William the Conqueror,* 231–33.

nore.[4] Orderic tells us that William raised a huge army and laid seige to the terrorized garrison.[5] Despite this, the garrison held out bravely enough to attract the attention of other adversaries of Duke William. The Angevins, possibly as early as the May gathering at Angers, decided to send forces to reinforce the rebels at Dol. By September Angevin troops were facing William at Dol.[6]

Dol is located near the northern coast of Brittany not far from Mont-Saint-Michel where the peninsula joins the mainland. To be effective the Angevin force had to muster somewhere on Anjou's northwest frontier, quite possibly in the environs of Craon or Château-Gontier, the latter held by Robert's son-in-law Rainald. From either of these bases it was feasible to move north through either Mayenne, whose lord Geoffrey was an Angevin *fidelis,* however erratic, or Vitré, held by Robert, the father of Robert's daughter-in-law.[7] The Angevins could not have travelled safely further to the west through Brittany, through Rennes for example, since Count Hoel of Brittany was cooperating with Duke William in besieging Dol.[8] Obviously the resources of Robert's honor were essential to the conduct of the campaign and he very likely played a major role in its planning and staging. Whether he personally took the field cannot be ascertained, but he probably did.

There is no doubt that Robert's brother Guy was active on the diplomatic front. An essential element of the Angevin strategy was an alliance with King Philip against the Normans. On 14 October the king appeared at Poitiers to seek aid from Duke Geoffrey of Aquitaine against William at Dol. By the king's own testimony he came in such haste that he did not even bring the royal seal.[9] Guy of Nevers was among the very high ranking personages attending King Philip and Duke Geoffrey. He appears to have been the ranking Angevin magnate at the gathering and likely was Fulk's representative. This makes good

---

4. Douglas, *William the Conqueror,* 234.

5. Orderic 2: 350–53.

6. "Annales de Renaud," 88. For the date, see Halphen, *Comté d'Anjou,* 182, n. 1.

7. As shown in Chapter Three, Robert of Vitré had concluded an alliance with Robert the Burgundian and could be expected to offer aid.

8. "Annales de Renaud," 88; Halphen, *Comté d'Anjou,* 182.

9. Besly, *Hist. des comtes de Poictou,* 365–66bis; Prou, *Rec. des actes de Philippe Ier,* 215–21, nos. 83 and 84.

sense because his brother was the key factor in the operations in the west of Maine, while he himself was high in the counsels of Fulk Rechin and cousin to the king. His role as de facto count of Vendôme had ended in January of the previous year when Count Burchard III had come of age, so he was at liberty to play the role of legate.[10] It is possible that Robert's younger son Robert Vestrol was present: certainly he appears a few years later as an important member of Duke Guy-Geoffrey's entourage.[11] The elder Robert and his family were clearly renewing their ties with the house of Poitou at this time. Guy's presence in Poitiers at the meeting between duke and king can not be seen as fortuitous but must be viewed in the light of Angevin interests.

While it is unclear how successful Philip's appeal for support from Duke Geoffrey was, there is no doubt about the final outcome of the ensuing military expedition. The Anglo-Saxon chronicle puts it succinctly, "King William . . . led a force to Brittany and besieged the castle of Dol; but the Bretons held it until the king came from France, and then King William went away and lost there both men and horses and incalculable treasure."[12] The Angevin chronicles say explicitly that Dol was defended by Angevin knights and that Duke William's siege machines were burnt in the Norman retreat.[13] The Norman historian Orderic adds that when William heard of the size of the approaching relief force he hastily withdrew after negotiations with the garrison, who were unaware that they were about to be saved. Yet even Orderic admits that the Norman retreat was so mismanaged that "the soldiers abandoned tents and baggage, with vessels and arms and furnishings of all kinds."[14] In the assessment of David Douglas, William's defeat at

10. Johnson, *Prayer*, 78, and *Cartul. Trinité de Vendôme*, 1: 392, no. 247.

11. *Cartul. Saintongeais de Trinité de Vendôme*, no. 33, 4 September 1078; *Chartes de Cluny*, 4: no. 3580, 11 January 1081; Besly, *Histoire des comtes de Poitou*, 387–89, 10 July 1083; "Livre noir de St-Florent," Bib. nat., n.a. lat. 1930, fol 85v–86v, 1083–1086; *Cartul. de St-Cyprien*, 201, no. 322, 1056–1086; *Cartulaire du Bas-Poitou*, ed. Paul Marchegay (Les Roches-Baritant, 1877), 15–17, no. 9, 15 January 1092. Although listed as "Robert the Burgundian," this is unlikely to be the elder Robert. For Robert Vestrol's role in the Poitevin court, see Richard, *Comtes de Poitou*, 1: 379, who names him as one of five men who usually compose Guy-Geoffrey's "cour judicaire," implying a level of legal expertise comparable to his father's in the Angevin court.

12. *Anglo-Saxon Chronicle*, 158.

13. "Annales de Renaud," 88.

14. Orderic, 2: 350–53. For a critical review of Orderic's account, see Douglas, *William the Conqueror*, 402–3.

Dol was "the first serious military check that he had suffered in France for more than twenty years, and its importance has been unduly minimized."[15]

Having so successfully beaten back the Normans on Robert's northwestern march, Count Fulk now quickly moved to counter an internal defection that directly threatened Robert's position in the east at Sablé. Following the Sarthe River from Sablé towards the east one comes to the castle of Malicorne, held from Robert by the *dominus* Waldin (see map). South and slightly east of Sablé one rides a little over twenty kilometers to arrive at the castle of Durtal, held from Robert by Marcoard of Daumeray.[16] These three strongholds held by men loyal to Robert form a lopsided square whose forth corner is the castle of La Flèche, less than twenty kilometers south of Malicorne and only about thirteen kilometers east of Durtal. Originally part of Maine, it came under the control of Lancelin I of Beaugency when he married Paula, the daughter of Count Herbert Wake-Dog of Maine.[17] Lancelin, a supporter of Count Odo II of Blois, had turned his allegiance to Fulk Nerra so that his son, John of La Flèche, could be styled "the most powerful of the Angevin lords" by Orderic Vitalis.[18] It is probably John who was responsible for the construction of an unusually strong fortress at the site since the annals of Renaud refer to it as "John's Fosse."[19] Most importantly John's wife was the daughter of Count Hugh I of Maine. Perhaps with ambitions for greater independence, John by the time of the siege of Dol had repudiated his allegiance to Count Fulk and had allied himself with Duke William. He thus became a general threat to Angevin interests in Maine and a particular threat to Robert at the very core of his honor.

Almost as soon as the Angevin-French alliance had defeated William

15. *William the Conqueror,* 234.

16. For Malicorne and Durtal, see Bertrand de Broussillon, *Craon,* no. 34; *Cartul. de St-Aubin,* 1: 189, no. 165, and 377–79, no. 329, 2: 353, no. 880; Gustave de Lestang, "La chatellenie et les premiers seigneurs de Malicorne au XIe et au XIIe siècle," *Revue historique et archéologique du Maine* 7 (1880): 247–303.

17. Charles de Montzey, *Histoire de La Flèche et de ses seigneurs: 1re période—1050–1589* (Le Mans and Paris: R. Pellechat and H. Champion, 1877) 1: 14, n.1.

18. "Potentissimus Andegavorum," Orderic, 2: 308. A contemporary charter calls John a "vir nobilis et miles egregius," *Cartul. St-Aubin,* 2: no. 746.

19. "Fissa Johannis" in the "Annales de Renaud," 88; Montzey, *La Flèche,* 12–13.

at Dol, Count Fulk led an attack against La Flèche either very late in 1076 or early 1077.[20] The assault apparently was nearly simultaneous with the fighting at Dol.[21] If so, in making such a combined attack on two widely separated fronts, Fulk, or rather his military commanders of whom Robert was foremost, displayed a tactical skill he (or they) is seldom credited as having.[22]

Despite this tactical sophistication, the attack failed when Fulk was "struck in the leg by a horse when he besieged La Flèche," as a contemporary charter explains.[23] Fulk, "gravely wounded, had himself transported by boat from the army to Angers via the River Loir."[24] At the port of Corzé, Fulk and his companions were very nearly killed in a boating accident and were saved only by the quick action of Girard Folet the provost of Angers. This indicates that the retreat by boat began near La Flèche and continued downriver through Durtal before reaching Corzé. Durtal was obviously the most practical staging area for both the original attack and the retreat. Robert's stronghold of Malicorne would also have been a logical and convenient place for Angevin forces to gather for an assault on La Flèche. In any case, it is highly unlikely that Robert or his most important men were not closely involved in the attack on a rebel stronghold in the midst of his own castles.

Despite this setback the Angevins could still benefit from their victory at Dol. The Angevins in alliance with the French had brought the Norman advance to a standstill, and in 1077 Duke William made peace with King Philip.[25] It would be most unlikely for Philip to conclude a treaty with William without a similar pact being made on behalf of his ally Count Fulk. Indeed, a charter from Saint-Vincent-du-Mans dated

20. The dates usually given for this attack are confused. The best reconstruction of the chronology is found in "Appendix E: The chronology of King William's campaigns between 1073 and 1081," in Douglas, *William the Conqueror*, 401–7. Cf. Halphen, 182–83.

21. Guillot, *Comte d'Anjou*, 1: 120. "Foulques le Réchin, laissant à Dol les siens accaparer les forces du Conquérant, tente aussitôt de s'emparer . . . La Flèche."

22. Bradbury, "Fulk Rechin," 34, highlights the skill Fulk displayed against the Normans in Maine.

23. Dom Housseau, III, no. 989. "Comes Fulco percussus est in cruse a quodam caballo cum obsideret Fissam Johannis." Cf. Guillot, *Comte d'Anjou*, 2: C 316; Halphen, *Comté d'Anjou*, 183 and no. 233.

24. Dom Housseau, III, no. 989. "Fortiter vulneratus fecit se de exercitu navigio Andecavis asportari per fluvium Leuge."

25. *Anglo-Saxon Chronicle*, "E," 159.

from before 5 November 1080 states that it was done "in the time when King William undertook a peace treaty with Count Fulk of Anjou near *Castellum Vallium.*"[26]

Perhaps the peace allowed Robert the time to absorb a personal loss. Robert's wife Advisa the White, whose marriage had given him Sablé and who was instrumental in his donation of the churches there to Marmoutier, was dead. On November 1077, Robert made a donation to the Trinity of Vendôme expressly so that the monks there would add the names of his brother Henry, his wife Advisa, and his son to their obituaries.[27] This is not a generalized donation for the souls of persons yet alive and indicates that Henry, Advisa, and perhaps one or more of Robert's sons were already dead.[28] By 13 March 1079 Robert had remarried. Little is known of Bertha, his second wife, except that her dowry probably included Noyen, about nineteen kilometers east of Sablé.[29]

At this point Robert's family in Nevers suffered a disaster that suggests they were playing a role in Angevin affairs through their loyalty to King Philip. As a counterbalance to the alliance between the Angevins and the king, William encouraged disaffection among Philip's own clients. One of these who allied himself with the Norman duke was Hugh of Le Puiset, viscount of Chartres. In 1079 Philip lost patience with Hugh's rebelliousness and attacked his stronghold at Le Puiset. Robert the Burgundian's brother Count William of Nevers led a powerful force including William's son Robert, bishop of Auxerre, to the king's aid. The siege of Le Puiset ended when Hugh made a sudden sortie that put the royalist force to flight and captured Count William, Bishop Robert, Lancelin of Beaugency, and one hun-

---

26. *Cartul. S. Vincent du Mans*, no. 99. Cf. Douglas, 405–6, and Halphen, *Comté d'Anjou*, 183, who observes that the place name is too frequent in the region to locate specifically. See also C. W. David, *Robert Curthose, Duke of Normandy* (Cambridge: Harvard University Press, 1920), 32–33 who downplays the Angevin achievement.

27. *Cartul. Trinité de Vendôme*, 1: 413–14, no. 264.

28. Henry only appears in one act, dating from 1056–1059, and may have been dead for some time, *Cartul. Saint-Aubin*, 2: 171–74, no. 677.

29. *Cartul. Trinité de Vendôme*, 1: 428–29, no. 276. Noyen was held from Robert by Rainard of Amné and does not appear among Robert's holdings until after 1080, *Cartul. Saint-Vincent*, 216–17, no. 364. Later Bertha approves an agreement between Robert and the monks of Saint-Vincent du Mans regarding a church at Noyen, which implies that she had a personal claim to it. See ibid., 217–18, no. 366.

dred knights. They were not released until they had paid a heavy ransom.[30]

The presence of Lancelin III of Beaugency with Robert's brother and nephew is particularly interesting, for he was the nephew of John of La Flèche. His grandfather, Lancelin I had been active from the late 1020s until perhaps 1054 in the Vendômois.[31] Robert had known this Lancelin's sons, John of La Flèche and Lancelin II, from as early as 1046–1052.[32] Robert's great-aunt Agnes had also had amicable dealings with Lancelin I.[33] Guy of Nevers while regent of Vendôme would have had continual contact with the family. Now the two families drew closer together. At about the time of the disastrous expedition to Le Puiset, Count William's younger son Rainald married Lancelin's daughter.[34]

Robert the Burgundian now showed a great interest in his new relative. He travelled east at least three times, witnessing acts of Lancelin on 1 June 1079 at Vendôme, 2 March 1080, and finally 12 July 1081 at Beaugency.[35] It is possible that this Robert the Burgundian was actually Robert's son, Robert Vestrol, which would still represent a high degree of family interest in the house of Beaugency. At no other time in the elder Robert's life is there any evidence for his family associating with Lancelin III of Beaugency at Vendôme or anywhere else. One trip might have been on account of his nephew's wedding, but not all three. Possibly it represents family efforts to succor the prisoners at Le Puiset, including Robert's brother Count William and the lord of Beaugency, but the dates are uncertain. Since the Angevins launched a second assault on La Flèche in 1081, however, it is tempting to see Robert's con-

30. Lespinasse, *Nivernais*, 1: 247–48; Augustin Fliche, *La règne de Philippe Ier, Roi de France (1060–1108)* (Paris: Société Française, 1912), 313–15. I am indebted to Mr. Christopher Crockett of Bloomington, Indiana for sharing his unpublished manuscript on the family of Le Puiset with me.

31. Guillot, *Comte d'Anjou*, 1: 120, n. 539 and 39, n. 187. For charters, Guillot, 2: C 57, C 116. See also the dated, but still useful Montzey, *La Flèche*, 12–15.

32. See *Cartul. Trinité de Vendôme*, 1: 155–56, no. 85 where Robert, as Countess Agnes's nephew witnessed a confirmation by "the sons of Lancelin."

33. Countess Agnes bought the church of Saint-Bienheué de Vendôme from him and convinced him to donate serfs to the Trinity of Vendôme. See *Cartul. Trinité de Vendôme*, 1: 42–44, no. 22 and 135–37, no. 74.

34. Rainald's son would succeed his grandfather as William II count of Nevers. For the marriage, see Bouchard, *Sword*, 346.

35. *Cartul. Trinité de Vendôme*, 1: 431–36, no. 279; 1: 455–59, no. 299; 2: no. 30l.

tacts with Beaugency as part of an Angevin diplomatic initiative. Lancelin certainly suffered, along with Robert's kin, during the siege of Le Puiset on behalf of King Philip, who was allied to the Angevins. Robert's interest may reflect an effort to exert pressure on John through more loyal members of his clan. If so, the results were all the Angevins could have hoped.

It was an established Angevin practice when the legitimate *dominus* of a castle was to be deposed by the count for infidelity to replace him with a loyal member of the same family. Geoffrey Martel did this at Château-Renault in the Touraine when he had evicted Wicher, the man who held the fortress, and replaced him with Rainald of Château-Gontier, Wicher's uncle.[36] In this way a man of doubtful loyalty was removed, but the same family retained control of the castle.

Possibly with such an arrangement in mind, Count Fulk and his forces moved up for the second assault on La Flèche in 1081. This time at least an Angevin account survives, the chronicle called "de Renaud" which says that

Fulk the Young, count of the Angevins, besieged the castle called "John's Fosse" [La Flèche], took it and burnt it. The castle had already rebelled against Fulk many times and William, king of the English, had previously shaken it loose from the count after gathering a huge force. Challenged by Fulk to war, King William retreated after giving hostages for his good faith, including his own brother the count of Mortain, his son and many others.[37]

Although Orderic conflates the two attacks discussed above into one, it seems that the details he adds actually refer to the 1081 assault. In this account Orderic avoids mentioning that the castle was actually destroyed and simply says that John sent to Duke William for reinforcements as soon as he learned that Count Fulk was preparing to attack. This obscures what was a major Angevin military achievement in tak-

---

36. See Guillot, *Comte d'Anjou*, 1: 346 and 328–29 for the case of Château-Renault. Guillot discusses several other instances where Geoffrey Martel used this technique. See Ile-Bouchard, p. 333 and Château-du-Loir, p. 335.

37. "Annales de Renaud," 88. ". . . et comes Andecavorum Fulcho Junior obsedit castrum quoddam quod Fissa Johannis dicitur atque cepit necnon succendit; quod jam sibi multoties antea rebellaverat; quod rex Anglorum ei antea, gente maxima congregate, excusserat Willelmus. Qui et ipse a Fulcone bello lacessitus, obsidibus pacis pro fide datis fratre suo, consule videlicet Mauritanie, et filio suo et multis aliis, recessit."

ing La Flèche.[38] Orderic adds that William immediately sent a strong force to add to John's own garrison. This news greatly disturbed Count Fulk, but "concentrating his scattered forces he invested John's castle."[39] Given the location of La Flèche, surrounded on the north, northwest, and west by Robert's castles, there can again be no doubt that Robert and his men were part of the massing Angevin force. A contingent of Bretons under Count Hoel (no longer allied with the Normans) also joined the Angevins for the assault. In response Duke William raised a large force of Normans and English, Orderic claims 60,000 knights, and led them to the relief of La Flèche. Even allowing for the obvious exaggeration, this was clearly a major military effort by both sides.

The Angevin-Breton force stood its ground and prepared to fight, a fact that Orderic treats as surprising. He claims the Angevins burnt their boats after crossing the Loire so that their unreliable troops would be forced to fight.[40] In any case La Flèche already had been destroyed and Duke William was not willing to continue the struggle. Among the Normans who urged peace was William of Évreux, who may already have been married to Robert the Burgundian's niece Hewise.[41] Lengthy negotiations at *Blancalanda* or *Brueria,* a spot about five kilometers from La Flèche, produced an agreement.[42] According to Orderic, Count Fulk now accepted the long standing Norman claim that the countship of Maine belonged by right to the king's son, Robert Curthose.[43] This was something the Angevins had been prepared to do since 1063. In the intervening twenty years Robert Curthose had matured into "a young man possessed of the cruder feudal virtues," in Douglas's memorable description, but one "devoid both of statesman-

---

38. Montzey, *La Flèche,* 37, stresses the skill and power displayed by Fulk in taking such a strong fortress.

39. Orderic, 2: 308–9.

40. Orderic, 2: 308–9. Oderic's account does not entirely make sense, since the Angevins should already have been on the north side of the *Loir* river facing the Normans. See Halphen, *Comté d'Anjou,* 184 n. 1 for discussion. Kate Norgate, *England Under the Angevin Kings,* 2 vols. (London and New York: Macmillan, 1887), 1: 265–67, examines the siege and attempts to explain this detail.

41. Orderic, 2: 310–11. For Helwise see Orderic, 4: 212–13.

42. Montzey, *La Flèche,* 36, identifies it as Blanche-Lande, also called "lande de Brouère."

43. Orderic, 2: 310–11.

ship and sagacity."[44] The Angevins were well aware of Curthose's character since in 1078–1079 he had foolishly revolted against his father. William's temporary defeat at the hands of his son was probably the cause of much amusement among the Angevins.[45]

Robert the Burgundian and the other Angevin *fideles* on the Manceau march must have viewed the prospect of such a man guarding Norman interests in Maine with equanimity, if not outright approval. This was all the more true since as part of the peace treaty Curthose had lawfully given his homage to Fulk "as a lesser man to a greater."[46] There was also a general amnesty for Angevins like John who had joined the Normans and men of Maine who had fought for Count Fulk.[47]

From Robert's perspective this treaty must have seemed a greater success than is generally recognized. The danger on his eastern flank from La Flèche was neutralized when John renewed his allegiance to the Angevin count, apparently with sincerity. John of La Flèche himself would become a monk of St-Aubin around 1097 during his last illness at Château-Gontier, indicating close ties with Robert's daughter and son-in-law. He would be buried in the abbey's chapter house in Angers, a loyal Angevin at last.[48] John's son Helias soon become the lord of La Flèche and would prove a staunch ally for Robert and the Angevins. This is odd, for Helias had two elder brothers who were passed over. One, Gauzbert, was in Le Mans and may be presumed to have been loyal to the Normans like his father.[49] He was not acceptable to the Angevins, and was supplanted by his younger brother. John, or someone powerful within his clan, had made a great concession to Angevin

---

44. *William the Conqueror*, 236–37.

45. Douglas, *William the Conqueror*, 238–39. Orderic's opinion of Robert Curthose was scathing, see, e.g., 3: 102–3 and 106–7.

46. "Denique Rodbertus Fulconi debitum homagium ut minor maiori legaliter impendit." My translation of the Latin is blunter regarding Curthose's inferior position than Chibnall's translation: "Robert did homage to Fulk as a vassal to his lord," in Orderic, 2: 310–11.

47. Ibid.

48. For John's reconciliation with Fulk, see Guillot, *Comte d'Anjou*, 1: 120 n. 542. John's death was around 1097, according to *Cartul. St-Aubin*, 2: no. 748. Helias attended his funeral at Angers; see ibid., no. 749. After the reconciliation of 1081, Hugh, brother of Waldin of Malicorne, one of Robert's men, appears in John's entourage. Ibid., nos. 746 and 747.

49. Montzey, *Histoire de La Flèche*, 44 and 67.

interests. Robert the Burgundian's ties with the Beaugency branch of the clan now acquire new significance. Whoever made the arrangements, and Robert is the most likely person, restored the situation on Robert's northeastern flank.

Furthermore Maine would now be ruled by Robert Curthose, who had sworn to Fulk as his subordinate. Not only had Curthose given little indication of his father's skill and ruthless energy, he was known to have often quarrelled with his father and on one occasion to have taken up arms against him. The pact between Count Fulk and Duke William did much to strengthen the situation in Maine for Robert.

Despite the success of the treaty of *Blancalanda,* a new dispute broke out almost immediately when Bishop Arnold of Le Mans died on 29 November 1081.[50] While Robert may have felt considerable satisfaction at the demise of the man who had caused him so much trouble, the problem of the episcopal succession once again threatened to disrupt the status quo on the Angevin march. Duke William was determined to install his own nominee in the see of Le Mans, in this case Hoel the Breton, a clerk in William's own chapel.[51] As a protégé of Bishop Arnold closely attached to William's personal service, he could be expected to be as scrupulous in maintaining Norman interests in Maine as had been his predecessor.[52] According to the *Actus pontificum,* Count Fulk opposed this move, supposedly threatening Archbishop Radulf of Tours, thus preventing him from consecrating Hoel. This was not, however, a repeat of Geoffrey the Bearded's intemperate treatment of the archbishop of Tours. Even though Pope Gregory VII ordered Radulf to proceed with the consecration, nothing was done for nearly four years. The Archbishop of Rouen finally consecrated Hoel as bishop of Le Mans on 21 April 1085.[53]

Pope Gregory's letter to Radulf is remarkably hostile towards the

50. "Annales de Vendôme," 65; *Actus pontificum,* 382.

51. Orderic, 2: 300. Orderic says that Hoel was so emaciated and poorly dressed when William first saw him that his chaplain was hard put to talk him into the nomination. This seems unlikely.

52. The author of the *Actus pontificum,* 383, who knew Hoel personally, says that he was raised by Arnold.

53. *Actus pontificum,* 383; Halphen, *Comté d'Anjou,* 185–86; Latouche, *Maine,* 39; Guillot, *Comte d'Anjou,* 1: 120–21. Pope Gregory's letter to Archbishop Radulf is published by Léopold Delisle, "'Trois lettres de Grégoire VII,'" *Bibliothèque de l'École des Chartes* 26 (1865): 559.

archbishop, even allowing for Hildebrandine overstatement. He begins by virtually accusing Radulf of being an Angevin tool, saying

We hear that your fraternity, swayed by worldly fear, declines the laying on of hands for the bishop-elect of Le Mans [Hoel], who desires to be consecrated by you and whose consecration pertains to the jurisdiction of your church. You are fearful, specifically, lest you offend the count of Anjou on this account. This matter is far from what it ought to be for priestly, and even more so for papal, dignity.[54]

After a brief quote from Pope Gregory the Great, the pope bluntly commands Radulf to consecrate the bishop elect immediately, and threatened that if he did not,

By our apostolic authority we advise and order your prudence to consecrate the bishop-elect, lest you violate canonical procedure. Putting aside the occasion of a secular offense, refuse and neglect this no further. Finally, it is better that you fear lest, if you consider it better to be terrified than to follow justice and [Hoel] is consecrated by someone else, as would be fair, the church of Tours through your hesitation (let it not be!) comes to feel a loss of its honor.[55]

None of this sounds as if the pope were addressing a man who was being prevented by force from carrying out his duty. Pope Gregory believed that Radulf was not resisting the count's demands very strenuously and we may doubt that the archbishop fully supported Hoel's election in the first place. This would explain the long delayed consecration. It is certain that on 6 January 1084, more than a year before the issue of Hoel's consecration was resolved, Archbishop Radulf was on good enough terms with Fulk to attend a meeting of his court at Angers.[56] A bitter split between count and archbishop would have

54. Delisle, "Trois lettres," 559. "Audivimus quod Cenomanensi electo, cujus consecratio ad jus tuae ecclesiae pertinet, consecrari per te cupienti, fraternitas tua mundani timoris intuitu imponere manum renuerit, metuens scilicet ne propter hoc comes Angegavensis offenderetur; quae res a sacerdotali, praecipue pontificali, sublimitate quam procul esse debeat . . ."

55. Ibid. "Deinde prudentiam tuam monemus et apostolica auctoritate praecipimus ut praelibatum electum consecrare, nisi canonica ratio contradicat, postposita saecularis offensionis occasione, non ulterius recuses aut negligas. Denique potius tibi timendum est ne, si magis pavori quam justiciae obsequi deliberaveris, et ille, sicut aequum fuerit, ab alio consecretur, et Turonensis ecclesia per tuam segnitiem, quod absit, honoris sui detrimentum sentire incipiat."

56. Bib. nat., Dom Housseau, III, no. 829.

caused Robert grave concern, as it apparently did at the time of Geoffrey the Bearded. The tone of Gregory's letter, however, and the fact that Radulf did not heed it, seems to argue for a more sanguine attitude on Radulf's part. There is, therefore, no need to see a major split between Robert's policy of cooperation with the archbishop of Tours and his count's determination to maintain control over the see of Le Mans. Although Robert could not have known it at the time, he would come to virtually coopt the new bishop to his own ends.

The ecclesiastical struggle over Hoel's consecration foreshadowed an intense military effort on Robert's part. As long as William the Conqueror remained alive and could call upon the military resources of both Normandy and England he would pose a threat to Robert's territory on the Maine-Anjou border. By 1083, Robert was willing to risk a direct military confrontation with the Conqueror in an effort to deflect the threat. Once again Robert's actions revolved around the twin concerns of loyalty to the Angevin count and his own family connections. Hubert of Sainte-Suzanne, viscount of Le Mans, had married Robert's niece Ermengarde, the daughter of his brother William count of Nevers on 6 December 1067.[57] Hubert was also the nephew of Geoffrey of Sablé, so he was the cousin of Robert's first wife Advisa the White.[58]

As Orderic, usually biased against the Angevins, tells the story, Hubert gave offense to Duke William in numerous unspecified ways. As a consequence Hubert had to abandon his castle of Beaumont-le-Vicomte and Fresnay-sur-Sarthe. Becoming a "public enemy" *(publicus hostis)*, Hubert retreated with his wife and followers to his castle of Sainte-Suzanne. This fortress, which is actually about thirty-five kilometers north of Sablé, was said by Orderic to be built "on the frontiers of Maine and Anjou," a phrase that indicates the Norman writer's understanding that the northern frontier of Anjou had migrated north, thanks in part to Robert's efforts.[59] The eleventh century fortress still stands, walled three meters thick atop a formidable ridge from which

57. Orderic, 4: 46–47. A charter of Saint-Martin de Bellême dated 6 December 1067 has among the witness list. "Signum Guillelmi, comitis Nivernemsis [sic], qui ipso die filiam suam donavit Usberto, vicecomiti cenomanorum." See Prou, *Rec. des actes de Philippe Ier,* 134–37, no. 50.

58. Bertrand de Broussillon, *Craon,* 1: 23.

59. Orderic, 4: 46–47. ". . . in confinio Cenomannensium."

one looks down on the surrounding countryside. From such a strong-hold Hubert could easily harass the Normans "who were busy protecting the county of Maine."[60]

Hubert's action must be seen in conjunction with the role of Robert Curthose. As has been noted, the Angevins, if not the Manceaux, were willing to accept Curthose as count of Maine as long as he acknowledged Count Fulk as his overlord. Shortly after 18 July 1083 the situation changed when Curthose rebelled once again against his father and went into exile.[61] Presumably this left William and his agents effectively governing Maine, a prospect that could not have appealed to Robert the Burgundian. At some point after 2 November 1083, Hubert and Robert began military operations against the Normans.[62]

Fortunately the ensuing campaign caught Orderic's imagination so that he provides the only account of Robert as a military leader. When the local Norman leaders complained of Hubert's depredations, Orderic explains:

The king quickly raised an army of Normans, summoned those among the men of Maine who were loyal to him and advanced on the enemy country with a strong force. But he could not blockade the castle of Sainte-Suzanne, which was made inaccessible by the crags and a thick growth of creepers surrounding it, neither could he bring effective pressure on his enemy in the castle, since Hubert was strong enough to procure supplies and controlled many entrances and exits. The king therefore built a castle in the valley of Beugy, posted a strong force of men-at-arms there to contain the enemy and himself returned to Normandy.[63]

Earthworks presumed to be remains of the siege camp at Beugy are still in evidence some 800 meters from the keep. There William left his household troops commanded by Count Alan the Red. His well supplied troops, however, were facing more than the troops of Sainte-Suzanne's garrison.

60. Orderic, 4: 46–47.

61. David, *Robert Curthose*, 36.

62. The exact dates for the siege of Sainte-Suzanne are uncertain. Orderic, 4: 46–47, places the outbreak immediately after the death of Queen Matilda on 2 November 1083. See Chibnall's n. 3, Orderic, 4: 45.

63. Orderic, 4: 48–49.

Experienced knights had flocked to Hubert from Aquitaine and Burgundy and other French provinces and were striving with all their might to help him and show their worth. As a result the castle of Sainte-Suzanne was stocked with booty taken from the defenders of Beugy and each day became better equipped for defence. Wealthy Norman and English lords were frequently captured and Hubert the vicomte and Robert the Burgundian, whose niece he had married, and their other supporters made an honorable fortune out of the ransoms of these men. In this way Hubert kept the Normans at bay for three years, growing rich at the expense of his enemies and remaining unvanquished.[64]

Robert's participation must be viewed within the context of the broader Angevin concerns in Maine. In fact, Robert was in Angers for Count Fulk's Christmas court, where a highly significant meeting of the count's court took place on 6 January 1084.[65] On that date a dispute was settled between the abbeys of Saint-Florent and Saint-Nicolas with over two hundred men as witnesses. Among the "judges" of the case was Archbishop Radulf of Tours, obviously on friendly terms with the count despite the controversy over Hoel's consecration. Bishop Geoffrey of Angers was there, as well as the abbots of the Trinity of Vendôme, Saint-Pierre de Fosse, and Saint-Pierre of Bourgueil. The three main lay judges, listed separately from the others, are Count Fulk, Robert the Burgundian, and Geoffrey of Mayenne. Their presence as well as that of Fulk of Matheflon, Girorius of Beaupréau, and many other knights, along with two hundred other witnesses, indicates that this was a major gathering of Angevin ecclesiastical and military leaders. Robert and Geoffrey were, of course, Fulk's chief *fideles* in Maine and the situation there must have been a major topic of discussion. Whether or not Hubert was already in defiance of Norman rule, it must have been after this meeting in Angers, and with the approval of Count Fulk, that Robert moved his own forces to Sainte-Suzanne. His role in Fulk's entourage and his actions at the siege confirm Halphen's interpretation that "it was not without the agreement of the count of Anjou, and perhaps his complicity" that the revolt took place.[66]

64. Ibid.
65. Bib. nat., Dom Housseau, III, no. 829.
66. Halphen, *Comté d'Anjou*, 186. ". . . ce ne fut pas sans l'assentiment du comte d'Anjou et peut-être sa complicité qu'un nouveau soulèvement des grands manceaux se produisit."

Robert's role was not a mere chivalric beau-geste, but a reasoned military response to the Norman threat carried out in consultation with his count.

The fighting around Sainte-Suzanne has often been characterized as a minor operation,[67] but J. O. Prestwich's analysis of Orderic's account reveals that it was a major military effort by the Normans. The Conqueror had entrusted the campaign against Hubert and Robert to the picked troops of his personal household, the *familia regis*. From the high rank of the commanders, including Alan the Red, count of Brittany and lord of Richmond, Prestwich concludes that a considerable force was involved, one "lavishly supplied with food and money."[68] Despite this massive effort, the Normans were never able to do any serious harm to either Hubert or Robert. As far as is known, and Orderic's account is both informed and detailed, no attempt was made to attack Sablé, or any other of Robert's possessions. The Normans never succeeded in isolating Sainte-Suzanne, nor did they ever extend their operations beyond the immediate vicinity.

In Orderic's account Aquitainians and Burgundians figure prominently among the defenders. Robert's son, Robert Vestrol, was a close associate of the count of Poitou during this period, while Robert and Count Guy-Geoffrey were cousins. There is little other reason to account for the participation of Aquitainian troops so far north. The presence of Burgundians at the siege is easily explained: Count William of Nevers was both Robert's brother and Hubert's father-in-law. It begins to appear as if the entire campaign against the Normans centered around the Burgundian clan at Sablé.

This may explain why the Norman offensive was so ineffectual. As long as Robert and his supporters, some from as far away as Aquitaine and Burgundy, could move with impunity from their bases around

67. David, *Robert Curthose*, 35, for example, calls it merely "a very troublesome local insurrection," while Douglas barely comments on it and Guillot does not mention it at all.

68. J. O. Prestwich, "The Military Household of the Norman King's," *English Historical Review* 96 (1981): 10. Prestwich also describes the background of the commanders to demonstrate their high standing among William's forces. In Sainte-Suzanne today signs proudly proclaim it the site of William the Conqueror's only defeat. Robert the Burgundian is not mentioned, nor is he mentioned in the informative pamphlet, "Sainte-Suzanne, A Medieval Town," put out by the ministry of culture for the Pays de la Loire.

Sablé to resupply Sainte-Suzanne, the stronghold was impregnable. It looks formidable enough as it is. From Sablé Robert's forces would have about a seventeen-kilometer ride to Brûlon, held by Robert, and another seventeen kilometer ride on to Sainte-Suzanne. The Normans, on the other hand, were unable to attack Sablé itself. Unlike Mayenne, which had been taken by the Normans in the past, Sablé was an integral part of the Angevin defense system, well supported on every side now that La Flèche had been brought back into the Angevin fold. An attack on Robert at Sablé would have probably been beyond Norman capabilities, and in any case would have involved them in open hostilities with the count of Anjou. Taking all this into account, it appears that the main leader of the war against the Normans was not Hubert, but Robert, headquartered in the nearly impregnable fortress of Sablé and backed by the archbishop of Tours, the monastery of Marmoutier, and the counts of Anjou, Poitou, and Nevers.

The fighting dragged on for at least two years with Robert and Hubert inflicting heavy losses on the Normans. Orderic gives a brief description of the nature of the fighting and the casualties, several of whom he lists by name. One of these, Richer of Laigle, was struck in the eye by an arrow shot from ambush during one attack. He managed to survive just long enough to pardon the young boy who had shot him and who was about to be slaughtered by his outraged complanions. A large Norman force seeking revenge then assaulted the garrison of Sainte-Suzanne but was defeated with yet more casualties. One important Norman commander, William count of Évreux, was taken prisoner in this action.[69]

William of Évreux's appearance here is ironic, since he had played a key role in the treaty of *Blancalanda* and may already have been married to another of Robert's nieces, Hewise of Nevers.[70] When this marriage took place is unknown; it could just as well have been after the siege. It is possible that while William was his prisoner Robert came to know the man and helped arrange the marriage.

Sometime between 23 May 1085 and 20 April 1086 the Normans de-

69. Orderic, 4: 48–51.
70. Orderic, 4: 212, n. 5.

cided that it would be better to conclude a peace with Hubert rather than to risk further disasters.[71] Orderic claims that when William learned of the extent of the casualties he pardoned Hubert for all his offenses. Hubert also received a safe-conduct to cross the Channel to England for the final negotiations. William guaranteed that Hubert would receive all his father's inheritance.[72] From Orderic's account there can be no doubt that Hubert considered the settlement a victory. Having fought against the Normans for two years, Hubert's hold on his lands was guaranteed by the Norman duke. Unfortunately, there is no word on what Robert received, if anything, in the peace treaty. He had performed a great military feat, had grown rich off booty and ransom, and had seriously weakened William's position in Maine. The Normans gained nothing from Robert in return.

71. Orderic, 4: 52–53, makes it clear that the Norman forces in the field were the ones who wanted peace. A charter presumed to date from 23 May 1085–20 April 1086 in *Cartul. de Saint-Vincent du Mans,* no. 492 was enacted "at the time Vicomte Hubert of Sainte-Suzanne made peace and concord with the English King."

72. Orderic, 4: 52–53.

CHAPTER SEVEN

Triumph at Le Mans

Robert would never again be troubled by William, king of the English and duke of the Normans. For the next year or so William was preoccupied with troubles in England and Normandy. After a particularly brutal campaign in the Vexin, the Conqueror fell ill or was injured and died on 9 September 1087. An event of such magnitude would obviously effect the political situation on the Maine/Anjou border. The Angevin struggle for Maine now entered a new phase.

Robert Curthose, acknowledged count of Maine, was in rebellion against his father at the time of his death. Despite this the Conqueror did not disinherit his son, who became duke of Normandy as well as count of Maine. His younger brother William Rufus became king of England.[1] Under Curthose's weak control Normandy lapsed into a state of chaos.[2] In Orderic's harsh judgement Curthose "was so idle and frivolous that he never governed justly and effectively as he ought to have done."[3] The Normans in England, preferring the milder rule of Curthose, attempted to revolt against William Rufus. Once William had put down this revolt he remained implacably hostile to his brother on the continent.[4]

For Robert and the other Angevin *fideles* in Maine, such as Geoffrey of Mayenne and Helias of La Flèche, the failure of Curthose to exert a

1. David, *Robert Curthose*, 40–41. Douglas, *William the Conqueror*, 360–61.
2. David, *Robert Curthose*, 43–44.
3. Orderic, 4: 110–11.
4. David, *Robert Curthose*, 49–53. For a differing, and not very convincing, opinion, see Frank Barlow, *William Rufus* (Berkeley: University of California Press, 1983), 70–73 and 263.

strong presence in Maine was a welcome relief to the years of warfare and uncertainty under William the Conqueror. For this reason, if for no other, they were willing to support him as the legitimate count of Maine, especially since Curthose always acknowledged that he held Maine from the count of Anjou.[5]

This attitude towards Curthose was clearly demonstrated in 1088 when he led an army to Le Mans to overawe any potential opposition to his rule. When the Normans arrived at Le Mans, probably in August, they were met by rejoicing crowds of clergy and citizens. According to Orderic, "after hearing his messages Geoffrey of Mayenne, Robert the Burgundian, Helias son of John [of La Flèche] and many others answered the summons, ready for the duke's service."[6] This comment is significant. Here are the three men Orderic viewed as the key to Maine, and all three are *fideles* of the count of Anjou. Geoffrey held the northwest of the county, while Robert and Helias between them dominated the southern portion of Maine. Men of this standing, who had consistently fended off efforts by the Conqueror to master them, would only have submitted to Curthose because it suited their purposes. Just as their lord, Fulk Rechin, had accepted Curthose as a subordinate, they were willing to work in his behalf as count of Maine.

Orderic implies that the three Angevin magnates joined with Curthose's Norman forces to attack rebels in northeast Maine. Paradoxically this would not be inconsistent with Robert's Angevin loyalty. The rebels were a faction led by the house of Bellême which was still a major power on the eastern flank of the Maine/Normandy border. By this point the Bellême had completely removed themselves from both Angevin and Norman alliances. Curbing the growing power of the dangerously independent Bellême family can be seen as an important goal for the Angevin party in Maine represented by Robert, Geoffrey, and Helias. For the moment at least their interests coincided with the duke of Normandy's, who from the Angevin point of view was acting as an avowed subordinate of their count.

By 1 September the combined force of Normans and Manceaux,

---

5. Orderic, who generally presents the Norman point of view, at least for affairs on the continent, never questioned Fulk Rechin's title as overlord of Maine. See Orderic, 2: 306–7, "Fulk resented the lordship of the Normans in Maine . . . a county that was rightfully his."

6. Orderic, 4: 154–55.

presumably including the three Angevin lords named by Orderic, had marched on the castle of Ballon, held by Pagan of Mondoubleau.[7] After some inconclusive combat the garrison made peace with Curthose and the ducal army moved on to the Bellême stronghold of Saint-Cénari. There the garrison resisted until starvation led to the fall of the castle. The captured castellan and many other prisoners were blinded or otherwise mutilated by the angry duke.

At this point Geoffrey of Mayenne and other Manceaux leaders *(tribuni)* approached the duke. Since Orderic had linked Geoffrey, Robert, and Helias together as the only leaders of the Manceaux named in his previous passage, it seems likely that Robert is to be understood as one of these *"tribuni."* They presented to Curthose a young knight named Robert Giroie, begging that the duke accept Giroie into his service and restore to him the castle of Saint-Céneri, which had been held by his father "by hereditary right *(hereditarius ius)."* The duke graciously granted their request and gave Giroie the castle of Saint-Cénari.[8]

This has several implications, especially if Robert were one of Giroie's patrons. Giroie's father, called Robert fitz Giroie, was from a Breton family established on the Maine/Normandy border earlier in the century. This Robert fitz Giroie died in 1060 after rebelling against Duke William on behalf of Geoffrey Martel.[9] In addition, Robert Giroie's aunt Adalais had married Salomon of Sablé, a high ranking member of Robert the Burgundian's entourage.[10] In this light Geoffrey of Mayenne's request has a very specific point. A major fortress facing the Bellême would henceforth be in the hands of a man whose father had fought for Geoffrey Martel and whose uncle by marriage was a loyal supporter of Robert the Burgundian. Robert and his Angevin allies were using their service to Robert Curthose to install one more pro-Angevin *dominus* in Maine in place of the dangerously independent Bellême family.

Shortly after this the castellans of Bellême and Alençon began to

7. Orderic, 4: 154–55; for Pagan, see Latouche, *Maine,* 40; for the date, David, *Robert Curthose,* 70 n. 1.

8. Orderic, 4: 154–55.

9. Orderic, 2: 78–81 and Chibnall's note on the date, 6 February 1060. Orderic claims that Robert was poisoned accidentally by his wife, but see Douglas, *William the Conqueror,* 408–15.

10. Orderic, 2: 30–31 and Chibnall's genealogy of the family between pages 370–71. For Salomon of Sablé, see *Cartul. Trinité de Vendôme,* 1: 271–73, no. 157 and 428–29, no. 276.

consider surrendering to the ducal forces after hearing of the mutila-
tions at Saint-Cénari. "However, Duke Robert," Orderic claims, "soon
abandoned his show of energy and, giving way to voluptuousness, sank
back with relief into idle dalliance, and disbanded his army, sending all
his men home."[11] Possibly Robert and the other Angevin allies simply
did not want a deathblow dealt to the Bellême. They may have assumed, correctly as it happens, that the Bellême would now cause
more trouble in Normandy than in Maine.[12] Whether this is so or not,
Robert returned to his march, having cemented his ties with Curthose,
brushed back the threat from Bellême, and overseen the installation of
a pro-Angevin lord at Saint-Céneri.

If this picture of Angevin cooperation with Duke Robert Curthose,
led by Robert the Burgundian, Geoffrey of Mayenne, and Helias of La
Flèche, is correct, than any effort on the part of local Manceaux lords
against the duke would be met with Angevin resistance. In fact, this is
exactly what happened, although Orderic presents the story in such a
bizarre fashion that it has generally been disregarded.[13]

According to Orderic the men of Maine grew restless under Norman rule when they learned of the chaos that was engulfing Normandy under Curthose's misrule. Hearing of their plan to revolt,
Curthose sent to Count Fulk and asked him to restrain the Manceaux.
At his request Fulk actually came to visit the duke in Normandy, where
he found him convalescing from an illness. Fulk thereupon told the
duke that he would prevent the revolt, but only if he received Bertrada
daughter of Simon of Montfort, whom he loved as his wife. Curthose
had to make enormous concessions to the lady's guardian, Count
William of Évreux, but finally the marriage was arranged. In return
Fulk persuaded the Manceaux to postpone their planned rebellion for a
year.[14]

At first glance Fulk's motive seems preposterous, but if we look be-

11. Orderic, 4: 156–57.

12. For a graphic description of the havoc Robert of Bellême is supposed to have caused
the duchy, see Orderic, 4: 158–63. This destruction apparently reached no further into Maine
than the stronghold of Saint-Cénari, which may have been exactly what the Angevins had intended.

13. David, *Robert Curthose*, 70, judged Orderic's version "hardly credible."

14. Orderic, 4: 184–87.

yond the surface of the story as told by a writer who regarded Fulk Rechin with disgust, there is actually nothing unlikely about it.[15] As has been suggested, Angevin policy supported Curthose as count of Maine, which is precisely what is going on in Orderic's account. This being so, what could be more natural than Fulk visiting with his ailing ally for "several discussions on peace and alliance."[16] This was probably the main point of the meeting, which was called to head off a rebellion in Maine. At the time Fulk was unmarried, although he had been married at least twice before. There is nothing inherently unlikely about an alliance being sealed with a marriage arrangement and that is probably all that should be read into it. Bertrada had been raised by Hewise, Robert's niece, so it is likely that Robert played some role in the lengthy negotiations needed to overcome William of Évreux's opposition. Robert certainly was with Curthose at about this time. A notice for an act at Sablé dated 29 August 1092 says that in 1090 the lord of Sablé was away "serving the count of Normandy."[17] In the context of Orderic's story it is clear that Robert would have been furthering Angevin interests by attending Curthose. Politics on the Maine border had more to do with this marriage than Orderic knows or admits.

Despite the understanding with Curthose, Fulk was only able to keep the Manceaux under control until 1090. Here we may very well see a disagreement among the Angevin *fideles* in Maine, since it appears that Robert the Burgundian, Geoffrey of Mayenne, and Helias of La Flèche all reacted differently to the revolt. This apparent split, however, may simply be due to the nature of our sources: the *Actus pontificum* and Orderic's history. Each of these works has a particular point of

15. Orderic, 4: 186–93. "Count Fulk was a man with many reprehensible, even scandalous, habits, and gave way to many pestilential vices." This sentence introduces a lengthy diatribe against everything from Fulk's personal taste in shoes to the fashion of men using curling irons.

16. Orderic, 4: 184–85. Orderic mentions these discussions as the prelude to Fulk's request for Bertrada.

17. "Anno ab incarnatione Domini MXC, defuncto nobilissimo rege Anglorum, Willelmmo seniore, principatum Normannie Rotbertus, ejus filius, obtinuit. Igitur, circa illud tempus, cum Rotbertus Burgundio vetulus, ad serviendum Rotberto comiti in Normanniam perrexisset." *Cartul. St-Aubin* 2: 252–53, no. 879, original in Archives Maine-et-Loire, H 110, no. 113. Duke William, however, died in 1087. The dating clause seems to mean that in 1090 Robert the Burgundian left to serve Robert Curthose. In his absence one of his knights brought a claim against St-Aubin that was not resolved until 29 August 1092, after Robert had returned.

view and neither is sympathetic or knowledgeable about Angevin affairs.

As it is, Helias, either on his own or with the approval of Count Fulk, began to claim the countship of Maine on the grounds that his mother Paula was the sister of Count Hugh IV of Maine.[18] He seized the castle of Ballon and used it as a base to attack the citizens of Le Mans who resisted him.[19] Bishop Hoel of Le Mans in particular steadfastly refused to cooperate with Helias because of his loyalty to Robert Curthose. Helias seized the bishop while he was riding about his diocese and imprisoned him at La Flèche.[20] This produced a sharp reaction among the citizens of Le Mans who took down all the holy images from the churches, blocking the doors and preventing all church services. In the face of such popular demonstrations Helias yielded and released Bishop Hoel.[21]

This incident, as presented by the *Actus pontificum,* may represent an attempt at seizing the county that had the full support of Count Fulk and Robert the Burgundian. The attempt misfired when it failed to carry Le Mans, and above all, the popular bishop of Le Mans. By imprisoning the bishop, Helias outraged public opinion to such an extent that he realized he could not rule. It may be that as long as Hoel remained loyal to Curthose, the Angevins who had accepted Curthose as Count of Maine were not willing wholeheartedly to back Helias. It is also possible that Helias was acting completely on his own.

A separate stage of the struggle now began when Geoffrey of Mayenne, the other Angevin *fidelis* in Maine, sent numerous legates to Italy to seek out Hugh, the son of Azzo of Este, to offer him the

18. *Actus pontificum,* 385. Orderic, 4: 194–95, makes Helias merely one of the rebelling Manceaux, and by no means the ringleader. For Helias's descent see Latouche, *Maine,* Appendix III, 113–15.

19. *Actus pontificum,* 385. Hugh, a much beloved knight of Fulk Rechin, was from Ballon and held the forest of Chambiers from Hubert of Durtal, probably with Robert the Burgundian as overlord. See Bib. nat., ms. lat. 12696, fol 264r–v, 1083–27 March 1094.

20. Orderic and the *Actus pontificum* seem to disagree on the timing of events. The *Actus pontificum,* 385, presents Helias's role as the first element of the revolt, carried out on his own. Orderic, 4: 194–95, presents the revolt in Maine as a general insurrection in which Helias plays a subordinate role and only captures Hoel after the bishop had excommunicated the principle rebels. Since the author of the *Actus pontificum* was an eyewitness, his account may be given considerably more weight. See Latouche, *Maine,* 2.

21. Both *Actus pontificum,* 386, and Orderic, 4: 194–95, agree on the popular reaction.

countship. This was the same Hugh who as a young boy had been offered the countship by the Manceaux in 1069.[22] Geoffrey must have thought that Hugh, having been supported by the Manceaux once before, might be more acceptable to them than Helias. He may have viewed Hugh as a suitable tool for the Angevins or, possibly, he simply sought to install the son of his former lover for his own purposes.

Whatever Geoffrey's motivations, his legates were successful in convincing Hugh to come to Maine. By 13 April 1091 Hugh had reached Tours and shortly after travelled to Maine.[23] It is difficult to see how Hugh could have passed through Tours, Anjou's second capital, if his claim to the countship were not at least tolerated by the Angevins. When near Le Mans the nobles of the city, "counting their oaths of fidelity to Count Robert as nothing, ran out to meet him at the castle of Chartre-sur-le-Loir."[24] He was welcomed, Orderic adds, by Geoffrey of Mayenne, Helias, and other citizens (*cives*) and castellans (*oppidani*).[25] Orderic does not mention Robert the Burgundian and he may not have been present.

Bishop Hoel, fearing he was in danger, departed the city in haste and went to Count Robert in Normandy. Curthose, however, was so sunk in "inertia and sensual pleasures" that he made no response to Hoel's pleas for action. As the author of the *Actus pontificum* put it, "he did not appear to care, except that the office of bishop remain in his domain."[26] This moment of disillusionment seems to have permanently weakened Hoel's loyalty to Curthose.

When Hoel returned to Le Mans he found that Hugh had so far established his control that it was not safe to enter the city. Staying at the monastery of Saint-Vincent he contented himself with communicating with Hugh by messengers. Hugh was able to encourage a faction within the church of Le Mans hostile to Hoel, headed by the canon Hilgot,

22. *Actus pontificum*, 386.

23. At Tours Hugh renounced the property taken by his father from the monks of Marmoutier. See Bib. nat., coll. Baluze 76 fol. 14. Since he did not use the title of count, Latouche, *Maine*, 41 n. 10, assumes he was still on his way to Le Mans.

24. *Actus pontificum*, 386.

25. Orderic, 4: 194–95.

26. *Actus. pont.*, 386. "Non enim curare videbatur, nisi ut episcopatus tantum in ejus dominio remaneret."

to set up a rival bishop. The situation within the city continued to deteriorate to the point where Hoel was willing to appeal to the last of the great Angevin lords in Maine, Robert the Burgundian. Hoel's supporters within the church gathered up the episcopal treasury and fled in secret to Sablé where the treasure was put under a safe guard.[27]

Robert had been a more subtle and patient politician than his colleagues. Having watched first Helias and then Geoffrey make their attempts at seizing the countship, Robert had bided his time and somehow made an alliance with Bishop Hoel. Possibly this was done with the influence of Archbishop Radulf of Tours, since Hoel was very close to the archbishop and often consulted him on church business.[28] When Hoel had no one to turn to Robert offered him his aid. From this point on it is evident that Hoel trusted Robert and relied upon him for support. Sablé, and the nearby abbey of Solesmes, became the headquarters for the pro-Hoel faction of the Manceau church.[29] As Helias's failure to hold Le Mans had shown Robert, the bishop held the key to Le Mans. Now the bishop, or at least his treasury, was in Robert's complete control.

After Hoel had satisfied himself that everything was secure at Sablé, he departed for England to solicit aid from William Rufus. This was by November 1091 at the latest.[30] Some of his clerics remaining in Sablé maintained communication with their supporters and relatives within the city. Despite harassment from the anti-Hoel forces, sympathetic women from Le Mans even managed to carry supplies to Sablé.[31] Robert was able to keep well informed on developments in Le Mans.

Robert soon travelled south to consult with Fulk Rechin. He was with the count at Montbazon between 29 January and 6 February.[32] On 17 February he was present at the count's court at Saumur to judge a case involving Saint-Florent.[33] Again it is evident that no matter what

27. *Actus pontificum*, 388. No other source mentions this extraordinary development.

28. *Actus pontificum*, 384.

29. The wording of the *Actus pontificum* is not clear, but it implies that Hoel himself may have gone to Sablé and was there when his loyal clerics arrived with the treasury.

30. The *Actus pontificum*, 390, states that Hoel was gone for nearly four months and later returned to Sablé in time for Easter, which fell on 28 March in 1092. Latouche, *Maine*, 42 n. 6.

31. Gradulf, the young brother of one of these clerics, was captured by the anti-Hoel forces and killed. See *Actus pontificum*, 389.

32. Guillot, *Comte d'Anjou*, 2: C 367.

33. Archives Maine-et-Loire, H 1840, no. 13.

relations Robert had with either Curthose or Bishop Hoel, he remained an important member of the Angevin court and kept in close contact with Count Fulk.

Shortly after Robert's appearance at Saumur, Hoel returned to Maine and found Le Mans on the verge of civil war between those who supported him and those supporting Hugh and his clerics. The bishop retreated to Solesmes two miles from Sablé and remained there long enough to celebrate Easter on 28 March 1092 and Pentecost on 16 May. So many people flocked to these services from Le Mans that "the inhabitants of this isolated hamlet were amazed."[34] Clearly this could only have been done under Robert's express protection.

By this time popular resentment against Hilgot and his master the pseudo-count Hugh had reached such an explosive level that Hugh decided to make peace with the bishop. Any negotiating with Hoel would surely involve Robert, his chief supporter among the nobility and protector of the episcopal treasury at this moment. On 28 June Hoel was welcomed back to Le Mans by a huge crowd that rushed out to meet him three or four miles from the city.[35] To mark his reconciliation with Hoel, Count Hugh made a public confirmation in the cathedral of donations made to the church by his predecessors as well as donations of his own.[36] Those clerics who had opposed the bishop were forced to beg for forgiveness.[37]

This effectively ended the rule of Hugh, the son of Azzo, although it still remained for Robert and the Angevin party to consolidate their victory. A hint of Robert's personal settlement may be seen in an act that almost certainly took place on 14 July 1092. Bishop Hoel and Abbot Rannulf of Saint-Vincent-du-Mans travelled once again to Sablé to end a dispute that had arisen between the abbot and Robert over the church of Saint-Germain of Noyen, one of the few times Robert was ever at odds with a monastery. In return for giving up his claim on the church Robert received sixty *solidi* of coins and the promise that the monks would commemorate the deaths of his father, his mother, Robert him-

---

34. *Actus pontificum*, 391. "Ita ut privati vici incole urbani conventus frequentiam mirarentur."

35. *Actus pontificum*, 392. For the date, see Latouche, *Maine*, 44.

36. Latouche, *Maine*, no. 42 of his catalogue of acts; *Actus pontificum*, 391.

37. *Actus pontificum*, 391.

self, and Count Geoffrey Martel.[38] After three decades Robert still remembered his benefactor.

Of more importance for Robert, although his role in it is uncertain, was the disposition of the countship of Le Mans. Hugh had made himself thoroughly unpopular and must have realized his position was untenable.[39] He allowed his kinsman, Helias of La Flèche, to talk him into selling him the title of count for 10,000 *solidi*.[40] Hugh immediately departed for Italy and Helias became count of Maine.

This event crowned all Robert's efforts on behalf of Count Fulk and for the protection of his honor in southern Maine. After years of fighting, legal maneuvering, and patient negotiating, Robert now saw an Angevin *fidelis* as count of Maine. The family of Le Flèche had been faithful to the house of Anjou ever since Fulk had burnt down their castle and concluded a peace with William the Conqueror. Bishop Hoel of Le Mans now owed Robert a great debt while feeling he owed Duke Robert absolutely nothing.[41] Henceforth he would cooperate amicably with both Helias and Fulk Rechin.[42]

Almost as soon as Helias received the title Robert travelled with him to Angers. There, shortly before 27 July, Robert assisted Count Fulk in a public donation of right over the land of Monnaie to Saint-Nicolas d'Angers. Helias attested the act with the title of count of Maine. As a mark of special favor Fulk allowed Robert publicly to kiss his hand for making the donation.[43]

---

38. *Cartul. St-Vincent*, no. 366, dated "II idus julii," i.e. 14 July. Hoel was elected bishop after the death of Bishop Arnold on 29 November 1081. Hoel's election was strongly opposed by Fulk Rechin who sought to reestablish the Angevin right of election held by Geoffrey Martel. For this reason it hardly seems likely that Robert would have recognized Hoel as bishop before his official consecration at Rouen in 1085. See Halphen, *Comté d'Anjou*, 185–86. The latest possible date would be 1092, the last full year that the witness, Geoffrey the *cantor*, held his office at Saint-Maurice, *Cartul. noir*, liii.

39. Orderic, 4: 195, sums up the scorn the Manceaux came to have for Hugh, saying "he was foolish, cowardly, and idle, and had no idea how to hold the reins of office."

40. *Actus pontificum*, 393. Orderic, 4: 198–99, provides the amount. He also provides an entertaining account of Helias convincing Hugh that Le Mans was a very dangerous place for him to remain.

41. David, *Robert Curthose*, 73.

42. For his cooperation with Fulk, see Halphen, *Comté d'Anjou*, 187 n. 8.

43. Le Peletier, *Epitome*, 49–50. For significance of the kiss, see Koziol, *Begging Pardon*, 6, 111, and 255.

CHAPTER EIGHT

Robert and the Crusade

Late in the unusually hot and dry summer of 1095 Robert, along with nearly everyone else in the Angevin-Maine region, became aware that important events were occurring within the hierarchy of the church, events that increasingly involved the French and would ultimately lead Robert on his last great military expedition.[1] He learned that Urban II, the Roman Pope, had crossed the Alps and was calling for a council of bishops, abbots, and other important clergy to take place at Clermont. Indeed, Robert's brother Guy may even have been present when Urban visited la Chaise-Dieu in the second half of August, although he had been serving at Saint-Nicaise de Reims since 1090.[2] Soon leaders of the church whom Robert knew well from long experience were preparing to make their way to Clermont. They included Bishop Geoffrey of Angers, Archbishop Radulf II of Tours, Bishop Hoel of Le Mans, Abbot Bernard of Marmoutier, Abbot Geoffrey of the Trinity of Vendôme,

---

1. After this chapter was first drafted, Jonathan Riley-Smith's *The First Crusaders: 1095–1131* (Cambridge: Cambridge University Press, 1997) appeared, in which the author identifies every First Crusader revealed in the extant documentation. In doing so he describes Robert the Burgundian's role in some detail. While nothing is out of line with the picture presented here, Riley-Smith's ability to place Robert within the broader context has been of great benefit, as was his interpretation of Urban's program, and I have made frequent use of this work.

2. Urban was at la Chaise-Dieu at least from 18 August until 25 August. See René Crozet, "Le voyage d'Urban II et ses négotiations avec le clergé de France (1095–1096)," *Revue historique* 179 (1937), 277, and *Gallia christiana* 2: 331. Guy was a monk there by 11 January 1081; see *Rec. des chartes de Cluny*, 4: 715–16, no. 3580. He was sent to Saint-Nicaise by Abbot Seguin in an effort to reform it. He became abbot of Saint-Nicaise when Abbot John departed for the crusade. See Pierre-Roger Gaussin, *L'Abbaye de la Chaise-Dieu (1043–1518)* (Paris: Éditions Cujas, 1962), 137.

Abbot Noel of Saint-Nicolas d'Angers, and Abbot William of Saint-Florent. Joining with others from all over France they answered Urban's summons and attended the Council at Clermont that lasted from 18 to 28 November.[3]

It would not have required much time for word of this council to reach the old lord of Sablé. The returning Bishop Geoffrey and his entourage would certainly have brought the news to Angers and from there travellers could quickly inform the surrounding territory. Abbot Bernard of Marmoutier would have taken special care to inform his monks at Sablé of the results of the council. More intimately, Abbot Geoffrey of Vendôme was a kinsman (perhaps a grandson, probably a nephew) who was particularly close to Robert's son Rainald, having spent time at Craon as a boy.[4] Robert could therefore have heard fairly accurate accounts of what Urban had said at Clermont. However Robert heard the news, as a high ranking member of the armsbearing class, a man who had in major part gained his fortune and reputation by his military prowess, he would have been most interested by the speech Urban was reported to have made on 27 November. This was Urban's first public appeal for an armed expedition to free Jerusalem from the Turks.[5] It was an appeal that would lead to an ever expanding wave of enthusiasm radiating out from the key stopping points of Urban's journey until the movement of armed men responding would become the mass movement now known as the First Crusade. Robert

---

3. The best summary of the sessions and their participants is found in Robert Somerville, "The Council of Clermont (1095) and Latin Christian Society," *Archivum historiae pontificiae* 12 (1974): 55–90. For the participants listed here see especially 74–76. Cf. Crozet, "Voyage d'Urban II," 285 and *Gal. christ.* 14: 73, 290, and 562.

4. Geoffrey of Vendôme, *Geoffroy de Vendôme: Oevres*, ed. and trans. Geneviève Giordanengo (Brepols: CNRS Editions, 1996), 56–58, letter 31, written to Rainald sometime before 16 December 1101. Geoffrey mentions a one-eyed person "whom I remember seeing in your court as a child."

5. There are so many different versions of this speech that it is difficult to know exactly what was said. A solid reconstruction of the main points based on the versions of Fulcher of Chartres, Robert the Monk, Baldric of Dol, Guibert of Nogent, and William of Malmesbury is D. C. Munro, "The Speech of Pope Urban II at Clermont, 1095," *American Historical Review* 11 (1906): 231–42. Carl Erdmann, *Die Entstehung des Kreuzzugsgedankens* (Stuttgart: W. Kohlhammer Verlag, 1935) argued that Urban did not call for a military expedition to free the Holy Sepulchre itself. However, H. E. J. Cowdrey, in "Pope Urban II's Preaching of the First Crusade," *History* 55 (1970): 177–88, persuasively demonstrated that this was precisely Urban's intention. Riley-Smith follows this interpretation in *First Crusaders*, 54–56 and 60–64.

was not immune to this fervor even though he was at least 65 and probably older.

Either with the returning prelates or messengers dispatched later Urban sent word that he was coming to Angers to deliver his message personally. A monk of Saint-Aubin named Milo, an important member of the papal entourage, probably made the arrangements.[6] Before reaching Angers Urban spent Christmas at Limoges and then travelled to Poitiers on 13 January 1096, where he stayed for the rest of the month.[7] Urban arrived at Angers by 6 February, the day his chancellery produced several letters dated from that town.[8]

The central purpose of the papal visit seems to have been to reconcile Fulk Rechin to the pope and to induce him, or at least some of his followers, to go on the proposed expedition to the Holy Land.[9] To do this Urban was prepared to do great honor to the count and to his chief supporters, most especially the Burgundian clan at Craon and Sablé. At the specific request of Count Fulk and "other friends of the monastery,"[10] Urban rededicated the church of Saint-Nicolas d'Angers and translated the body of Robert's old patron, Geoffrey Martel, into the nave of the church amid great ceremony. At some point the pope presented Fulk with the golden flower he carried. The count was so delighted that he promptly ordered that henceforth he and his successors would carry the flower on every Palm Sunday.[11] The crowds were so great that a contemporary remarked, "you would have thought the whole mass of the world had poured into the church."[12] On the same

6. Milo supposedly led the pope to Angers. See Somerville, "Council of Clermont," 81 and n. 181 referring to the "Annales de Renaud," 14.

7. Crozet, "Voyage de Urban," 295, and G-Régis Cregut, *Le concile de Clermont en 1095 et la première croisade* (Clermont-Ferrand: Lib. Catholique, 1895), 141.

8. Migne, *Patrologia Latina*, 151: 445–47, nos. 171–73, all "data Andegavi VIII Idus Februarii."

9. See Riley-Smith, *First Crusaders*, 59–60, for useful comments on this visit and Urban's dealings with Fulk.

10. Le Pelletier, *Epitome*, 43. "Rogatu fulconis eiusdem civitatis comitis, amicorumque aliorum eiusdem Monasterii Monachorum." Robert and his son Rainald had always had a special dedication to Saint-Nicolas and they might very well be among these *amici*.

11. Fulk Rechin, "Fragmentum historiae," 381. The entry is translated in Riley-Smith, *First Crusaders*, 59. This event is mentioned in Bib. nat., Dom Housseau III, no. 1018.

12. Baldric of Dol, "Vita B. Roberti de Arbissello," in *Patrologia Latina*, 162: 1050. "Celebrare ibi habuit [Urbanus] solemnem cujusdam ecclesiae dedicationem, ad quam confluxisse putares totam orbis amplitudinem."

day Count Fulk and William of Orléans with his son Hunard made gifts of land to the monastery.[13]

Robert appears in none of these acts. Considering his rank and intimacy with the count it is unlikely that he would have been absent from the ceremonies if he had been in Angers at the time or overlooked if present.[14] Surely he would have enjoyed the honor given to Geoffrey Martel. In his stead the family was represented at Angers by Rainald of Craon who played a notable part in the activities surrounding Urban's visit.[15] This is evident from the fact that Urban displayed a marked favor toward Rainald and his father throughout his progress through Anjou. Rainald had become the patron of a wondering preacher of great local renown, Robert d'Arbrissel, who had established himself as a hermit in the forest of Craon as early as 1093.[16] In later years d'Arbrissel would gain much fame and notoriety as the founder of the abbey of Fontevraud. It is likely that Rainald, with Fulk's approval, had arranged for d'Arbrissel to preach at the dedication of Saint-Nicolas. Urban was so impressed with what he heard that he commissioned the hermit to preach his appeal for an expedition to the Holy Land.[17] This could not help but enhance the prestige not only of d'Arbrissel, but of his patron Rainald of Craon as well. It also marks the family's continuing concern and influence within the highest reaches of the Church.

Urban showed his appreciation of Rainald's efforts in more concrete ways. The day after the great consecration of Saint-Nicolas, 11 Febru-

---

13. Le Pelletier, *Epitome*, 64–65 and 43–44. The gifts included land in the forest of Les Échats, for which see Le Pelletier, *Epitome*, 30–32, and Bib. nat., Dom Housseau, 13₁, no. 9504.

14. Angot, *Généalogies féodales*, 730, assumed that Robert did not attend the pope in Angers because he was busy preparing for Urban's expected arrival at Sablé.

15. There was perhaps one other member of the family present. One of the witnesses to Fulk's gift on 10 February was a *Gosfridus Burgundus*; see Le Pelletier, *Epitome*, 65. He may have simply been from Burgundy, but by this time the term *Burgundus* is used almost as a family name for Robert and his children. Robert had a son named Geoffrey but he is so rarely attested that it is assumed he died young. Possibly this is the son.

16. Baldric of Dol, "Vita B. Roberti," 162: 1049; Bertrand de Broussillon, *Maison de Craon*, 26. For Rainald's relationship with this remarkable figure, see W. Scott Jessee, "Robert d'Arbrissel: Aristocratic Patronage and the Question of Heresy," *Journal of Medieval History* 20 (1994): 221–35.

17. Baldric of Dol, "Vita B. Roberti," 1050–51. "Robertum loqui praecepit . . . cujus verba valde papae complacuerunt . . . imperat denique et injungit ei praedicationis officium." Baldric claimed that the pope himself asked to hear d'Arbrissel preach, but it seems more likely that the local arrangement committee suggested it.

ary, Rainald and his three sons, Mauricius, Henry, and Robert went to the episcopal chamber and there made the official donation of a piece of land in the woods near the castle of Craon to found a church of Augustinian canons dedicated to the Virgin Mary. The church would be known as *Sancta Maria de Bosca* and later simply as La Roë. The importance of both the donation and the donor is underlined by the stature of those members of the papal entourage who attested it. Aside from the bishop of Angers there was Archbishop Hugh of Lyon, Archbishop Amatus of Bordeaux (the papal legate), Bishop Ivo of Chartres, Bishop Hoel of Le Mans, and Bishop Walter of Albi.[18]

As if this august assemblage were not enough, the next day, 12 February, the pope himself confirmed Rainald's charter of concession by laying his hands upon it in another, less public, ceremony in the greater chamber of the Angevin bishop. Bishop Geoffrey was again present as well as other members of the papal entourage, including Cardinals Teuzo, Albert, and Rangerius, Archdeacon Ingelramnus of Soissons, and Milo, the monk of Saint-Aubin.[19] The entire concession would be confirmed yet again at the council of Tours, 21 March 1096.[20] Acceding to the requests for recognition from laymen such as Count Fulk and Rainald was apparently a calculated tactic to win their support.

Robert the Burgundian, waiting in his stronghold at Sablé, was to have the opportunity to hear this exhortation full force, face to face. Urban himself came to Sablé after leaving Angers, probably on 13 February. On the 14th he issued a papal order, a *privilegium*, at Sablé confirming the properties of Saint-Nicolas.[21] One can only imagine what the

18. "Data Andegavis III idus Febroarii, in crastina dedicationis basilice Beati Nicholai." Cartulary of La Roë, Archives Mayenne, H 1, fol. 3, no. I; copy by Paul Marchegay, Archives Maine-et-Loire, H 1, p. 1, no. 1. Published in *Gallia christiana*, 15: 151, no. 10. A photographic copy of this cartulary is in the Library of Congress, Washington, DC.

19. Ibid. "Facta igitur hac concesione a Raginaldo Credonensi firmata est hoc carta in superiori camera Gaufridi Andegavensis episcopi Junioris per impositionem manus Urbani secundi pape, et per beati Petri auctoritatem pridie idus febroarii." For complete identification of the members of the papal entourage see Somerville, "Council of Clermont," 80–81.

20. Cartulary of La Roë, no. 1. "Hec secunda sanctio facta est Turonensi concilio apostolico viro missam devotissime celebrante, XII° Kalendas aprilis . . . anno MXCVI." Guillot, *Comte d'Anjou*, 2: C 392, treats all three acts under the date 11 March 1096.

21. *Patrologia Latina*, 151: 447–49 and Le Pelletier, *Epitome*, 25–27. "Datum apud Sableulium per manum Joannis, sanctae Romanae Ecclesiae diaconi cardinalis, XVI Kalend. Martias, indict. IV, anno Domini 1096, pontificatus autem domini Urbani II papae VIII." The act is discussed in Ménage, *Histoire de Sablé*, 82.

visit meant to Robert, a man who had labored his entire life to maintain good relations with the Church and yet had seen himself and all those dependent upon him placed under an episcopal interdict.

The papal entourage must have been enormous. From the act of papal confirmation Robert's son had secured in Angers and other sources, we know that it included at least three cardinals, the papal chancellor John of Gaëta (the future Pope Gelasius II), two other Cardinal-deacons, Milo of Saint-Aubin who had recently been made a Cardinal, and the archdeacon of Soissons. There were undoubtedly other officials and assistants, as well as a staff of scribes and administrative personnel to carry on the demands of administration and diplomacy.[22] The papal visitation was not only a mark of Robert's prestige and importance but also a tribute to the substantial resources on which he could draw to provide lodging and sustenance for such a crowd.

The visit gave the lord of Sablé an opportunity to hear more of Urban's vision of a military pilgrimage to the Holy Land. What Urban said to Robert is, of course, unknown, but by 22 August Robert is said to have been wanting to go to Jerusalem.[23] In an act of the same year Robert himself says that he was "going to Jerusalem."[24] In this respect Robert mirrors the reaction to what the nobility of the region heard, or thought they heard, from Urban: an exhortation to participate in a military expedition to Jerusalem. Fulk Rechin put it exactly this way in his little chronicle, "the Roman Pope Urban came to Anjou and urged our people to go to Jerusalem and subdue the heathen nation that had seized that city and all the land of the Christians as far as Constantinople."[25]

Fulk emphatically placed the emphasis on the armed expedition to

---

22. Somerville, "Council of Clermont," 81–82; and Riley-Smith, *First Crusaders,* 57.

23. Bib. nat., ms. fr. 22450, fol. 161r. "Robertus Burgundio qui tunc Jerusalem ire volebat."

24. Bib. nat., ma. lat.. 17126, fol. 168 published in *Cartul. de St-Aubin,* 2: 353, no. 880. "Ego Rotbertus Burgundus, iturus Jerosalimam." There was no Latin term for Crusade until the thirteenth century when *crux, crusata,* and *croseria* came into use. In Robert's time more general terms like *iter, expeditio,* and *peregrinatio* were used. See Cowdrey, "Urban's Preaching," 179, note 6.

25. "Fragmentum historiae," 237–38. ". . . venit Andegavim papa Romanus Urbanus et ammoniut gentem nostram ut irent Jerusalem qui civitatem illam et totam terram christianorum usque Constantinopolim occupaverant." For the emphasis on the armed expedition, see Cowdrey, "Urban's Preaching," 181.

Jerusalem. This was the message that Urban brought to Angers, that Robert d'Arbrissel was to preach, and that ultimately would lead hundreds of Angevins, Manceaux, and Normans temporarily to lay aside their differences to take up the cross and travel to the Holy Land. That the pilgrimage was understood to be an armed expedition is evident from an Angevin charter of 23 June 1096, which characterized the time it was written as

the year in which an innumerable crowd went to Jerusalem to expel the persecution of the Muslims' perfidy, namely in the year following Pope Urban's visit to Angers.[26]

It is clear that Urban was seen in the Angevin region as exhorting, even ordering, members of the military class to go to Jerusalem and free it from the Turks.

Yet Robert's decision to heed this call is surprising since he was at least 65 and probably 70, at least a decade older than the redoubtable Count Raymond of Toulouse, who would have a difficult time on the Crusade, being noticeably sicker than younger members of the expedition.[27] Nor could Robert have regarded the rigors of the the proposed journey lightly. Contrary to the usual image of Crusaders taking the vow with little idea of the geography involved, Robert would have had few illusions as to either the distances or the expense involved. Travel, even long and arduous travel, was virtually a way of life for the nobles of western France at this time.[28] Robert's own son Rainald, for example, had travelled as far as Rome sometime before 1084 and would have told his father the details of the long journey.[29] Robert had his own knowledge about Jerusalem. It is likely that the father-in-law of Robert's nephew, Lancelin of Beaugency, had already gone on pilgrimage to the

---

26. *Cartul. noir,* no. 65; Guillot, *Comte d'Anjou,* 2: C 397. "Anno Domini MXCVI . . . anno quo innumerabilis populus ibat in Hierusalem ad depellendam pincenatorum perfidiae persecutionem; scilicet secundo anno quo Urbanus papa Andegavum visitavit." In the Paschal year Pope Urban's visit would be in 1095 and 23 June would be in 1096.

27. Frederic Duncalf, "The First Crusade: Clermont to Constantinople," in *A History of the Crusades,* ed. Kenneth M. Setton, 5 vols. (Madison: University of Wisconsin Press, 1969), 1: 272. In many ways Raymond's age and motivation parallel Robert's. See John Hugh Hill and Laurita Littleton Hill, *Raymond IV Count of Toulouse* (Syracuse: Syracuse University Press, 1962), 36–39.

28. Van Luyn, "*Milites* dans la France," 41.

29. *Cartul. manceau,* 2: 78–79, no. 8.

Holy Land when Robert visited him in the 1070s.[30] As a young man entering the Angevin court, Robert had the opportunity to meet the survivors of two Angevin pilgrimages to Jerusalem: the last pilgrimage of Count Fulk Nerra in 1040 and that of Countess Hildegard in 1045–1046. Robert would certainly have remembered that both count and countess died on these trips.[31] Hildegard's *vicarius*, Stabilis, had gone with her and survived to tell the Angevin court about their journey.[32] Robert knew the man, still living after 1067 when he was present at a judgement by the Burgundian.[33] Fulk's journeys had left a more concrete remembrance in the structure of the abbey of Beaulieu-lès-Loches. Adorned by the count with sculptures perhaps inspired by examples seen on the way to Jerusalem, it contained a piece of stone that Fulk had filched from the Holy Sepulchre itself. At many points in his long life Robert could have reached out and touched a portion of the sacred city.[34]

Yet Robert was determined to go to Jerusalem. The religious convictions Robert had displayed in the past now left Robert susceptible to the pope's appeal. Perhaps Urban simply repeated the main points of the message first heard at Clermont, minus the lavish praise for the Franks since his listener was a Burgundian.[35] Appeals for aid from the East had reached Rome and Urban believed this aid was necessary. Jerusalem itself was a holy place beyond all others so that it would be God's work to rescue it from the Muslims. Members of the military class (such as

30. In the 1070s Lancelin had built a church dedicated to the Holy Sepulchre, implying he had been there; see Riley-Smith, *First Crusaders*, 33. The act is in *Cartul. Trinité de Vendôme*, 2: 3–6.

31. Fulk Nerra made at least four pilgrimages to Jerusalem. See Bernard S. Bachrach, "The Pilgrimages of Fulk Nerra, Count of the Angevins, 987–1040," in *Religion, Culture and Society in the Early Middle Ages* (Kalamazoo: 1987), 205–17. Such an unusual feat must have made a deep impression on the Angevin nobility. For Countess Hildegard's pilgrimage, see Guillot, *Comte d'Anjou*, 2: 159–60 and 181, nos. C 242 and C 275. Members of both expeditions would have returned to Anjou during the time Robert first appears in Geoffrey Martel's entourage.

32. *Cartul. du Ronceray*, no. 47, and Guillot, *Comte d'Anjou*, 2: C 329. "Stabilem vicarium qui de familia comitisse Hyldeardis fuerat et cum ea Jerosolium ierat."

33. *Cartul. du Ronceray*, no. 244.

34. Bernard S. Bachrach, "The Combat Sculptures of Fulk Nerra's 'Battle Abbey,'" *Haskins Society Journal* 3 (1991): 76 and 69–70.

35. Riley-Smith, *First Crusaders*, 64, observes that Urban would have tuned this part of his message to the ethnic identity of his audience.

Robert) ought to fight only righteous wars and not remain mired in iniquitous wars with fellow Christians. Considering Robert's career, this would presumably have had special resonance for him.[36] Many scholars have argued that Urban had called for grants of plenary indulgence and a full remission of sins, but a careful scrutiny of crusader charters, including Robert's, has convinced Riley-Smith that Urban was defining a revolutionary new type of pilgrimage, a penitential war. "There can be no doubt that the crusaders understood that they were performing a penance and that the exercise they were embarking on could contribute to their future salvation."[37] Otherwise, however, the charters reflect neither an understanding of a total forgiveness of sins offered nor of the opportunity of martyrdom. Arduous military service in an expedition to free Jerusalem would aid in their salvation but only in the sense of a penance sufficient to cover the sins they had committed.[38] As a crusader from Le Mans put it:

Considering that God has spared me, steeped in many and great sins, and has given me time for penance, and fearing that the weight of my sins will deprive me of a share in the heavenly kingdom, I . . . wish to seek that sepulchre from which our redemption, having overcome death, wished to rise.[39]

This concentration on Jerusalem as the locus for penance seems to have been the chief factor in Robert's decision.[40] His goal was a specific place of deep religious significance to his contemporaries. Jerusalem was, in fact, Christ's *patria*, his native land. The sheer number of eleventh century pilgrimages (such as Count Fulk's and Countess Hildegard's) had accustomed the people of France to regard the Holy Land as their own distant homeland.[41] Recent research has shown that the regaining of Jerusalem was the major thrust of Urban's message

---

36. Based on Munro's reconstruction in "Speech of Urban II," 242. For a deeper examination of Urban's call at Clermont see Jonathan Riley-Smith, *The First Crusade and the Idea of Crusading* (London: Athlone Press, 1986), 13–30, and his latest work, *First Crusaders*, 60–75.

37. Riley-Smith, *First Crusaders*, 69.

38. Bull, *Knightly Piety*, 167–70, says much the same—Urban did not offer the later medieval indulgence.

39. *Cartul. St. Vincent du Mans*, I: col. 69; translated in Riley-Smith, *Idea of Crusade*, 23.

40. This was true of most of the first crusaders. See Joshua Prawer, *The World of the Crusaders* (New York: History Book Club, 1972), 16.

41. Paul Rousset, *Histoire d'une idéologie: La Croisade* (Lausanne: L'Age d'homme, 1983), 28.

and of those responding from the very beginning. The *patria* must be restored to Christian rule.[42] Indeed, this was Count Fulk's own assessment of Urban's message in the passage cited above. Robert expressed this idea with straightforward simplicity: he was "going to Jerusalem."

This preoccupation with a specific geographic place is clearly reflected in a charter executed at Marmoutier for Robert two years later as he made his final preparations. How much of the wording is due to Robert's own feelings and how much from that of the monks is problematical, but it is unlikely that Robert was so unsophisticated in his approach to written documents that he would have allowed it to stand if it did not reflect his own ideas.[43] In the prologue Robert dwelt on mankind's fall and expulsion from Paradise into "the tearful valley of exile." It was Jesus, "the Second Adam," who "restored man to life and homeland *(patria)*." The rest of the prologue contains the commonplace idea that sins should be redeemed by gifts to the poor, represented in this case by the monks of Marmoutier.[44] The use of the word *patria,* a concrete, temporal homeland, in association with Paradise lost and then regained almost certainly reflects Robert's preoccupation with regaining Jerusalem, Christ's *patria.* As Robert's document states, the "son of God . . . clearly demonstrated that he himself was the way by which we would not only return to the *patria* of Paradise but would also be conveyed to angelic fellowship."[45] In Robert's case, this restoration and return is associated not with military action but with the redemption of sin through charitable gifts.

This is hardly surprising when one considers Robert's advanced age. He was not a young knight seeking a sanctified use of arms but a man at the end of a long life seeking salvation. In Robert's mind, then, the

---

42. Most notably, Riley-Smith concluded that there is "overwhelming evidence, above all in the charters of departing crusaders, for Jerusalem being a prime goal from the start." See *Crusades: Short History,* 7. He examines this in more detail in *First Crusaders,* 23–39.

43. Riley-Smith, *First Crusaders,* 5, cites one case of a pilgrim departing in 1101 having his charter of donation to an abbey read out and explained to him in the vernacular. Bull, *Knightly Piety,* 155, also accepts the charter evidence as reflecting the views of the lay donors.

44. *Cartul. manceau,* 2: 86–89, no. 13. A French translation is in Lalubie, *Baronnie médiévale,* 117–18.

45. *Cartul. manceau,* 2: 86–89, no. 13. A document from the abbey of Molesme in Burgundy carries a very similar prologue, but without the mention of Christ's *patria.* See Bouchard, *Sword,* 226. Perhaps the concern with *patria* reflects Robert's own ideas.

regaining of the *patria* is linked directly with eternal salvation, the "angelic fellowship." In this respect an important attraction would have been Urban's promise of such salvation through the war-pilgrimage. It was the motive that overshadowed all others. Urban himself had planted the idea that the journey to Jerusalem would be "satisfactory," that is, so demanding that it would satisfy the penance required to atone for the crusader's sins. This was not a full plenary indulgence as once thought.[46] As Guibert de Nogent, for one, put it, knights could attain salvation by going on crusade as surely as they could by taking monastic vows.[47]

Robert shared this interpretation: if he went on the crusade it would bring him closer to salvation. He links redemption of his evil deeds with charitable acts to monasteries and his own trip to Jerusalem:

I, Robert the Burgundian . . . listening to the leaders of the holy Church so that I have no doubts and struggling to redeem my sins, the evil of which I am well aware, through charitable acts notify the whole world that . . . when at last I wished to go to Jerusalem and was preparing the things necessary for my journey I made a donation [to the monastery of Marmoutier].[48]

Despite modern attempts to rationalize crusading zeal in terms of economic gain, colonial exploitation, or simple land hunger of growing families, Robert the Burgundian is quite explicit and we should not doubt that in his case the quest for redemption was a genuine motivation. It would certainly be in keeping with the remarkable efforts

46. Bull, *Knightly Piety*, 167–71. For the view that Urban was actually talking about a full indulgence, see Hans Eberhard Mayer, *The Crusades*, 2d ed., trans. John Gillingham (Oxford: Oxford University Press, 1988), 23. For other views, see Jean Richard, "Urbain II, la prédication de la croisade et la définition de l'indulgence," in *Deus qui mutat tempora: Menschen und Institutionen im Wandel des Mittelalters*, ed. Ernst-Dieter Hehl, et al. (Sigmaringen: J. Thorbecke, 1987), 129–35; Daniel Norman, "Indulgences and the Holy War," in Setton, *History of the Crusades* 4: 8–16; Ronald C. Finucane, *Soldiers of the Faith: Crusaders and Moslems at War* (New York: St. Martin's Press, 1983), 20 and 36–37.

47. Guibert de Nogent, "Gesta Dei per Francos," *Recueil des historiens des croisades: Historiens occidentaux*, 5 vols. (Paris: Imprimerie nationale, 1844–1895) 4: 124. For commentary, see Bull, *Knightly Piety*, 171, and Riley-Smith, *First Crusaders*, 95. Orderic makes the same point, 5: 16–18.

48. *Cartul. manceau*, 2: 86–89. "Ego Rotbertus, scilicet Allobrox . . . ab Ecclesie sancte rectoribus audiens et ita esse non dubitans et peccata mea, quorum male conscius sum, elemosynis redimere satagens, notificio universis quod . . . cum tandem ire in Jerusalem vellem et itineri meo necessaria prepararem, . . . feci donationem."

Robert made throughout his life to look after the spiritual welfare of the castle and community of Sablé while cultivating the warmest relations with the monks of Marmoutier and other abbeys. Indeed, Marmoutier kept a priory at Sablé, complete with a house for their abbot. Robert had several family members, a brother, a nephew, and a daughter, who entered holy orders. His eldest son was the patron of a renowned charismatic preacher, while Robert himself had his own chaplain and was on familiar terms with a succession of abbots and archbishops. There was a constant interchange of ideas between Robert and members of the Church. Robert was not a simple soul, credulously accepting whatever more sophisticated churchmen told him. He had his own understanding of his faith, he had seen the Pope in person, and it moved him to go to Jerusalem for the good of his soul.

For Robert, if he were typical of the attitudes observed by Marcus Bull in his study of the First Crusaders in southern France, fear of the afterlife was a very real concern. Heaven and Hell were real destinations envisioned in concrete terms. To Bull's crusaders Heaven was the heavenly "homeland"—once again the term used by Robert—and Hell a place of perpetual torment. Judgement at some future point would decide their fate; until then their souls would wait in a place that was neither heaven nor hell but a place of torture and pain until they had expiated their earthly sins. A man like Robert, judge, commander, patron overseeing the fate of dependents, would necessarily amass an enormous weight of sin in this life. All of Robert's gifts to the Church were an effort to enlist the aid of monks to help lighten his burden. Urban's call for an armed pilgrimage allowed him and others to redress the balance, to escape time in the half-way realm of death before Judgement.[49] For people of the time this fate was real to a degree that is difficult for moderns to grasp. Robert's whole program of gift-giving as reconstructed here bears witness to the fact that he shared this view.

Seen in this light, an essential element of Robert's preparation, indeed one of the *necessaria* for the journey that he mentioned, was the bestowing of gifts on the monasteries that had already received numerous gifts from the Burgundian. From the time Urban left Sablé to travel

---

49. Bull, *Knightly Piety*, 186–94.

to Le Mans until Robert actually got underway in early 1098, this is a major preoccupation of Robert's acts.

In 1096, for example, almost certainly after Urban's visit, Robert took care to settle his accounts with the monastery of Saint-Aubin concerning land at Brion in a series of closely connected acts. The monks had been paying rent to Robert for land to build on. They now took the opportunity to buy the land outright for a payment of seven pounds. Robert and his son Rainald accepted this payment in the count's court in Angers.[50] Afterwards Geoffrey of Brion, who held the place from Robert, likewise travelled to Angers, apparently at Robert's urging. There, in Saint-Aubin's chapter house, he conceded and confirmed all that the monks had acquired or would acquire in his holding of Brion. Like his *dominus,* Geoffrey received a payment: a horse worth 100 *solidi.*[51]

After this all the parties travelled to Brion, some thirty kilometers east of Angers and nearly fifty kilometers south of Sablé, for another round of ceremonial acts. *Dominus* Robert and his wife Bertha made another general grant of everything the monastery already held in Robert's *feodum,* as well as at Durtal, Lion-d'Angers, Pincé, and *Castele- to.* This act was evidently part of an imposing ceremony at Brion in which the charter of Geoffrey of Brion's concession was read out in Robert's presence in order to have it formally recognized before the many witnesses. Bishop Lambert of Arras, recently returned from the Council of Clermont, was among those present.[52] It is known that Lambert traveled with what may have been an unusually large entourage, so the gathering at Brion must have been quite impressive.[53] Presumably Robert's outlay for such a gathering was equally impressive. To add to the expense Robert also gave Saint-Nicolas land near the

50. *Cartul. de St-Aubin,* 1: 440–41, no. 381. Count Fulk and many other barons were present, indicating the importance of the act.

51. *Cartul. de St-Aubin,* 1: 441–42, no. 382. In contrast to Robert's act this was performed virtually in private. There was only one lay witness, "solus Walterius de Monte Rotundo vidit, quia solus cum eo erat." There are two versions of this document. The witness is found only in a late twelfth century copy, cartulary of Saint-Aubin, Bib. d'Angers, ms 829, fol. 127. The second version is from the seventeenth century, cartulary of Brion, Archives Maine-et-Loire, H 224, fol. 10.

52. *Cartul. de St-Aubin,* 1: 441–42.

53. Somerville, "Council of Clermont," 79–80.

essarts of Maisnil that included the right to use wood taken from the woods of Brion.[54] All this suggests that the public nature and splendor of this complex of acts was linked to Robert's intention to go to Jerusalem, although this is not explicitly stated.

It is important to note the payments that Robert and Geoffrey received for their generosity. It is evident that elements of these pious donations were, in fact, often outright sales used to raise money for the journey to the Holy Land. This was a common way to raise money, for the Church was one of the few institutions with ready cash. An associate of Robert, the knight Fulk of Matheflon, for example, received 1100 *solidi* from the monks of Saint-Nicolas for the concession of the tithe of Azé when he set off for Jerusalem. Fulcard of Rochfort likewise handed over to the monks his estate as a gage for a loan.[55] Money was a major preoccupation, in general, for the Crusaders as "each one hastened to convert into money everything that he did not need for the journey," as one contemporary put it.[56] Expenses are difficult to estimate, but it may have cost a common knight four or five times his annual income to go on the crusade.[57] So many sales and mortgages were made by crusaders that contemporaries noted that prices dropped throughout *Francia*.[58]

Unfortunately Robert's further efforts to finance his journey are undocumented. It may be that Robert's wealth was so great, or so well managed, that he did not need to resort to the expedients mentioned above. More likely it is simply that the steps he took to equip his expedition have left no documentation.[59]

---

54. Bib. nat., Dom Housseau, 13₁, no. 9632.

55. *Gal. christ.*, 14: col. 673. For arrangements made by manceaux crusaders, see David, *Robert Curthose*, "Appendix D: Robert's Companions on Crusade," 221–29.

56. Guibert, "Gesta Dei", 141.

57. Riley-Smith, *Crusades: Short History*, 12. For raising money see Fred A. Cazel, Jr., "Financing the Crusades," in Setton, *History of the Crusades*, 4: 116–49; and Riley-Smith, *First Crusaders*, 109–23.

58. Finucane, *Soldiers of the Faith*, 42–43.

59. This is not surprising. Many acts have been lost and others would have generated no written agreement even when involving large sums of money. Godfrey duke of Lower Lorraine, for example, raised 7,000 marks of silver by mortgaging his castle to the bishop of Liège, an act that has left no documentation except a passing mention in Orderic, 5: 208. Even more telling, there is no official record of the treaty of 1096 in which King William Rufus agreed to pay his brother Robert Curthose 10,000 marks of silver in return for the duchy of Normandy at the time of Curthose's departure. It may never have been written down. See Barlow, *William Rufus*, 363.

Whatever preparations Robert made in the two years that he delayed his departure, his role as a *dominus* in the Angevin court continued. On 22 August 1096, he took his place at the head of the knights in Angers attesting a comital act in favor of Saint-Nicolas. A few days later, when the monks of Saint-Aubin contested this donation, Count Fulk ordered Robert the Burgundian and Rainald of Château-Gontier to implement a judicial meeting between the two monasteries.[60] On 11 May of the following year he ended a dispute between Saint-Nicolas and Rainald of Brionneau.[61] Before leaving in 1098 he took part in a judgement in the episcopal court at Angers involving the same monastery and Aimeric of Trèves. He next participated in the judicial meeting held for this and other disputes at Saumur. This was a major judgement attended by Count Fulk, Bishop Geoffrey of Angers, Bishop Marbod of Rennes, and many other barons.[62]

The Norman threat to Maine is a more likely cause of Robert's delay, however, than the press of responsibility within the Angevin court. For awhile it looked as if a *modus vivendi* had been worked out by which Helias of La Flèche was count of Maine closely allied to the count of Anjou. As long as a disinterested Robert Curthose sat as Duke, Norman claims to Maine could be ignored. The wave of enthusiasm for going to Jerusalem that swept through the region in Urban's wake threw this comfortable situation into complete confusion. Both Helias of La Flèche and Robert Curthose decided, like Robert the Burgundian, to take up the crusading cross. This immediately created political problems that endangered the Burgundian's own plans. Duke Robert, in order to finance his expedition and to protect his position in Normandy, placed his duchy along with his claim to Maine in the hands of his brother, King William Rufus of England. In return he received 10,000 marks of silver. When King William heard the terms his brother proposed, "he was overjoyed and gave his wholehearted approval."[63] William had every reason to be pleased. More aggressive than his brother, he now had the opportunity to consolidate his hold over Normandy and to extend Norman claims over Maine in his own name.[64]

60. Le Pelletier, *Epitome*, 30–32.   61. Bib. nat., Dom Housseau, 13₁, no. 9504.
62. Bib. nat., Dom Housseau, 3, no. 1001.   63. Orderic, 5: 27.
64. For William's attitude toward Normandy and Maine, see Barlow, *William Rufus*, 367–79.

Helias's plans were almost immediately effected by the new determination and energy of the Norman leadership. In September 1096 at
Rouen he asked William for a guarantee of peace so he could go to
Jerusalem. As Orderic has it the king supposedly replied in some heat,
"Go where you choose, but surrender the city of Le Mans and the
whole county of Maine to me, for I intend to hold all that my father
held," and threatened to push his claim "with swords and lances and
showers of missiles."[65] Whether or not William actually uttered these
words, the expressed intention probably reflects what people of the region thought, including Robert, watching the situation from the border. Helias understandably cancelled his plans for travelling and retired
into Maine to prepare his defenses.[66]

Shortly thereafter, in late September or early October, Duke Robert
left for the Holy Land with a large expedition. While it contained at
least some Manceaux, many more must have followed Helias in re-
nouncing the journey.[67] For two years after the departure of the crusaders Robert the Burgundian waited while the English king made no
move to exert his authority over Maine. The charters give no evidence
of any particular concern on his part regarding the safety of Sablé or
the general political situation in Maine. Possibly he felt that William
would be no more of a problem than his brother. More likely he was
perfectly aware that throughout 1097 the king was too busy with wars
against the Welsh, the Scots, and above all the French to bother with
Maine.[68]

The question arises though: knowing Rufus's intentions, why did
Robert leave at the precise moment that he did after waiting for two
years? One possible explanation for Robert's decision remains. Robert
must have known that by the end of October 1097 the crusaders at the

---

65. Orderic, 5: 231 and note. Chibnall stresses in the note that these "imaginary speeches"
reflected contemporary viewpoints and were not mere rhetorical flourishes.

66. Orderic, 5: 233.

67. For the duke's companions see David, *Robert Curthose*, 93–95 and Appendix D, 221–29.
David cites the evidence of charters for Manceaux lords who raised money to go on the crusade but as Chibnall says (Orderic, 5: 110, n.1), it is uncertain whether any of them left after
Helias decided to stay in the face of William's threat. One who certainly did change his mind
was Pagan of Mondoubleau. He supposedly left with the duke (David, 223, 225), but was still
in Maine in 1098 (Orderic, 5: 243, n. 4).

68. Orderic, 5: 233, and Chibnall's n. 1, 232.

great siege of Antioch had written home urgently asking for reinforcements by the next Easter, 28 March 1098.[69] The crusaders remained concerned about the large number of people who, like Robert, had taken
the oath but had not yet set out. In January 1098 they excommunicated
them and asked the bishops of the west to do the same.[70] The timing
fits in precisely with the date of Robert's departure in 1098, which occurred before Easter since an act dated 23 February 1098 refers to the
year as "the year in which Robert the Burgundian and Rainald of
Château-Gontier made for Jerusalem."[71]

If Robert needed the call from the crusaders to get underway, he
was not alone. He used a curious term in one of his charters to refer to
his journey, proclaiming, "I, Robert the Burgundian, *dominus* of the castle of Sablé, am going to Jerusalem with the army of the Christians,
that is, the second expedition, which was made in the year 1098."[72] This
expression, *secunda profectio,* implies that Robert saw himself as only a
part of a larger expedition of the Christian army. Enough men in the
region must have answered the calls for reinforcements in the first few
months of 1098 to warrant this description.[73]

By the beginning of 1098 Robert's preparations were coming to an
end in any case. It was on Robert's mind to make a special donation to
Marmoutier, the monastery that had always been particularly close to
him, so that in his own words, "God may protect me safe and un-
harmed in going and returning."[74] Abbot Bernard of Marmoutier, who
maintained his own residence at Sablé, travelled to the castle to receive

69. Heinrich Hagenmeyer, *Chronologie de la primiere croisade* (Paris: E. Leroux, 1902), 106.
There is, of course, no way of knowing if Robert heard of these letters, but the crusaders
clearly intended that their request be disseminated throughout the Christian West and
Robert had good sources of information.

70. Riley-Smith, *First Crusade*, 23.

71. Bertrand de Broussillon, *Maison de Craon*, 1: 50, no. 84. ". . . anno quod Rotbertus Burgundus et Rainaldus de Castro Gunterii Hierosolimam petierunt."

72. *Cartul. manceaux*, 2: 89–91, no. 14. "Notum sit omnibus quod ego Rotbertus Bur-
gondus, Sablolii castri dominus, vadens in Jerusalem cum exercitu christianorum in secunda
scilicet profectione que facta est anno ab Incarnatione Domini MXCVII." The year 1097 here
is a Paschal year, that is, 1098 new style. The word *profectio* would resonate with Robert's intent focus on reaching Jerusalem: it is the word used repeatedly in the Vulgate Bible for the Israelites marching to the promised land under Moses.

73. Riley-Smith, *First Crusaders*, 109.

74. *Cartul. manceau*, 2: 86–89. ". . . et ut Deus sanum et incolumen in eundo et redueundo
me custodiret."

Robert's gift in person.[75] The gift consisted of five arpents of vineyards on the River Vaige and a burg that Robert and Bertha had begun to construct in a vineyard belonging to a man called Ermenfred. Robert was careful to protect his wife's interest, however. The monks were not to receive full ownership until after her death.

Although the donation of both properties was publicly approved by Robert's son Robert Vestrol as well as Robert's wife, it is clear that the younger Robert objected to generosity on such a lavish scale from his father. As Robert later told the monks at Marmoutier, "in the beginning I had retained the customs of the burg of Saint-Nicolas in Sablé and had wished to give them to the monks there but inasmuch as the monks were intent on maintaining peace and concord, they did not wish to accept the customs because they felt that my son Robert was reluctant to relinquish them."[76] For the moment this portion of the gift was set aside for Robert to deal with later.

Robert's eldest son, Rainald, on the other hand, was much more agreeable. He "conceded to my grace"[77] as Robert put it and as *dominus* of Craon authorized in advance all the charitable gifts that his father might make on his journey. Robert was careful to note though, that "Rainald's brother Robert may have no payment of money for this concession."[78] The old lord was losing patience with his son's obstinence.

When all Robert's final preparations were completed and he was at last ready to depart, he added two *mansurae* of land at Bellenoe to the gift for the monks to possess immediately. By this time Abbot Bernard had returned to Marmoutier, so Alfred, prior of the cell at Sablé, received the donation.[79]

Once this act was completed Robert assembled his followers and set out for the Holy Land. While one would expect that Robert and his son-in-law would have travelled together, there is no evidence in the

75. *Cartul. manceau*, 2: 86–89. The abbot's house is called *domus sua*.

76. *Cartul. manceau*, 2: 89–91, no. 14. "Costumas etiam in burgo Sancti Nicolai Sabloliensis mihi a principio retinueram, et quas eis dare Sablolii volueram sed ipsi eas utpote monachi paci studentes et concordie suscipere noluerunt eo quod filium meum sepedictum Rotbertum invitum concedere senserant."

77. "Consesserat mei gratia," *Cartul. manceau*, 2: 86–89.

78. Ibid. "Frater suus Rotbertus pro concessione nullam haberet pecunie mercedem."

79. Ibid.

charters that they did so. Nevertheless their combined entourages would have made a considerable body of men embarking from the northwestern corner of the Angevin defensive structure.[80] Among Robert's companions at least as far as Tours, and probably for the whole trip,[81] were his chaplain Barthelemy,[82] Harduin of Vione whom Robert called "one of my nobles who was going with me to Jerusalem,"[83] Drogo of Trogné, Alberic Guarnerius's son, Arnulf of Sées, Rainald of *Baicum*, Walterius of Saint-Loup, Harduin of *Monteborri*, Geoffrey of Daumeray, and Picard Jordon's son.

From Sablé Robert seems to have travelled to Angers with his sons Rainald and Robert. A very cryptic notice published only in the seventeenth century by Giles Ménage states that "when Robert proceeded to Jerusalem" he made a donation to Saint-Nicolas d'Angers in the presence of Abbot Lambert.[84] Unless the abbot had travelled to Sablé himself, this implies that Robert with his sons Rainald and Robert Vestrol, who gave their consent, were in Angers at Saint-Nicolas to make this donation. It would certainly make sense that Robert would visit Angers to settle his final donations to the monasteries of Saint-Nicolas and Saint-Aubin and to take formal leave of his lord Count Fulk, just as Rainald of Château-Gontier did.[85] From Angers he set out for Tours and the abbey of Marmoutier without his sons.

Robert's next documented stop was at the abbey of Marmoutier of Saint-Martin near Tours. If Robert had gotten underway by 23 February, he arrived at Marmoutier by 25 March.[86] It was at Marmoutier that

---

80. John France, "Patronage and the Appeal of the First Crusade," in *The First Crusade: Origins and Impact*, ed. Jonathan Phillips (Manchester and New York: Manchester University Press), 5–20, discusses the influence of lords, or the heads of a *mouvance* as he calls them, on the participation of men within their patronage.

81. Robert's last recorded stop on his way to the Holy Land was at Marmoutier where these men witnessed a series of acts. Their names are given in the last two charters cited.

82. This is the only appearance of Barthelemy as Robert's chaplain. His predecessor may have been the chaplain Fulk in *Cartul. de St-Vincent*, no. 366.

83. *Cartul. manceau*, 2: 86–89. "Unus procerum meorum qui mecum in Jerusalem ibat."

84. Ménage, *Histoire de Sablé*, 82. "Dedit R. Burgundio cum perrexit Hierusalem." Ménage, the only source for this notice, cites a no longer extant work.

85. "Gesta consulum Andegavorum," 149. "Rainaldus, jam vetulus, cruce facta, licentia comitis Jersolimis perrexit."

86. Guillot, *Comte d'Anjou*, 2: C 403, shows that Robert departed from Marmoutier by 28 March 1098. *Cartul. manceau*, 2: 86–89, no. 13, makes it clear he spent at least three days there before this date, so that he arrived 25 March at the latest.

the monks carefully wrote down Robert's own account of his gifts to the monastery providing the details of Robert's final preparations.[87] When Robert arrived at the abbey he found that Abbot Lambert was "absent by chance,"[88] but Radulf of Chartres, the prior, hastened to receive him "honorably" and "reverently."[89] This perhaps implies that Robert had left in some haste, without taking the time to make sure that the abbot would be there for him. The next day, Robert tells us, "I went into their chapter house and before all those who were present I humbly begged the monks that they might mention my memory to God in their prayers."[90] He then brought up the gifts he had already made earlier at Sablé to the monastery and formally confirmed and authorized them.[91] Robert was still troubled by the reluctance of the monks to accept his gift of the revenue of the burg of Saint-Nicolas in the face of his son's disapproval. Now, while Robert Vestrol was absent and could not object, the Burgundian made the grant of the revenue and even added three *mansurae* of property at La Lande, "for compassion of this son of mine."[92]

To symbolize the gifts of that day Robert then gave Prior Radulf a gold signet ring, a gift from his daughter. After the prior accepted the ring from Robert's hand he returned it, so that Robert could send it back "in place of a *signum* to those of his people who remained behind at Sablé."[93] With this act Robert was literally, as well as symbolically, handing over his authority with his seal.

"The next day," Robert continues, "I placed upon the alter of the church of Marmoutier the domaine of all those properties that I had given and conceded the day before in the chapter house."[94] Still con-

---

87. *Cartul. manceau*, 2: 86–91, nos. 13 and 14.

88. *Cartul. manceau*, 2: 86–89. "Abbas tunc forte absens."

89. "A monachis honorice susceptus essem," in *Cartul. manceau*, 2: 86–89, and "susceptus a monachis ipsius loci reverenter," in *Cartul. manceau*, 2: 89–91, no. 14.

90. *Cartul. manceau*, 2: 86–89. "Veni in capitulum ipsorum et coram universis qui aderant et quos ut in orationibus suis ad Deum mei momores forent suppliciter oraveram." *Cartul. manceau*, 2: 89–91, no. 14, is a slightly more detailed account of the same act.

91. *Cartul. manceau*, 2: 86–89. "Confirmans et auctorizans."

92. *Cartul. manceau*, 2: 89–91, no. 14. "In misericordia tamen ipsius filii mei."

93. *Cartul. manceau*, 2: 86–89. "Eo quod ipsum [anulum] ad meos remanserant remissurus essem loco signi."

94. *Cartul. manceau*, 2: 89–91, no. 14. "In crastino quoque altero posui super altare dominicum ecclesie ipsius loci omnium que pridie in capitulo dederam et concesseram."

cerned about his younger son's reluctance to agree to part of this donation, Robert made one last try to settle the matter. "From whence I be-
seeched my often mentioned son Robert by letter that he willingly approve this donation of mine for the sake of God and my gratitude."[95]
This dispatch of the letter, and presumably the signet ring, is Robert
the Burgundian's last recorded act.

Robert's testimony continues, however, for he was not the only crusader from Sablé taking the precaution of gaining the monk's goodwill.
"It should also be known that one of my nobles who was going with
me to Jerusalem, named Harduin of Vione, donated to God and Saint
Martin."[96] Harduin did this expressly "so that God might deign to guide
him and return him safe and sound to his own people."[97]

At some point after this act Robert and his company set out for the
Holy Land. Tours may have been the staging area for crusaders from
the region leaving on the "second expedition." Perhaps Rainald of
Château-Gontier joined up with Robert only at this point, for he certainly took no part in the acts performed at Marmoutier. These acts
have the appearance of a special, private ritual, reserved for the men of
Sablé and their lord and intended to mark them apart by stressing their
special relationship with Saint Martin of Marmoutier.

Robert's departure with his own men in company with Rainald of
Château-Gontier and his entourage came at almost the precise moment
when William Rufus, having completed his campaign against the
French in the Vexin, turned his attention towards Maine. In a sudden attack in the bad weather of February, the king attempted to take Count
Helias's castle at Dangeul. Although the assault misfired, William's chief
ally, Robert of Bellême, strengthened the garrisons of his own strongholds and continued the struggle.[98] It was not for nothing that Robert

95. *Cartul. manceau*, 2: 89–91, no. 14. ". . . donum et concessonem unde et sepefatum
filium meum Rotbertum per literas rogavi ut libenter annueret propter Deum et mei gratiam
huic mee donationi."

96. *Cartul. manceau*, 2: 86–89. "Sciendum etiam quod unus procerum meorum qui
mecum in Jerusalem ibat, nomine Harduinus de Vionio, dedit Deo et beato Martino, et sub
eisdem testibus obtulit super illud idem altare, censum octo denariorum quem ei solvebant
annis singulis monachi de vinea Inferneti, sita Sablolii."

97. *Cartul. manceau*, 2: 91–92, no. 15. ". . . ut Deus eum sanum et incolumem ducere et re-
ducere ad suos dignaretur." The words are not Robert's but those of an impersonal notice of
the act.

98. Orderic, 5: 232–35. Cf. Latouche, *Maine*, 46.

and the other Angevins had worked so hard with Robert Curthose to curb the power of the Bellême. It is uncertain if Robert was even aware of this attack when he set out. Indeed, he may already have been underway when it occurred. Certainly it did not deter him, although the presence of such an aggressive and hostile force would have been troubling. For a few months Norman plans sputtered futilely, but in April Robert of Bellême captured Count Helias in an ambush and handed him over to King William.[99] This signalled a massive incursion into Maine by the Normans. To block them Count Fulk hurried to Le Mans where he hastily installed a strong Angevin garrison. While a number of important Manceaux lords went over to the Normans, William broke off the campaign and retired into Normandy. Later in the year Fulk realized that he could not hold Le Mans in the face of another Norman attack and concluded a peace treaty with William that secured Helias's liberty while the king took possession of Le Mans.[100] Helias's liberty was obviously of great importance to the Angevins. There was nothing more for the nobles of Maine to do but submit. Orderic specifically names among those now willing to obey William's commands Viscount Radulf, Geoffrey of Mayenne, and Robert the Burgundian.[101]

Thus the lord of Sablé slipped under the control of William Rufus, at least for a time. By "Robert the Burgundian" Robert's son Robert Vestrol is clearly meant. What became of the father is unknown. If he survived the journey to the Holy Land, which is by no means certain given the conditions of travel and his advanced age, he would have arrived in time to take part in the capture of Jerusalem on 15 July 1099.[102] By the time his eldest son Rainald died in 1102, his grandson Alard was styled *senior* of Château-Gontier, indicating that people were aware that his father Rainald was already dead.[103] Years later another son of Rainald,

99. Orderic 5: 238–39; Latouche, *Maine*, 47.

100. Latouche, *Maine*, 47–50; Orderic 5: 244–47.

101. Orderic, 5: 250–51. "Radulfus vicecomes et Gosfredus de Meduana Rodbertus Burgundio aliique totius provinciae proceres regi confederati sunt, redditisque munitionibus datis ab eo legibus sollerter obsecundarunt."

102. Hagenmeyer, *Chronologie*, 250. Riley-Smith, *First Crusaders*, 37, cites the case of a pilgrim in 1026 reaching Jerusalem in just over five months and another in 1058 making the round trip in about a year.

103. "Cartul. of La Roë," 8–9, no. 8. Angot, *Généalogies féodales*, 189, felt this indicated that Rainald's death was known by this date.

himself leaving on crusade, would speak of his father in terms that could conceivably apply as well to his grandfather Robert the Burgundian: "He died gloriously in the service of God at the Holy Sepulchre."[104]

104. *Cartul. noir*, no. 147, dated 1120–1123. ". . . in servitio Domini, ad sanctum sepulchrum laudabilem finem adeptus est."

Conclusion

Robert's legacy was the extension and maintenance of Angevin domination over the county of Maine. In 1098 he was so confident of the strength of this domination that he departed for Jerusalem fully convinced that his holdings south of Le Mans were safe. The apparent failure of this assessment when William Rufus attacked almost the moment Robert departed was just that: apparent, not real. Although temporarily shaken by Rufus, Robert's achievement in maintaining Craon and Sablé as Angevin strongholds free from Norman domination for nearly half a century was never in serious danger. The Normans and their allies the Bellêmes, while having their moments of success, never penetrated to southern Maine and the core of Robert's honor. King William accomplished considerably less than his father. The story is a familiar one of great victories for the Normans, at least as told by their own chroniclers, that somehow never managed to have any lasting result in Maine. The quantity and quality of Norman historical writing should not mislead us. They tell only the Norman side of events. As in Robert's time, lower Maine remained Angevin, the bishop of Le Mans was pro-Angevin, and the people of Le Mans were anti-Norman. However much William Rufus might have hammered away at Angevin control, Helias remained count. He also remained deeply involved in Angevin politics, playing the role of mentor to Fulk's son Geoffrey Martel II. It took barely three months for Count Fulk Rechin to recapture Le Mans and permanently restore his *fidelis* Helias to the countship of Maine when William Rufus died in August 1100. By 1106 even the ferocious Robert of Bellême had joined the Angevins, fighting alongside Fulk's son Geoffrey at the siege of Candé.[1]

Helias, the man Robert had helped gain the countship by securing the support of Bishop Hoel of Le Mans, then promised his daughter Erembourg to young Geoffrey Martel. When Geoffrey died in 1106, Erembourg was simply married to Rechin's second son, Fulk the Young, who became count of Anjou in 1109. Indeed, in a charter dated between 19 May 1106 and 14 April 1109, Fulk and his already married son are reported as acting in concert with "Count Helias under whose authority the county of Anjou was held at that time."[2] This marriage effectively united Maine and Anjou when Helias died the following year.[3] This was not the result of chance, nor of a fortuitous betrothal, but rather of political realities forged by half a century of struggle by the Angevins for control of Maine.

Helias and his friendship with Geoffrey Martel and later young Fulk are seen as the key to Angevin control but cannot be understood without an appreciation of the achievement of the Angevin *domini* and above all of Robert the Burgundian. Robert may have been instrumental in making Helias heir to his father's holdings despite two older brothers. It was certainly Robert who was the chief architect of the Norman defeat at Sainte-Suzanne and in co-opting the influential Bishop Hoel to the Angevin side. These steps were essential to creating Helias as count of Maine. Helias's close association with the Angevin cause must be understood within a political reality deeply influenced by the actions of the *dominus* of Craon and Sablé. Angevin power was simply too great for Helias to resist even if he wished. His own strong personal ties with Angevins, first with the older Robert and Fulk, then with their sons, would have led him to see himself as an Angevin in any case. We forget, perhaps, that for Helias, his daughter's marriage meant not the absorption of Maine by Anjou, but the opportunity for his descendants to rule Maine, Anjou, and Touraine.

1. Thompson, "Robert of Bellême," 277.

2. "Comes Helias sub cujus manu tunc temporis pagus Andegavensis habebatur." Bib. nat., Dom Housseau III, no 963, discussed in Guillot, *Comte d'Anjou* C 442.

3. Latouche, *Maine,* 49–51, and Halphen, 188–90, present well documented summaries of events. Barlow, *William Rufus,* 381–92, 402–6, provides a more detailed account from the Norman point of view.

Robert, to be sure, must have had his own personal assessment of his career, however opaque to us. Certainly by the common measure of his time he was a splendid success. He had moved from a subordinate to a trusted companion of the count of Anjou, from a knight to a *dominus* of many castles. For Robert himself, his paramount achievements may have been the building of his honor to pass on to his two eldest sons, the advancement of the Angevin cause against the Normans, and the care of his own and his family's souls by careful attention to the Church. These were the central concerns of his life as they have come down to us.

His honor, the lands, rights, and titles that made up his *casamentum,* is inextricably connected to the family. He had the opportunity to win his honor because of family connections; he built and protected it with a sense of his own family, his first wife Advisa not least of all. Inheritance through the female line explained the splitting of his honor between his two eldest sons. Rainald's wife carried the title of Craon with her blood; Robert Vestrol's mother passed title of Sablé to him. Having secured these titles, Robert was able to use kinship ties to protect them, as at Sainte-Suzanne and La Flèche. By Robert's departure, a huge swath of territory from Craon to Durtal was controlled by family members. Craon was held by his eldest son Rainald, a man of thirty years experience as *dominus* of that castle. The threat from the Bretons had long been diffused by Rainald's marriage to the daughter of the lord of Vitré. At Sablé Robert's younger son, Robert Vestrol, ruled in conjunction with Robert's second wife Bertha. Although less prone to follow his father's lead in maintaining cordial ties with the Church than his elder brother, Vestrol had the advantage of years of service in the court of Count Guy-Geoffrey of Poitou. Robert's grandson Alard was *dominus* of the neighboring castle of Château-Gontier, so vital to the strategic protection of Sablé and Craon.

This family-dominated core in turn was embedded into a web of strong alliances. In the west, the Breton lord Robert de Vitré was his eldest son's father-in-law. In Maine to the north his niece's husband was viscount of Le Mans and his ally Helias was count. Further north Robert even had a connection among the Normans with William of

Évreux, the husband of yet another niece. To the east, Lancelin of Beaugency was father-in-law to Robert's nephew. In the south was Robert's strongest ally, the support to all his success, the count of Anjou.

The powerful position of Robert's family existed within the context of loyalty to the counts of Anjou. It is the central contention of this study that however shaken he may have been on occasion, Robert remained loyal to the house of Anjou. He himself said he owed his honor to Count Geoffrey Martel and he commemorated Geoffrey's memory to the end of his life. Robert probably could not separate in his own mind his family interests from those of the count of Anjou. In fact, in the person of his great-aunt Agnes, they were literally related, as more distantly he was related to both Geoffrey the Bearded and Fulk Rechin.

Robert's loyalty to the counts of Anjou was more than that of a warrior, living for the thrill of battle, the enhancement of his chivalric reputation, and the petty greed satisfied by plunder and ransom. This is the assumption of much of the writing about the breakdown of the Angevin state during the civil war between Geoffrey the Bearded and Fulk Rechin. Such actions as, for example, the siege of Sainte-Suzanne, have been seen in this image of a dangerously independent nobility pursuing their own self aggrandizement in an endless round of petty wars. Robert was a careful and rational man who worked patiently at being a diplomat, judge, political figure, even a reformer of the Church. The siege of Sainte-Suzanne, far from being an heroic *beau geste* embodying chivalric ideals of a warrior elite, was a carefully thought out campaign waged with a clear-headed sense of political realities and backed by skillfully fostered alliances. The campaign makes perfect sense in relation to Angevin long term interests on their border with the Normans. If Robert personally led his followers on that occasion, it was because he had come to the conclusion that it would further the interests of the Angevins, most prominently, his own family. His actions with Robert Curthose and Bishop Hoel followed the same pattern.

Robert's role within the Angevin state had another side, probably of equal importance to him: his relationship with the Church. To ensure the spiritual health of himself and his family, Robert made a long series of rich donations for their souls to various monasteries and skillfully built strong ties with the archbishop of Tours and the monks of Marmoutier. Siding with the reform faction within the Church, he was willing to place the churches of Sablé under monastic control. Robert has left written testimony to his motivations for his donations and his preparation for his crusade and there is no need to doubt his sincerity. Nor should we take them at face value. His role as benefactor and reformer advanced his practical agenda as surely as his military campaigns. His ties with the Church were to the ecclesiastical establishments most associated with the Angevin state and the count of Anjou. His reform of his churches had an overt political aspect. It got them out from under the bishop of Le Mans. His confraternity with the wealthy and powerful Marmoutier resulted in genuine benefits. Robert, like many people of his time, probably saw no contradiction in a man benefitting both spiritually and materially from such actions.

About his role in the deposition of his lawful count, Geoffrey the Bearded, and how he used the situation to his own ends, he may have been more uncomfortable. When Robert saw his family's position threatened by Geoffrey's incompetence, he revealed himself as a ruthless master of realpolitik as he abandoned Geoffrey and threw his support behind Fulk Rechin. Robert skillfully manipulated the situation to his advantage, gaining lands, prestige, power, and independence. There can be no doubt that Robert, like other Angevin *domini,* emerged from the struggle more powerful and more independent.[4] This does not amount to a revolution, however, nor to a permanent weakening of the state Fulk Nerra and Geoffrey Martel had created. The balance of power between the count and his *domini* was severely shaken under Geoffrey the Bearded, then renegotiated under Fulk Rechin.

As his part of the renegotiation, Robert retained a distinct loyalty to the Angevins and to the family of his first lord, Geoffrey Martel. In return, he gained in status, power, and independence. This is the key to Robert's success. As long as he was paramount within Angevin affairs,

---

4. Guillot, *Comte d'Anjou,* 299–352, is ample proof of the increasing independence of Angevin castellans in a juridical sense with the growth of what he calls "les seigneuries châtelaines." It is not the juridical status of castles and castle commanders in question here, but the commanders' collective sense of an "Anjou" and their ability to project power.

and could use his position within the Angevin defensive net, Normans, Bretons, and Manceaux were no serious threat to him. While this loyalty may have wavered at times, it was never in serious doubt. During Robert's lifetime loyalty to the count of Anjou furthered his personal policy of building and protecting his honor. While both Fulk Rechin and Robert were alive, the count of Anjou was also loyal to Robert. The count owed Robert too much and was too dependent on him for it to be otherwise. As long as Robert could keep this axis healthy, neither the Normans nor any other enemy could seriously threaten him.

This fact tells us something about the Angevin state under Fulk Rechin that has been largely unappreciated. Fulk's regime is usually contrasted unfavorably with the Norman regime, where the king/duke was supposedly supreme.[5] In light of Robert the Burgundian's solid achievement in Maine, should we not ask why a looser, more decentralized state, with the count as "first among equals" is not an acceptable alternative? In judging eleventh century societies, is the best criteria for good government the amount of centralized authority a principality could exert over the local lords of the realm? K. F. Werner critiqued this view in 1992 when he pointed out that the fascination with strong central power was a nineteenth century ideal brought on by a reaction to the French Revolution.[6] The reality shown in this study argues that there could be great strength in a system such as Fulk and his barons constructed, if one can think in terms of Angevin leadership as the collective body of the upper nobility rather than the single body of the count.[7] The *domini* did not wreck the Angevin state. Fulk and his *fideles* were able to use force against any *domini*, such as John of La Flèche, who went too far. The Angevin system had functioned effectively, relying on loyal barons such as Robert operating with considerable independence, to face down the Normans and slowly extend their control

5. See, for example, Jacques Boussard, "Les institutions de l'empire Plantegenet," in *Histoire des institutions Francaises au Moyen Age*, eds. Ferdinand Lot and Robert Fawtier, vol. 1 (Paris: Presses Universitaires de France, 1957): 39–41.

6. Karl Ferdinand Werner, "Royaume et Regna: Le Pouvoir en France comme enjeu entre le roi et les grands," in *Pouvoirs et libertés au temps des premiers Capétiens*, ed. Elisabeth Magnou-Nortier and Pierre Desports (Maulévrier: Éditions Hérault, 1992), 25–26.

7. For Werner it is the nobles with their rights and liberties who make up the realm. Ibid., 29.

over the county. Fulk may have left much of the leadership in the hands of Robert, Helias, and other frontier lords, but this was no less of an achievement than the decades long process of conquering the Touraine begun by Fulk Nerra and only completed by Geoffrey Martel when Robert was yet a young man.[8]

This achievement was crucial to the assertion of Angevin power during the twelfth century. Fulk Rechin's descendants, the Plantagenets, would have a profound impact on the kingdoms of England and France. His grandson Geoffrey, married to a granddaughter of William the Conqueror, would conquer Normandy in the 1140s while his grandson Henry II would become king of England in 1154. Without Maine firmly within their power, the Plantagenets, no matter how much they may have wished later to downplay Fulk and his dangerously (from their point of view) independent nobility, would have had a drastically reduced power base from which to launch their struggle for control of Normandy and England. Far from weakening the Angevin state, this particular *dominus* played a crucial role in projecting Angevin authority into Maine and blocking the Norman advance. Without realizing it, the Plantagenets owed much to Robert the Burgundian and his loyalty to the house of Anjou.

---

8. "Fulk's achievement seems as important as either Fulk Nerra's or Geoffrey Martel's," Bradbury, "Fulk Rechin," 2.

Appendix: The Family of the Counts of Nevers

Once it was assumed by scholars that feudal ties had overwhelmed the pull of blood and birth.[1] This view has been replaced with a renewed appreciation of just how powerful family remained. Even William the Conqueror, as pragmatic a ruler as one could wish, relied for his most trusted associates not on feudal vassals but on his half-brother and a pair of cousins.[2] As historians traced the origins of powerful tenth and eleventh century families, it became clear that their power was based on nobility, and nobility was based on birth within a specific family whose members had held power at least since the times of Charles the Bald.[3] This continuity between the old Carolingian aristocracy and the aristocracy of the tenth and eleventh centuries has now been demonstrated by a number of scholars as a sign of the continuing importance of family status.[4]

Yet the continuity observed is that of kinship groups, not individuals. Men of relatively modest family backgrounds with ability, charisma, or simple good fortune could rise in society, but the ultimate, and nearly universally sought after, mark of success was marriage to a daughter of an established noble family.[5] Such

1. Marc Bloch, *Feudal Society*, trans. L. A. Manyon, 2 vols. (Chicago: University of Chicago Press, 1970), 142, 224–27, is the best known statement of the preponderance of feudal institutions over family relationships. This view was critiqued by Sydney Painter, "The Family and the Feudal System in Twelfth Century England," *Speculum* 35 (1960): 1–16, and Elizabeth A. R. Brown, "The Tyranny of a Construct: Feudalism and Historians of Medieval Europe," *American Historical Review* 79 (1974): 1063–88. T. N. Bisson, "Nobility and Family in Medieval France: A Review Essay," *French Historical Studies* 16 (Spring 1990): 597–613, brings the argument up to date and attempts to rehabilitate Bloch in general, but see Reynolds, *Fiefs and Vassals*.

2. For the importance of kinship among the Normans, see Searle, *Predatory Kinship*.

3. Van Luyn, "*Milites* dans la France," 206–7, also points out the important, though secondary, role of landed wealth in establishing access to power.

4. Karl Ferdinand Werner, "Untersuchungen zur Frühzeit des französischen Fürstentums," in *Die Welt als Geschichte* 17 (1958): 256–89, 19 (1959): 146–93, and 20 (1960): 87–119; "Bedeutende Adelsfamilien im Reich Karls des Grossen," in *Karl der Grosse-Lebenswerk und Nachleben*, vol. 1, *Persönlichkeit und Geschichte*, Helmut Beumann, ed. (Düsseldorf: Schwann, 1965), 83–142; Jaques Boussard, "L'origine des familes seigneuriales dans la région de la Loire moyenne," *Cahiers de civilization médiévale* 5 (1962): 303–22. For a summation of this work and further bibliography see Jane Martindale, "The French Aristocracy in the Early Middle Ages: A Reappraisal," *Past and Present* 75 (1977): 5–45.

5. Bouchard, "Origins of the French Nobility," 524–30. There is, of course, an analogous trend among women courting men of higher status and their offspring, legitimate or not, acquiring a higher social rank than their mothers. William the Conqueror is the most notable example of this.

an individual acquiring the outer trappings of nobility might therefore be a "new man" without suitably Carolingian credentials, but his children, by virtue of their maternal family, would be in full possession of such credentials. Robert the Burgundian's own family history as reconstructed in the twelfth century by Hugh of Poitiers in his *Origo et historia brevis nivernensium comitum* exemplifies many of these issues.

According to this account the family was founded by a Landric, nephew of the Poitevin bishop of Autun, Hildegarius. A quarter of the text is taken up with an account of how Hildegarius became bishop when an unnamed king of France spied him "sporting with some young woman" and was impressed with Hildegarius's cleverness.[6] Some time afterwards Bishop Hildegarius was called upon by Richard the Justiciar (923–936) to help lay siege to the castle of Metz-le-compte, the lair of brigands who ruthlessly preyed upon travellers passing through the Nivernais.[7] The bishop was accompanied by his nephew Landric who in the ensuing battle captured the fleeing *dominus* of Metz. After the brigand chief was hanged, Landric received the captured castle as his reward.

The new lord of Metz then married an Angevin woman who bore him a son named Bodo after his godfather, Bodo *de Montibus*. This godfather made the younger Bodo a handsome gift of land upon which Bodo established a castle called *Moncellis*, now Monceaux-le-Comte.[8] From this base Bodo extended the territory under his control and fathered a son named Landric.

This Landric was a man, Hugh tells us, of great liberality. His stronghold was located on the main pilgrimage route to Rome where he was accustomed to entertain all who travelled that way, noble and common alike. Finally Landric himself made the pilgrimage in the company of the counts of Poitou, Anjou, and Burgundy. When the pilgrims reached *Biterna*, probably Viterbo in Italy,[9] each count began to bid for Landric's services. The count of Burgundy won by granting Landric's request for the castle of Nevers, along with the rank of count. According to Hugh, the count responded to Landric, "I grant your wish and bestow upon you and your heirs hereafter the countship of Nevers in return for the right of homage."[10] In this way Landric became the first of his family to be made hereditary count of Nevers and took every opportunity to extend his boundaries.

Hugh was combining two important trends in genealogical reconstruction for the noble houses of the twelfth century. The family had deep roots in the Carolingian nobility, and yet Hugh felt the need to stress the "new man" stereotype. This latter was a constant feature of the new genealogies, even when the family had re-

6. "Origo," 236. "ludentum cum quadam juvencula."

7. Mirot, "Origines des premiers comtes," 9, and Huygens, "Origo," 236.

8. A few kilometers south of Metz-le-Compte. See Huygens, "Origo," 237 n. 101/102.

9. Huygens, "Origo," 237 n. 113.

10. "Origo," 238. "Concedo sicut vis, et comitatum Nivernis, salvo jure hominii, tibi et heredibus tuis deinceps tribuo."

spectable origins with members of an existing noble family, as here.[11] An important point is being made. The nobles, or their house scholars, were saying in effect: We are nobles because our ancestor was able to perform deeds that revealed his inherent nobility and raised him and his descendants above the common run. We are thus nobles because we are inherently superior *in fact*, as well as in blood.

So convincing was Hugh in stressing this "new man" version of the family origins that modern scholars have spoken of the Landrican family's "mediocre" or "unexulted" origins.[12] Yet this was not true, even in Hugh's perhaps fictional account. He described Hildegarius as one who "stood out" as the king's deacon and served as an official of the palace. Furthermore, he was personally selected by the king to be bishop of Autun.[13] In short, he was closely attached to the king's personal service and therefore probably from a distinguished family, perhaps one of royal blood.

This is even more true of the historical figure who served as the model for Hugh's Hildegarius: Bishop Adalgar of Autun. He is apparently the same Adalgar who appears early in the reign of Charles the Bald as a monk of Saint-Germain-des-Prés.[14] By 867 Adalgar was a *notarius* in the king's chancery.[15] In this office his personal influence was such that he could successfully petition the king to restore a church to the abbey of Saint-Sulpice.[16] By 875, at the latest, King Charles refers to him as "chancellor of our sacred palace and abbot of the monastery of Saint Peter and Paul . . . in the woods of Montier-en-Der."[17] Adalgar was further promoted to the episcopal seat of Autun by 23 February 877. He was able to request that King Charles give the royal monasteries of Flavigny and Corbigny to his church of Autun.[18] From that point on Adalgar simply acted as abbot of Flavigny, one of the wealthiest monasteries in Burgundy.[19]

Adalgar was remarkably assiduous in advancing the wealth of his church. In 877 he was careful to secure a confirmation of the possession of the two monasteries from Pope John VIII while attending the Council of Ravenna as an imperial dele-

---

11. The twelfth century "Gesta consulum Andegavorum," 26–29, for example, follows the same pattern in describing the descent of the counts of Anjou. Tertullus, the son of a mere forester, rose in rank by impressing King Charles the Bald and was given a bride from a powerful Burgundian magnate family from whom arose the house of Anjou. See also Bachrach, *Fulk Nerra*, 3–4.

12. Lot, "Chanson de Landri," 2; Bouchard, "Origins," 519.

13. "Origo," 236.

14. *Acts des Charles II*, 3: 58. While it is not certain, the editors accept this Adalgarius as the future Bishop of Autun.

15. *Actes des Charles II*, 2, no. 304, 30 October 867. "Adalgarius notarius." No. 338, August 866–April 870, has "A-dal-ga-rius clericus scripsi et subscripsi." He appears in a dozen other acts as notarius.

16. *Actes de Charles II*, 3: 91.

17. *Actes de Charles II*, 2: no. 382, 867–875 August. Here again Adalgar asks the king for a favor, this time for a grant of immunity for his monastery.

18. Ibid., no. 420. Also published in *Cartulaire de l'Église d'Autun*, 1: no. 7.

19. *Cartulary of Flavigny*, 73–75, no. 24.

gate.[20] In yet another charter of papal confirmation from the same year, he took pains to list much of the property he had taken from Flavigny.[21] In succeeding years he obtained confirmations of church properties from King Boso, brother-in-law of Charles and pretender to the throne of Burgundy,[22] King Carloman, who led the Carolingian restoration,[23] and King Odo,[24] all at his personal request. Adalgar's exactions on Flavigny, in particular, must have been severe. At his death the rector of that monastery was accused of poisoning the bishop even though Adalgar had personally rewarded the man with many gifts.[25] A man so successful in amassing power could well afford to advance the fortunes of younger kinsmen, as would have been expected. A churchman of such influence would most likely come from a magnate family and even if not, his elevation would have raised the fortunes of his family from that point on. Even if the family were already prominent in the Poitevin region, Adalgar's success in Burgundy would have allowed younger sons to make their mark in the east.

Unfortunately there is no surviving documentation to connect the historical Bishop Adalgar with the Landrican family. There is, in fact, evidence that members of this family were already in the eastern part of the *regnum Francorum* before the alleged events of Hugh's little history. A certain Landric, called "our faithful vassal" *(fidelis vassallus)* by Charles the Bald, was given the chapel of Saint-Albain in the Mâconnais with all its lands, houses, pastures, meadows, and dependent laborers by the king in 842.[26] Landric and his wife Hildesendis then gave the chapel to the cathedral of Mâcon.[27] Landric and Hildesendis could very well be the parents of the Landric, nephew of Adalgar, found in the *Origo et historia*. If so Hildesendis would most likely be the sister of Adalgar.[28] It is suggestive to recall that in the *Origo et historia* the name Adalgar is rendered as Hildegarius. The first element of the names of both the bishop of Autun and the wife of Landric are identical. As Werner has demonstrated, aristocratic families commonly used the repetition of names and portions of names almost as a distinctive badge of kinship.[29] Aside from this simi-

20. *Actes de Charles II*, 2, no. 30. Adalgar is present as "episcopus, missus etiam imperialis."

21. *Cartulary of Flavigny*, no. 23, pp. 69–72.

22. *Actes de Charles II*, 2: no. 17. Adalgar was one of the twenty-four bishops to sign the act of Mantailles, 15 October 879, that elected Boso.

23. *Actes de Charles II*, 2: no. 16.

24. *Actes de Charles II*, no. 24. For Adalgar's career in general, see Poupardin, *Le royaume de Provence sous les Carolingiens* (Paris, 1901; reprint ed., Geneva: Slatkine Reprints, 1974), 79 n.4, 99, 110 n. 7, 112–13, 128, 133 n. 4, and 333 n. 5.

25. *Cartulary of Flavigny*, no. 25, pp. 75–78. "This is a very curious case," as Bouchard comments, and although the accused rector was acquitted "the account still leaves the impression that he had indeed poisoned Adalgar."

26. *Actes de Charles II* 1: no. 10, 23 August 842.

27. *Cartulaire de Saint-Vincent de Mâcon*, ed. M.-C. Ragut (Mâcon, 1864), no. 60.

28. Bouchard, *Sword*, 341 n. 179. Lespinasse, *Nivernais*, 192, and Mirot, "Origines," believed that Landric was the bishop's brother.

29. Karl Ferdinand Werner, "Liens de parenté et noms de personne: un problème historique et

larity of names, however, there is no documentary evidence to confirm this part of the genealogy given in the *Origo et historia.*

What can be said, though, is that the origins of the counts of Nevers may go back to a supporter of Charles the Bald named Landric who held considerable land in the Mâconnais in the mid-ninth century and was probably related to the bishop of Autun. Even if we reject Hugh of Poitier's genealogy, the Landrican counts of Nevers are still a striking confirmation of the theory that eleventh century comital families had their origins in the Carolingian aristocracy of the eighth and ninth centuries. Robert the Burgundian came from just such a family.

---

méthodologique," in *Structures politiques du monde Franc (VIe–XIIe siècles): Études sur les origines de la France et de l'Allemagne* (London: Variorum Reprints, 1979), 26.

Bibliography

Manuscript Sources

The following represent repositories visited and manuscripts consulted either in the original or on microfilm copies with the exception of the manuscript in the British Museum.

Archives départmentales de Maine-et-Loire
> G 842
>> 39 H2; 40 H 1; 61 H 1 (Cartulary of la Roë); H 110; H 224 (Cartulary of Brion); H 289; H 360; H 1773; H 1777; H 1840; H 3368; H 3370; H 3652; H 3712; H 3713 (Livre blanc de St-Florent); H 3714 (Livre d'argent de St-Florent); H 3715 (Livre rouge de St-Florent);

Archives départmentales d'Indre-et-Loire
> H 270; H 306; H 1002

Archives départmentales de la Sarthe
> H 267; H 359

Bibliothèque nationale, Paris
> Collection Touraine Anjou (Dom Housseau): vols. II1; II2; III; XII2; XIII
> Collection Moreau
> Collection Baluze: vols. 38; 47; 77; 139
> Collection De Camps
>> Ms. lat.: 5419; 54411; 54412; 54413; 54414; 5446; 5447; 10122; 11792; 12679; 12696; 12700; 12780; 12878 (Dom le Michel); 12879; 12880; 12875; 13820; 13900; 17049; 17126
>> N. a. lat.: 1930 (Livre noir de St-Florent); 1935; 1939; 2588; 7433;
>> N. a. fr.: 7433; 22225; 22329; 22450

British Museum, London
> "Cartulaire de l'abbaye de Quimperlé," ms. Egerton 2802

Published Primary Sources

Acta pontificum romanorum inedita: Urkunden der Päpste vom Jahre 748 bis zum Jahre 1198. Ed. J. V. Pflugk-Harttung. Tübingen: Franz Fues, 1881.

Actus pontificum Cenomannis in urbe degentium. Eds. Gustave Busson and Ambroise Ledru. Archives historiques du Maine, vol. 2. Le Mans: Siège de la Société, 1902.

Adalbaron of Laon. "Rythmus satiricus." In "Les Poèmes de Adalbaron." Ed. G. A. Hückel. In *Mélanges d'histoire du Moyen Age*, Vol. 13. Paris, 1901.

———. "Rythmus satiricus." In Claude Hohl, "Landri de Nevers dans l'histoire et dans le *Girart de Roussillon*." Published in *Chanson de geste et le mythe Carolingian: Mélanges René Louis,* vol. 2. Saint-Père-sous-Vézelay: Musée archéologique regional, 1982.

Amoin. "Gesta francorum." In *De regum procerumque francorum origine gestis clarissimis usque ad Philippum Augustum.* Paris: Badius Ascensius, 1514.

Anglo-Saxon Chronicle. Ed. and trans. Dorothy Whitelock. London: Eyre and Spottiswoode, 1961.

"Annales de Renaud." In *Recueil d'annales angevines et vendômoises.*

"Annales de Saint-Aubin." In *Recuiel d'annales angevines et vendômoises.*

"Annales de Saint-Serge." In *Recueil d'annales angevines et vendoômoises.*

"Annales de Vendôme." In *Recueil d'annales angevines et vendômoises.*

"Annales Nivernensis." In *Monumenta Germania Historia, scriptores,* vol. 13, p. 89.

"Annales Vezeliacenses," in *Monumenta Vizeliacensia: textes relatifs à l'histoire de l'abbaye de Vézelay.* Ed. R. B. C. Huygens. Corpus Christianorum continuatio mediaevalis, vol. 42. Turnhout: Brepols, 1976.

Baldric of Dol. "Vita b. Roberti de Arbissello." In *Patrologiae latina,* 162: 14–15.

Barbier de Montault. "Charte le l'an 1096 relative à l'abbaye de Saint-Nicolas des Angers." *Repertoire archéologique de l'Anjou* (1862): 55–58.

Cartulaire blésois de Marmoutier. Ed. Charles Métais. Blois: E. Moreau, 1891.

Cartulaire d'Assé-le-Riboul. Ed. Arthur Bertrand de Broussillon. Archives historiques du Maine, vol. 3. Le Mans: Socété des archives historique du Maine, 1903.

Cartulaire d'Azé et du Géneteil. Ed. M. du Brossay. Archives historique du Maine, vol. 3. Le Mans: Société des archives historiques du Maine, 1903.

Cartulaire de Château-du-Loir. Ed. Eugène Valée. Archives historiques du Maine, vol. 6. Le Mans: Société des archives historiques du Maine, 1905.

Cartulaire de Cormery. Ed. J. Bourassé. Tours and Paris: Guilland-Verger and Dumoulin, 1861.

Cartulaire de l'abbaye cardinale de la Trinité de Vendôme. 5 vols. Ed. Charles Métais. Vendôme: Clovis Ripé, 1893–1894.

Cartulaire de l'abbaye de Noyers. Ed. C. Chevealier. Mémoires de la Société archéologique de Touraine, vol. 22. Tours: Guilland-Verger, George-Joubert, 1872.

Cartulaire de l'abbaye de Saint-Aubin d'Angers. Ed. Arthur Bertrand de Broussillon. Documents historiques sur l'Anjou, vols. 1–3. Paris: A. Picard, 1903.

Cartulaire de l'abbaye de Sainte-Croix de Quimperlé. Ed. Léon Maitre and Paul de Berthou. 2d ed. Paris: H. Champion, n.d.

Cartulaire de l'abbaye du Ronceray d'Angers. Ed. Paul Marchegay. Archives d'Anjou, vol. 3. Paris: A. Picard, 1900.

Cartulaire de l'abbayes de Saint-Pierre de la Couture et de Saint-Pierre de Solesmes. Ed. Benedictines of Solesmes. Le Mans: Monnoyer, 1881.

Cartulaire de l'Église d'Autun. Ed. Anatole de Charmasse. Vol. 1. Paris: Auguste Durand, 1875.

Cartulaire de l'Évêché du Mans (965–1786). Ed. Arthur Bertrand de Broussillon. Archives historiques du Maine, vol. 9. Le Mans: Société des archives historiques du Maine, 1908.

Cartulaire de Marmoutier pour le vendômois. Ed. Trémault. Vendôme: Clovis Ripé, 1893.

Cartulaire de Marmoutier pour le Dunois. Ed. Émile Mabille. Châteaudun: Henri Lecesne, 1874.

Cartulaire de Saint-Cyprien de Poitiers. Ed. L. Redet. Poitiers, 1874.

Cartulaire de Saint-Cyr de Nevers. Ed. René de Lespinasse. Paris: Chez Champion, 1916.

Cartulaire de Saint-Laud d'Angers. Ed. A. Planchenault. Angers: Germain and Grassin, 1903.

Cartulaire de Saint-Maur-sur-Loire. Ed. Paul Marchegay. Archives d'Anjou, vol. 1. Angers: Charles Labussière, 1843.

Cartulaire de Saint-Victeur au Mans. Ed. Paul de Farcy. Paris: Alphonse Picard et Fils, 1895.

Cartulaire de Saint-Vincent de Mâcon. Ed. M.-C. Ragut. Mâcon: Imprimerie d'É. Protat, 1864.

Cartulaire de Saint-Vincent du Mans. Ed. S. Menjot d'Elbenne. Le Mans: A. de Saint-Denis, 1888–1913.

Cartulaire du Bas-Poitou. Ed. Paul Marchegay. Les Roches-Baritant, 1877.

Cartulaire manceau de Marmoutier. Vols. 1–2. Ed. E. T. Laurain. Laval: Librairie Goupil, 1945.

Cartulaire noir de la cathédrale d'Angers. Ed. Charles Urseau. Documents historiques du l'Anjou, vol. 5. Angers: Germain and G. Grassin, 1908.

Cartulary of Flavigny, 717–1113, Ed. Constance Brittain Bouchard. Cambridge, Mass.: Medieval Academy of America, 1995.

Chartes de Saint-Julien de Tours (1002–1227). Ed. L.-J. Denis. Archives historiques du Maine, vol. 12. Le Mans: Société des archives historiques du Maine, 1912.

Chartes et documents pour servir a l'histoire de l'abbaye de Saint-Maixent. Ed. Alfred Richard. 2 vols. Archives historiques du Poitou, vol. 16 and 17. Poitiers: Typographie Oudin, 1886.

Chartes vendômoises. Ed. Charles Métais. Vendôme: Société archéologique, scientifique et littéraire du Vendômois, 1905.

"Chronicon Sancti Maxentii Pictavensis." In *Chroniques des églises d'Anjou*.

"Chronicon Sancti Sergii Andegavensis," in *Chroniques des églises d'Anjou*.

Chronique de Nantes (570 environ–1049). Ed. René Merlot. Paris: A. Picard, 1869.

Chronique de Parcé. Ed. H. de Barranger. Archives Departmentales de la Sarthe: Inventaires et Documents. Le Mans: Imprimerie Monnoyer, 1953.

Chroniques des comtes d'Anjou ed des seigneurs d'Amboise. Ed. Louis Halphen and René Poupardin. Paris: A. Picard, 1913.

Chroniques des églises d'Anjou. Ed. Paul Marchegay and Émile Mabille. Paris: Jules Renouard, 1869.

Ecclesiastical History of Orderic Vitalis. 6 vols. Ed. and trans. by Marjorie Chibnall. Oxford: Clarendon Press, 1969–1973.

Fulk Réchin. "Fragmentum historiae Andegavensis." In *Chroniques des comtes d'Anjou et des seigneurs*.

Gallia Christiana in Provincias Ecclesisticas Distributa. Vols. 2, 4, 14. Paris: Typoghrphia Regia: Didot Fratres, 1744, 1853.

"Gesta Ambaziensium dominorum." In *Chroniques des comtes d'Anjou et des seigneurs d'Amboise*.

"Gesta consulum Andegavorum." In *Chroniques des comtes d'Anjou et des seigneurs d'Amboise*.

Geoffrey of Vendôme, *Geoffroy de Vendôme: Oevres*. Ed. and trans. Geneviève Giordanengo. Brepols: CNRS Editions, 1996.

Gregory VII, "Trois lettres de Grégoire VII et la Bibliotheca rerum germanorum de Philippe Jaffé." Ed. Léopold Delisle. *Bibliothèque de l'École des Chartes* 26 (1865): 556–561.

Guibert de Nogent. "Gesta Dei per Francos." In *Recueil des historiens des croisades: Historiens occidentaux*, 5 vols. Paris: Imprimerie nationale, 1844–1895.

Hugh of Fleury. "Modernorum regum Francorum liber." In *Recueil des historiens des Gauls et de Francs*. Vol.12. Ed. Léopold Delisle. Paris: V. Palmé, 1877.

Le Pelletier, Laurent. *Rerum scitu dignissimarum a prima fundatione monasterii S. Nicolai Andegavensis ad hunc usque diem, epitome, necnon eiusdem monasterii abbatum series*. Angers: Adamum Mauger, 1635.

Livre des serfs de Marmoutier. Ed. André Salmon. Tours: Ladavèze, 1864.

Maison de Craon: 1050–1480: Étude historique accompagné du cartulaire de Craon. Ed. Arthur Bertrand de Broussillon. 2 vols. Paris: Alphonse Picard et Fils, 1893.

Obituaire de la cathédrale d'Angers. Ed. Charles Urseau. Angers: Librairie Grassin, 1930.

"Obituaire de Saint-Serge." In *Recueil d'annales angevines et vendômoises*.

"Origo et historia brevis Nivernensium comitum," by Hugh of Poitiers. In *Monumenta Vizeliacensia: textes relatifs à l'histoire de l'abbaye de Vézelay*. Ed. R. B. C. Huygens. Corpus Christianorum continuatio mediaevalis, vol. 42. Turnhout: Brepols, 1976.

Papsturkunden 896–1046. Ed. Harald Zimmermann. 2 vols. Vienna: Verlag der Österreichischen Akademie der Wissenschaften, 1985.

Patrologiae cursus completus. Series Latina. Vols. 151, 157, 159, 162. Ed. J.-P. Migne. Paris: Garnier Fratres, 1880.

Premier et second libres des cartulaires de l'abbaye Saint-Serge et Saint-Bach d'Angers. Ed. Yves Chauvin. 2 vols. Angers: Presses de l'Université d'Angers, 1997.

Raoul Glaber. *Rodulfi Glabri Historiarum libri quinque*. In *Rodulfus Glaber Opera*. Ed. John France. Oxford: Oxford University Press, 1989.

Recueil d'annales angevines et vendômoises. Ed. Louis Halphen. Paris: Alphonse Picard et Fils, 1903.

Recueil des actes de Charles II, le Chauve, Roi de France. 3 vols. Ed. Arthur Giry, Maurice Prou, and Georges Tessier. Paris: Imprimerie nationale, 1943–1952.

Recueil des actes de Charles III le Simple, roi de France (893–923). Ed. Philippe Lauer. Chartes et diplômes relatifs à l'histoire de France. Paris: Imprimerie nationale, 1949.

Recueil des actes de Philippe Ier, Roi de France (1059–1108). Ed. Maurice Prou. Paris: Imprimerie nationale,

Recueil des chartes de l'abbaye de Cluny. Ed. Auguste Bernard and Alexandre Bruel. 6 vols. Paris: Imprimierie nationale, 1876–1903.

Recueill des historiens des Gaules et de la France. New edition by Léopold Delisle. Paris: Palmé, 1874.

Regesta pontificum romanorum ab condita ecclesia ad annum post christum natum MCX-CVIII. Vol. 1. Ed. Philippe Jaffé. Lipsiae: Veit et Comp., 1885.

Richer. *Histoire de France.* 2 vols. Ed. and trans. R. Latouche. Paris, 1937.

Wace. *The Conquest of England, from Wace's Poem of the Roman de Rou.* Trans. Alexander Malet. London: Bell and Daldy, 1860.

William of Jumièges. *The Gesta Normannorum ducem of William of Jumièges, Orderic Vitalis, and Robert of Torigni.* Ed. and trans. Elisabeth M. C. van Houts. Oxford: Clarendon Press, 1992.

William of Malmesbury. *Gesta regum Anglorum: The History of the English Kings.* Ed. and trans. R. A. B. Mynors. Completed by R. M. Thomson and M. Winterbottom. Oxford: Clarendon Press, 1998.

William of Poitiers, *The "Gesta Gvillelmi" of William of Poitiers.* Ed. and trans. R. H. C. Davis and Marjorie Chibnall. Oxford: Clarendon Press, 1998.

Select Bibliography of Secondary Sources

Angot, Alphonse. "Sablé." *Bulletin de la commission historique et archéologique de la Mayenne,* 2d series 35 (1919): 166–89.

———. *Généalogies féodales mayennaises de XIe au XIIIe siècle.* Laval: Goupil, 1942.

———. *Dictionnaire historique, topographique et biographique de la Mayenne.* 4 vols. Mayenne: Joseph Flach, 1962.

Bachrach, Bernard S. "A Study in Feudal Politics: Relations between Fulk Nerra and William the Great, 995–1030." *Viator* 7 (1976): 111–22.

———. "The Idea of the Angevin Empire." *Albion* 10 (1978): 293–99.

———. "The Angevin Strategy of Castle Building." *American Historical Review* 88 (June 1983): 533–60.

———. "Henry II and the Angevin Tradition of Family Hostility." *Albion* 16 (1984): 111–30.

———. "Enforcement of the *Forma Fidelitatis:* the Techniques Used by Fulk Nerra, Count of the Angevins." *Speculum* 59 (1984): 796–819.

———. "Geoffrey Greymantle, Count of the Angevins, 960–87: A Study in French Politics." *Studies in Medieval and Renaissance History* 7 (new series, 1985): 1–67.

———. "Pope Sergius IV and the Foundation of the Monastery at Beaulieu-lès-Loches." *Revue Bénédictine* 95 (1985): 258–63.

———. "The Pilgrimages of Fulk Nerra, Count of the Angevins, 987–1040." In *Religion, Culture and Society in the Early Middle Ages*. Kalamazoo: Medieval Institute Publications, 1987.

———. "The Combat Sculptures of Fulk Nerra's 'Battle Abbey'," *Haskins Society Journal* 3 (1991): 63–79.

———. *Fulk Nerra the Neo-Roman Counsul, 987–1040: A Political Biography of the Angevin Count*. Berkeley: University of California Press, 1993.

Baring-Gould, S. *Lives of the Saints*. 14 vols. Edinburgh: John Grant, 1914.

Barlow, Frank. *William Rufus*. Berkeley: University of California Press, 1983.

Barthélemy, Dominique. *L'Ordre seigneurial XIe–XIIe siècles* Vol. 3 of *Histoire de la France médiévale*. Paris: Seuil, 1990.

———. "La mutation féodale a-t-elle eu lieu?" *Annales Économies, sociétés, civilisations* 3 (1992): 767–77.

———. *La société dans le comté de Vendôme de l'an Mil au XIVe siècles*. Paris: Fayard, 1993.

Barton, R. E. "Lordship in Maine: Transformation, Service and Anger." *Anglo-Norman Studies XVII: Proceedings of the Battle Conference 1994*. Ed. Christopher Harper-Bill. 17: 41–63. Woodbridge, Boydell Press, 1995.

Bates, David. *Normandy Before 1066*. New York: Longman, 1982.

———. *William the Conqueror*. London: G. Philip, 1989.

Beech, George. *A Rural Society in Medieval France: The Gâtine of Poitou in the Eleventh and Twelfth Centuries*. Baltimore: John Hopkins Press, 1964.

Bertrand de Broussillon, Arthur. *La maison de Craon: 1050–1480: Étude historique accompangné du cartulaire de Craon*. 2 vols. Paris: A. Picard et Fils, 1893.

Besly, Jean. *Histoire des comtes de Poictou et des ducs de Guyenne, contenant ce qui s'est passé de plus mémorable en France depuis l'an 811 jusques au Roy Louis le Jeune*. Paris: R. Bertault, 1647.

Bisson, T. N. "Nobility and Family in Medieval France: A Review Essay." *French Historical Studies* 16 (Spring 1990): 597–613.

Blake, E. O. "The Formation of the 'Crusade Idea.'" *Journal of English History* 21 (1970): 11–31.

Bloch, Marc. *Feudal Society*. Trans. L. A. Manyon. 2 vols. Chicago: University of Chicago Press, 1970.

Bodard de la Jacopière, Didacus-Antoine de Charpentier de. *Chroniques craonaises*. 2d ed. Le Mans: Monnoyer, 1871.

Bouchard, Constance Brittain. "Laymen and Church Reform around the Year 1000: the Case of Otto-William, Count of Burgundy." *Journal of Medieval History* 5 (1979): 1–10.

———. "The Origins of the French Nobility: A Reassessment." *American Historical Review.* 86 (1981): 500–532.

————. *Sword, Miter and Cloister: Nobility and the Church in Burgundy, 980–1198.* Ithaca: Cornell University Press, 1986.

Bourdigné, Jehan de. *Hystoire agregative des annales et croniqies daniou.* Paris: C. de Boinge et C. Alexandre, 1529. Republished with modernized spellings and commentary as *Chroniques d'Anjou et du Maine par Jehan de Bourdigné.* New ed. 2 vols. Angers: Cosnier et Lachèse, 1842.

Bournazel, Eric and Jean-Pierre Poly. *La Mutation féodale Xe–XIIe siècle.* 2d ed. Paris: PUF, 1980. Translated by Caroline Higgit as *The Feudal Transformation, 900–1200.* New York: Holmes and Meier, 1991.

Boussard, Jacques. "La vie en Anjou aux XIe et XIIe siècles." *Le Moyen Âge* 56 (1950): 29–68.

————. "La seigneurie de Bellême aux Xe et XIe siècle." *Mélanges d'histoire du moyen âge dediés à la mémoire de Louis Halphen.* Paris: Presses Universitaires de France, 1951.

————. "Les institutions de l'empire Plantegenet." In *Histoire des institutions Francaises au moyen âge.* Ed. Ferdinand Lot and Robert Fawtier. 1: 35–59. Paris: Presses Universitaires de France, 1957.

————. "L'origine des familles seigneuriales dans la région de la Loire moyenne." *Cahiers de civilisation médiévale* 5 (1962): 303–22.

————. "Le éviction des tenants de Thibaut de Blois par Geoffroy Martel, comte d'Anjou, en 1044." *Le Moyen Âge* 69 (1963): 141–49.

Bouton, André. *Le Maine: Histoire Économique et sociale des origines au XIVe siècle.* 2d ed. Vol. 1. Le Mans: A. Bouton, 1975.

Bradbury, Jim. "Fulk le Réchin and the Origin of the Plantagenets." In *Studies in Medieval History Presented to R. Allen Brown.* Ed. Christopher Harper-Bill et al. Woodridge, Suffolk, and Wolfeboro, N.H.: Boydell Press, 1989.

Brown, Elizabeth A. R. "The Tyranny of a Construct: Feudalism and Historians of Medieval Europe." *American Historical Review* 79 (1974): 1063–88.

Bull, Marcus. *Knightly Piety and the Lay Response to the First Crusade: The Limousin and Gascony, c. 970–c. 1130.* Oxford: Clarendon Press, 1993.

————. "The Diplomatic of the First Crusade." In *The First Crusade: Origins and Impact.* Ed. Jonathan Philips. Manchester and New York: Manchester University Press, 1997): 35–54.

Chaume, Maurice. *Les Origines du duché de Bourgogne.* 2 vols. Dijon: Imprimerie Jobard, 1925.

Chevrier, E. "Notice sur les Églises de Sablé." *Revue historiqie et archéologique* 1 (1876): 399–424.

Chibnall, Marjorie. "Mercenaries and the *familia regis* under Henry I." *History* 62 (1977): 15–23.

Constable, Giles. "Medieval Charters as a Source for the History of the Crusades." In *Crusade and Settlement.* Ed. Peter W. Edbury. Cardiff: University College Cardiff Press, 1985.

Coolidge, Robert T. "Adalbero, Bishop of Laon." *Studies in Medieval and Renaissance History* 2 (1965): 1–114.

Cordonnier, Paul. "L'Ancien château de Sablé d'après un ancien plan." In "Sur les chemins autour de Sablé." *Revue historique et archéologique du Maine,* 2d series 45 (1966): 61–66.

Cowdrey, H. E. J. "Pope Urban II's Preaching of the First Crusade." *History* 55 (1970): 177–88.

Cregut, G-Régis. *Le concile de Clermont en 1095 et la première croisade.* Clermont-Ferrand: Librairie Catholique, 1895.

Crouch, David. *The Beaumont Twins: The Roots and Branches of Power in the Twelfth Century.* Cambridge: University Press, 1986.

———. *William Marshall: Court, Career, and Chivalry in the Angevin Empire, 1147–1219.* London and New York: Longman, 1990.

Crozet, René. "Le voyage d'Urban II et ses négociations avec le clergé de France (1095–1096). *Revue historique* 179 (1937): 271–310.

David, C. W. *Robert Curthose, Duke of Normandy.* Cambridge: Harvard University Press, 1920.

———. "Henri Ier, l'Empire et l'Anjou (1043–1056)." *Revue belge de philologie et d'histoire* 25 (1946–1947): 87–109.

———. *Études sur la naissance des principautés territoriales en France: IXe–Xe siècle.* Bruges: De Tempel, 1948.

———. "Une crise du pouvoir capétien (1032–1034)." *Miscellanea in memoriam Jan Frederick Niermeyer.* Groningen: J. B. Wolters, 1967: 137–48.

Dictionnaire de la langue française du seizieme siècle. Edmond Huguet, ed. Paris: H. Champion, 1925–1967.

Dillay, Madeleine. "Le régime de l'église privée du XIe au XIIIe siècle dans l'Anjou, le Maine, la Touraine." *Revue historique de droit français et étranger.* 4 series 4 (1925): 256–61.

Douglas, David C. *William the Conqueror: the Norman Impact upon Engalnd.* Berkeley: University of California Press, 1967.

Du Cange, Charles de Fresne. *Glossarium mediae et infimae Latinitatis.* 10 vols. Niort: L. Favre, 1883–1887.

Duby, Georges. *La sociéte aux XIe et XIIe siècles dans la région mâconnaise.* Paris: S.E.V.P.E.N., 1953.

———. *William Marshal: the Flower of Chivalry.* Trans. by Richard Howard. New York: Pantheon Books, 1985.

Dunbabin, Jean. *France in the Making, 843–1180.* Oxford: Oxford University Press, 1985.

Dupont, Étienne. *La participation de la Bretagne à la conquête de l'Angleterre par les Normands.* Paris: Duval, 1911.

Erdmann, Carl. *Die Entstehung des Kreuzzugsgedankens.* Stuttgart: W. Kohlhammer Verlag, 1935. Trans. by Marshall W. Baldwin and Walter Goffart. *The Origin of the Idea of Crusade.* Princeton: Princeton University Press, 1977.

Erdmann, Carl and N. Fickermann. *Briefsammlungen der Zeit Heinrichs IV.* Weimar: Hermann Böhlaus Nachfolger, 1950.

Fanning, Stephen. "From *Miles* to *Episcopus:* The Influence of the Family on the Career of Vulgrinus of Vendôme." *Medieval Prosopography* 4 (1983): 9–30.

———. *A Bishop and his World before the Gregorian Reform: Hubert of Angers, 1006–1047.* Philadelphia: American Philosophical Society, 1988.

Farmer, Sharon. *Communities of Saint Martin: Legend and Ritual in Medieval Tours.* Ithaca: Cornell University Press, 1991.

Finucane, Ronald C. *Soldiers of the Faith: Crusaders and Moslems at War.* New York: St. Martin's Press. 1983.

Fleury, Gabriel. "Les fortifications du Maine: La Tour Orbrindelle et le Mont-Barbet." *Revue historique et archéologique du Maine* 29 (1891): 136–54 and 279–303.

Fliche, Augustin. *La règne de Philippe Ier, Roi de France (1060–1108).* Paris: Société Française, 1912.

Fournier, Gabriel. *Le château dans la France médiévale: essai de sociologie monumentale.* Paris: Aubier Montaigne, 1978.

France, John. "Patronage and the Appeal of the First Crusade." In *The First Crusade: Origins and Impact.* Ed. Jonathan Phillips. Manchester and New York: Manchester University Press, 1997.

Gaussin, Pierre-Roger. *L'Abbaye de la Chaise-Dieu (1043–1518).* Paris: Éditions Cujas, 1962.

Genicot, Léopold. *Les généalogies.* Typologie des sources du Moyen Age Occidental. Turnhout: Brepols, 1975.

Gillingham, John. *Richard Coeur de Lion: Kingship, Chivalry and War in the Twelfth Centruy.* London: Hambledon Press, 1994.

Guillot, Olivier. *Le comte d'Anjou et son entourage au XIe siècle.* 2 vols. Paris: A. and J. Picard, 1972.

———. "A Reform of Investiture before the Investiture Struggle in Anjou, Normandy, and England." In *The Haskins Society Journal* 3 (1991): 81–100. London, 1991.

Guillotel, Hubert. "La place de Châteaubriant dans l'essor des châtellanies bretonnes (XIe–XIIe siècles)." *Mémoires de la Société d'Histoire et d'Archéologie de Bretagne* 66: 5–77.

Hagenmeyer, Heinrich. *Chronologie de la premiere croisade.* Paris: E. Leroux, 1902.

Halphen, Louis. *Le comté d'Anjou au XIe siècle.* Paris: A. Picard et Fils, 1906; reprint ed., Geneva: Slatkine-Megariots Reprints, 1974.

Hill, John Hugh and Laurita Littleton Hill. *Raymond IV Count of Touslouse.* Syracuse: Syracuse University Press, 1962.

Hohl, Claude. "Landri de Nevers dans l'histoire et dans le *Girart de Roussillon.*" In *Chanson de geste et le mythe Carolingian: Mélange René Louis,* vol. 2: 791–806. Saint-Père-sous-Vézelay, 1982.

Howe, John. "The Nobility's Reform of the Medieval Church." *American Historical Review* 93 (1988): 317–39.

Hückel, G. A. "Les poèmes de Adalberon." In *Mélanges d'histoire du Moyen Age.* Ed. Luchaire. Vol. 13. Paris: Felix Alcan, 1901.

Jessee, W. Scott. "A Missing Capetian Princess: Advisa Daughter of King Robert II of France." *Medieval Prosopography* 11 (1990): 1–16.

―――. "The Angevin Civil War and the Norman Conquest of 1066." *The Haskins Society Journal: Studies in Medieval History* 3 (1991): 101–9.

―――. "Robert d'Arbrissal: Aristocratic Patronage and the Question of Heresy," *Journal of Medieval Histroy* 20 (1994): 221–35.

―――. "The Family of Robert the Burgundian and the Creation of the Angevin March of Craon and Sablé." *Medieval Prosopography* 16 (1995): 31–67.

―――. "Urban Violence and the Coup d'Etat of Fulk le Réchin in Anjou, 1067." *The Haskins Society Journal: Studies in Medieval History* 7 (1997): 75–82.

Johnson, Penelope. *Prayer, Patronage and Power: The Abbey of la Trinité, Vendôme, 1032–1187.* New York: New York University Press, 1981.

Joubert, André. "La demolition des château de Craon et de Château-Gontier d'apres les documents inédits (1592–1657)." *Revue historique et archéologique du Maine* 17 (1885): 66–100.

Kleinclausz, Arthur. *Histoire de Bourgogne.* Paris: Hachette, 1924; reprint ed., Marseille: Lafitte Reprints, 1976.

Koziol, Geoffrey. *Begging Pardon and Favor: Ritual and Political Order in Early Medieval France.* Ithaca: Cornell University Press, 1992.

La Borderie, Arthur le Moyne de. *Histoire de Bretagne.* 3 vols. Paris: A. Picard, 1897.

Lalubie, Jacques. *Une baronnie médiévale: Sablé-sur-Sarthe de l'an 1000 à l'an 1500.* Sablé-sur-Sarthe: J. Lalubie, 1994.

Latouch, Robert. "La commune du Mans (1070)." *Mélanges d'histoire du moyen âge dédiés à la mémoire de Louis Halphen.* Paris: Presses Universitaires de France, 1951.

―――. *Histoire du comté du Maine: pendant le Xe et le XIe siècle.* Paris: H. Champion, 1910; reprint ed., Geneva: Slatkine Reprints, 1977.

Le Baud, Pierre. *Histoire de Bretagne avec les Chroniques des maison de Vitré et de Laval.* Paris: Gervais Alliot, 1638.

Le Patourel, John. *The Norman Empire.* Oxford: Clarendon Press, 1976.

―――. *Feudal Empires: Norman and Plantagenet.* London: Hambledon Press, 1984.

Ledru, M. A. "Une page de l'histoire de Sablé (1567–1589)." *Revue du Maine* 11 (1882): 80–102.

Lespinasse, René de. *Le Nivernais et les comtes de Nevers.* 3 vols. Paris: H. Champion, 1909–1914.

Lestang, Gustave de. "La chatellenie et les premiers seigneurs de Malicorne au XIe et au XIIe siècle." *Revue historique et archéologique du Maine* 7 (1880): 247–303.

Lewis, Andrew W. *Royal Succession in Capetian France: Studies on Familial Order and the State.* Cambridge: Harvard University Press, 1981.

Little, Lester K. and Barbara H. Rosenwein. *Debating the Middle Ages: Issues and Readings.* Malden and Oxford: Blackwell, 1998.

Lot, Ferdinand. *Études sur le règne de Hughes Capet et la fin du XIe siècle*. Fasc. 147 of Bibliothèque de l'École des hautes études, Sciences historiques et philologiques. Paris: É. Bouillon, 1903; reprint ed., Geneva: Slatkine, 1975.

———. *Les derniers Carolingians: Lothaire, Louis V, Charles de Lorraine, 954–991*. Paris: É. Bouillon; reprint ed., Geneva: Slatkine Reprints, 1975.

———. "La chanson de Landri." *Romania* 32 (1903): 1–17.

Martindale, Jane. "The French Aristocracy in the Early Middle Ages: a Reappraisal." *Past and Present* 75 (1977): 5–45.

Mayer, Hans Eberhard. *The Crusades*. Ed. and trans. John Gillingham. 2d ed. Oxford: Oxford University Press, 1988.

Ménage, Giles. *Histoire de Sablé: premiere partie*. Paris: Pierre le Petit, 1683.

———. *Second partie de l'histoire de Sablé*. Le Mans, 1844.

———. "Description de la ville de Sablé par Giles Ménage." *Revue de l'Anjou* 2 (1868): 93–103.

Mirot, Léon. "Les origines des premiers comtes héréditaires de Nevers." *Annales de Bourgogne* 17 (1945): 7–15.

Miyamatsu, Hironori. "Les premiers bourgeois d'Angers aux XIe et XIIe siècles." *Annales de Bretagne et des Pays de l'Ouest* 97 (1990): 1–11.

———. "A-t-il existé une commune à Angers au XIIe siècle?" *Journal of Medieval History* 21 (1995): 117–52.

Mollat, Guillaume. "La restitution des églises privées au patrimonie ecclésiastique en France du IXe au XIe siècle." *Revue historique de droit français et étranger*. 4th series 27 (1949): 399–423.

Montzey, Charles de. *Histoire de la Flèche et de ses seigneurs: 1er Période—1050–1589*. Le Mans and Paris: R. Pellechat and H. Champion, 1877.

Morice, Dom P. Hyacinthe. *Histoire ecclésiastique et civile de Bretagne*. Guingamp: Benjamin Jollivet, 1835.

Munro, D. C. "The Speech of Pope Urban II at Clermont, 1095." *American Historical Review* 11 (1906): 231–42.

Norgate, Kate. *England Under the Angevin Kings*, 2 vols. London and New York: Macmillan, 1887.

Owen, D. D. R. *Eleanor of Aquitaine: Queen and Legend*. Oxford: Blackwell, 1993.

Painter, Sidney. "The Family and the Feudal System in Twelfth Century England." *Speculum* 35 (1960): 1–16.

———. *William Marshal, Knight-errant, Baron, and Regent of England*. Baltimore: John Hopkins Press, 1933.

Petit, Ernest. *Histoire des ducs de Bourgogne de la race capétienne*. Paris: E. Thorin, 1885.

Pfister, Christian. *Études sur le règne de Robert le Pieux (996–1031)*. Paris: F. Viewig, 1885.

Port, Célestin. *Dictionnaire historique, géographique et biographique de Maine-et-Loire*. 3 vols. Paris: Dumoulin, 1878.

Poupardin, René. *Le royaume de Provence sous les Carolingiens (855–933)*. Paris: Librairie Bouillon, 1901; reprint ed., Geneva: Slatkine Reprints, 1974.

———. *Le Royaume de Bourgogne (885–1038): Étude sur les origines du royaume d'Arles*. Paris: H. Champion, 1907.

Prawer, Joshua. *The World of the Crusaders*. New York: History Book Club, 1972.

Prestwich, J. O. "The Military Household of the Norman Kings." *English Historical Review* 96 (1981): 1–35.

"Promenade pittoresque et archéologique dans la vallée de la Sarthe à travers le canton de Sablé." *Le Journal de Sablé* (15 September 1907).

Reynolds, Susan. *Kingdoms and Communities in Western Europe, 900–1300*. Oxford: Clarendon Press, 1984.

———. *Fiefs and Vassals: The Medieval Evidence Reinterpreted*. Oxford: Oxford University Press, 1994.

Richard, Alfred. *Histoire des comtes de Poitou*. 2 vols. Paris: A. Picard, 1903.

Richard, Jean. "Urbain II, la prédication de la croisade et la définition de l'indulgence." In *Deus qui mutat tempora: Menschen und Institutionen im Wandel des Mittelalters*. Ed. Ernst-Dieter Hehl. Sigmaringen: J. Thorbecke, 1987.

Rickard, Peter. *A History of the French Language*. 2d ed. London: Routledge, 1989.

Riley-Smith, Jonathan. *The Crusades: Idea and Reality, 1095–1274*. London, 1981.

———. *The First Crusade and the Idea of Crusading*. London: Athlone Press, 1986.

———. *The First Crusaders: 1095–1131*. Cambridge: Cambridge University Press, 1997.

Rosenthal, Joel T. "The Education of the Early Capetians." *Traditio* 25 (1969): 366–76.

Rosenwein, Barbara H. *To Be the Neighbor of Saint Peter: The Social Meaning of Cluny's Property, 909–1049*. Ithaca: Cornell University Press, 1989.

Round, John Horace. *Geoffrey de Mandeville: A Study of the Anarchy*. New York: Burt Franklin, 1892.

Rousset, Paul. *Histoire d'une idéologie: La Croisade*. Lausanne: L'Age d'homme, 1983.

Sassier, Yves. *Recherches sur le pouvoir comtal en Auxerrois du Xe au début du XIIe siècle*. Vol. 5 of *Cahiers d'Archéologie et d'histoire*. Auxerre: Société des Fouilles Archéologiques et des Monuments Historique de l'Yonne, 1980.

Setton, Kenneth M., ed. *A History of the Crusades*. 5 vols. Madison: University of Wisconsin Press, 1969.

Shopkow, Leah. *History and Community: Norman Historical Writing in the Eleventh and Twelfth Centuries*. Washington: The Catholic University of America Press, 1997.

Somerville, Robert. "The Council of Clermont (1095) and Latin Christian Society." *Archivum historiae pontificiae* 12 (1974): 55–90.

———. "The Council of Clermont and the First Crusade." *Studia Gratiana* 20 (1976).

Southern, R. W. *The Making of the Middle Ages*. New Haven: Yale University Press, 1968.

Stutz, Ulrich. "The Proprietary Church as an Element of Mediaeval Germanic Ecclesiastical Law." In *Mediaeval Germany, 911–1250: Essays by German Historians*. Ed. and trans. Geoffrey Barraclough. Oxford: Blackwell, 1938.

Tellenbach, Gerd. *Church, State and Christian Society at the Time of the Investiture Contest*. Trans. R. F. Bennett. Oxford: Blackwell, 1959.

Thompson, Kathleen. "Robert of Bellême Reconsidered." *Anglo-Norman Studies XIII: proceedings of the Battle Conference 1990* 13: 261–84. Ed. Marjorie Chibnall. Woodbridge: Boydell, 1991.

Tonnerre, Noël-Yves. *Naissance de la Bretagne: Géographie historique et structures sociales de la Bretagne méridionale*. Angers: Presses de l'Université d'Angers,1994.

Van Houts, Elisabeth. "Wace as Historian." In *Family Trees and the Roots of Politics: the Prosopography of Britain and France from the Tenth to the Twelfth Century*. Ed. K. S. B. Keats-Rohan. Woodbridge, Suffolk: Boydell Press, 1997.

Van Luyn, P. "Les *milites* dans la France du XIe siècle." *Moyen Age* 77 (1977): 1–9.

Vaughn, Sally N. *Anselm of Bec and Robert of Meulan: The Innocence of the Dove and the Wisdom of the Serpent*. Berkeley: University of California Press, 1987.

Werner, Karl Ferdinand. "Untersuchungen zur Frühzeit des französischen Fürstentums." *Die Welt als Geschichte* 17 (1958): 256–89; 19 (1959): 146–93; 20 (1960): 87–119.

———. "Bedeutende Adelsfamilien im Reich Karls des Grossen." *Karl der Grosse-Lebenswerk und Nachleben*. Vol. 1. Ed. Helmut Beumann. Düsseldorf: Verlag L. Schwann, 1965.

———. "Liens de parenté et noms de personne: un problème historique et méthodologique." In *Structures politiques du monde Franc (VIe–XIIe siècles): Études sur les origines de la France et de l'Allemagne*. London: Variorum Reprints, 1979.

———. "Royaume et Regna: Le Pouvoir en France comme enjeu entre le roi et les grands." In *Pouvoirs et libertés au temps des premiers Capétiens*, Ed. Elisabeth Magnou-Nortier and Pierre Desports. Maulévrier: Éditions Hérault, 1992.

White, Stephen D. "Pactum . . . *Legem Vincit et Amor Judicium,* the Settlement of disputes by Compromise in Eleventh-Century Western France." *American Journal of Legal History* 22 (1978): 281–308.

———. *Custom, Kinship, and Gifts to Saints: The "Laudatio Parentum" in Western France, 1050–1150*. Chapel Hill: University of North Carolina Press, 1988.

Ziezulewicz, William. "Sources of Reform in the Episcopate of Airard of Nantes, 1050–1054." *Ecclesiastical History* 4 (1996): 432–45.

Zimmermann, Harold. *Papstabsetzungen des Mittelalters*. Köln: Herman Böhlaus Nachf, 1968.

Index

*Robert the Burgundian and the Counts of Anjou,
ca. 1025–1098* was designed and composed in
Monotype Dante by Kachergis Book Design,
Pittsboro, North Carolina; and printed on 60-
pound Glatfelter and bound by Thomson-
Shore of Dexter, Michigan.